THE
# POWYS
JOURNAL

Volume XIII

# THE POWYS SOCIETY

*President* Glen Cavaliero

*Chairman* Richard Perceval Graves
*Hon. Treasurer* Michael J. French
*Hon. Secretary* Peter J. Foss

The Powys Society is a registered charity, No. 801332

The Powys Society was founded in 1967 to 'establish the true literary status of the Powys family through promotion of the reading and discussion of their works', in particular those of John Cowper Powys (1872–1963), Theodore Francis Powys (1875–1953), and Llewelyn Powys (1884–1939).

The Society publishes a journal and three newsletters a year, and has embarked on a publication programme. In addition it organises an annual weekend conference, occasional meetings, exhibitions, and walks in areas associated with the Powys family.

The Society is an international one, attracting scholars and non-academics from around the world, and welcomes everyone interested in learning more about this remarkable family.

Correspondence and membership enquiries should be addressed to the Hon. Secretary:

Dr Peter Foss
82 Linden Road, Gloucester GL1 5HD
(tel: 01452 304539)

Visit the Powys Society Web Site:
www.powys-society.org

# THE POWYS JOURNAL

## Volume XIII
## 2003

*Editor*
J. Lawrence Mitchell

*Contributing Editor*
Charles Lock

*The Powys Journal* is a publication of The Powys Society, appearing annually each summer. Its aim is to publish original material by the Powys family — in particular, John Cowper Powys, Theodore Francis Powys and Llewelyn Powys — and scholarly articles and other material relating to them and their circle. It also carries reviews of books by and about the Powys family and their circle.

*The Powys Journal* is grateful to the copyright holders of the individual estates and their literary agents for their permission to quote from the writings of John Cowper Powys, Theodore Francis Powys and Llewelyn Powys.

**mss for publication and correspondence** about the contents of the *Journal* should be addressed to the Editor, Professor J. Lawrence Mitchell, Department of English, Texas A & M University, College Station, Texas 77843–4227, USA; his e-mail address is <j-mitchell@tamu.edu>.

*The Powys Journal* has a refereeing policy, whereby material is submitted for independent reports, in which the anonymity of the author and the referee is preserved. mss should, therefore, be submitted in duplicate, or on disk in text-only format or RTF (as well as in your own wordprocessor) with one paper copy, with the name and address of the author on a separate sheet. mss will be acknowledged but cannot be returned unless accompanied by a stamped, self-addressed envelope. Authors of printed articles will receive two copies of the *Journal.*

Orders for copies of the *Journal* should be addressed to the Society's Publications Manager, Stephen Powys Marks, Hamilton's, Kilmersdon, near Bath, Somerset, BA3 5TE (tel. 01761 435134).

Cover and title-page design: Bev Craven

Typeset in Garamond
in PageMaker 6.5 on a Macintosh computer
by Stephen Powys Marks
Printed by Anthony Williams, printer (tel: 0117 986 0431)

ISSN 0962–7057
ISBN 1 874559 26 0

# CONTENTS

Editorial                                    7

Stephen Powys Marks
Powys Family Connections in
East Anglia                                  9

Susan Rands
The Powys-Fox Connection            40

Barbara Ozieblo
The Poet Gamel Woolsey:
The Creation of a Mythical
Middle-Earth                                53

Jacqueline Peltier
Llewelyn and Alyse Gregory:
A Correspondence with
Dr Marie Stopes                            77

Melvon L. Ankeny
Gladys Brown Ficke and
The Final Beauty                           95

J. Lawrence Mitchell
Theodore Powys and John
Death                                          120

Robin Wood
Resident Foreigners and Bards!
John Cowper Powys & James
Hanley in Wales                          144

Andrew Nash
Frank Swinnerton on John
Cowper Powys                            166

Paul Roberts
John Cowper Powys and The
Cambridge Summer Meetings      179

Peter Foss
An Inventory of the Llewelyn
Powys Holdings: Manuscripts
of Works (Part One)                    204

Kate Kavanagh
'In View of Glastonbury' and
writers' views on JCP:
The 2002 Conference                  235

REVIEWS

Charles Lock
On Biographical Proportions:
A review-essay (Fisherman's
Friend, A Poor Man's House,
Robert Gibbings)                        240

Donald Kerr
Unquiet world: The Life of Count
Geoffrey Potocki de Montalk
STEPHANIE DE MONTALK          248

Paul Christensen
Wet Leaves
PATRICIA V. DAWSON               251

Robin Wood
James Hanley: Modernism and
the Working Class
JOHN FORDHAM                       253

Advisory Board                         255

Notes on Contributors               256

*The Cowper Johnsons: a family gathering in the back garden of No 9 The Close, Norwich, 1910. The Revd C. F. Powys and Mary Cowper Powys née Johnson are second and third from the right (see note 12 on page 38).*
*(by courtesy of Anne and Catharine Cowper Johnson)*

# EDITORIAL

One of the obligations we owe the future is to ensure that the past is not forgotten. In this volume of *The Powys Journal*, history has certainly not been neglected. Susan Rands, for example, reveals a little-known connection between the Powys and the Fox families; and Peter Foss has given us another kind of historical document—a marvellously detailed inventory of the Llewelyn Powys manuscripts and typescripts, one of which (a gift from Alyse Gregory to George Sims, the bookdealer), I am happy to say, was recently acquired by the Cushing Library at Texas A&M University.

Despite JCP's idiosyncratic decision to omit any mention of women in his *Autobiography*, his success and that of other members of the Powys Circle crucially depended upon the beneficence of the fairer sex. John's letters and diaries, for example, reveal his almost total dependence upon Phyllis Playter; and Theodore relied upon Mrs Stracey for criticism of his early work and upon his wife, Violet, for everything else. In this issue, some of the women who gave of themselves so unselfishly receive a little welcome positive attention. Stephen Powys Marks takes us deep into the East Anglian ancestry of Mary Cowper Johnson, 'The Powys Mother', to whom Louis Wilkinson may have been a little unfair with his casual accusation, in *Welsh Ambassadors*, of 'mental masochism'. Jacqueline Peltier writes about the interesting exchanges between Dr Marie Stopes and Alyse Gregory who took up cautious correspondence after the death of Llewelyn. Barbara Ozieblo casts new light upon Gamel Woolsey, Llewelyn's 'Dittany Stone' of *Love and Death*, whose poetic talent seems to have gone lamentably unappreciated by Gerald Brenan, her husband, until after her death. It is worth remembering that, in his introduction to *The Collected Poems of Gamel Woolsey* (1984), Glen Cavaliero deems Woolsey's work 'not unworthy to stand beside ... [that of] such visionary poets as Edwin Muir and Kathleen Raine'.

International interest in 'The One Powys' remains reassuringly strong, on the evidence of our contributors to this issue who hail from Canada, Denmark, France, New Zealand, Spain, the United Kingdom, and the United States of America.                                        JLM

1930 — 1920 — 1910 — 1900 — 1890 — 1880 — 1870 — 1860 — 1850 — 1840 — 1830 — 1820 — 1810 — 1800

Charlotte Emra 1842

Revd Walter George Wilkinson 1929 1931
Lowestoft  Aldeburgh
Christabel Wilkinson 1869 1895 1906 1881
Louis Wilkinson 1968
1867

Revd Littleton Charles Powys 1872
Stalbridge
Amelia Moilliet 1790 1802
cc fellow  cc
Littleton Albert Powys 1890
Revd Charles Francis Powys 1843 cc
1838  1840
Revd Littleton Powys 1748 1825 cc

Shirley  Dorches.  Montacute
John Cowper Powys 1872 1963
Littleton Charles Powys 1874 1955 cc
Theodore Francis Powys 1875 1953 cc
Llewelyn Powys 1884 1939
sD Harting
1871

Mary Cowper Johnson (11 children) 1849
Catharine Cowper 'Kate' 1842
Revd William Cowper Johnson jun 'Cowper' 1844  Yaxham 1924
Maria Theodora 'Dora' 1845 1916
Eleanor Gertrude 1847
Annie Elizabeth 1864 1914
Henrietta Cowper 'Etta' 1855 1921
1856

Stalbr.  Marianne Patteson (7 children) 1962
Northwold 1893  1894
Revd John Barham Johnson  Yaxham
Henry Vaughan Johnson  Welborne 1894
1900

Revd John Patteson 1814 1873 cc
Revd William Cowper Johnson sen 1812 1820 1818 cc cc
John Staniforth Patteson 1781 1832
Anne Elizabeth Tasker (4 ch.) 1789 1808
1808
Revd John Johnson 1769 1788 1833
Yaxham & Welborne
Maria Dorothea Livius (6 children) 1864

EXPLANATION

Each person's life is represented by a horizontal line, with birth and death shown by vertical bars across it at the dates shown below. Vertical lines, drawn on the date of marriage shown to left of line, link parents, indicated by crosses at the intersections, and children marked by small circles.

cc denotes entry to Corpus Christi College, Cambridge in year marked by small bar below line.

STEPHEN POWYS MARKS

# Powys Family Connections in East Anglia

## INTRODUCTION

In May 1999 a small group of members of The Powys Society spent a most exhilarating weekend in East Anglia to see for themselves various places with well-known associations for the Powys family.[1] We visited Aldeburgh, Sweffham, Yaxham and Northwold, and stopped at several points between to hear a selection of readings from John Cowper Powys's *A Glastonbury Romance* and *Autobiography*, and from Littleton Powys's *The Joy of It*. Our President Glen Cavaliero and the present author had an evening each to instruct and entertain the company: this paper is a revised version of my talk. I distributed a collection of photocopied illustrations and also showed some books and original letters and photographs. We stayed at Hengrave Hall in Suffolk, an enormous Tudor mansion, almost like an Oxford college, which is run by nuns largely as a religious conference centre.

As I pointed out then, this is a literal, rather than a literary, account of the family connections in East Anglia, for which I prepared extensive genealogical material, including a diagram to show the overlapping lives of Wilkinsons, Powyses, Johnsons and Pattesons (revised version in *Figure 1*); this was in the form of a bar chart, a device which I employed first in *Newsletter* 43 to show the relationship of several Powys families;[2] another chart showed the very large number of members of these families who attended Corpus Christi College, Cambridge.[3] Pedigrees of the Johnson and Patteson families are printed on a fold-out sheet at the end of this volume.

*Figure 1    Powys family connections in East Anglia: A chronological chart.*

9

The most obvious and most important connection with East Anglia is the provenance and family of 'The Powys Mother', Mary Cowper Johnson (1843–1914; *Figure 2*), whose own forebears and relations had lived in the eastern counties, mainly in various parts of

*Figure 2   'The Powys Mother', Mary Cowper Powys, with Llewelyn, Marian and Philippa in Christening gown, 1886.*

Norfolk and in Norwich itself; Mary's father and many in his family were clergymen. Then there is the Cambridge connection; indeed, to a large extent its importance can be almost summed up as the 'Corpus Connection'. Then there are the connections which primarily involve T. F. Powys: the school in Suffolk run by Louis Wilkinson's father, attended by TFP for a year and a bit; and his farming experience, mainly in Suffolk, but also very briefly in Norfolk, over a period of nine years.

The most valuable source for the Johnsons, to which I owe a great deal, is the *magnum opus* of Catharine Mary Johnson (1896–1996), who called herself Mary Barham Johnson in honour of her parents (and was often called Mary BJ): *Letters and Diaries of the Norfolk Families of Donne and Johnson.*[4] In half a long lifetime's study of these families she drew on an enormous hoarded and safeguarded accumulation of the letters and diaries of those two families, mainly at the time in her own possession;[5] Mary BJ had inherited these papers from her mother Catharine Bodham Johnson, who lived to the even greater age of 105.

A small portion of the letters, largely connected with Mary Cowper Powys née Johnson, has come down to me via Lucy Penny, the youngest daughter of Mary Cowper Powys.[6] There has not been time to study these as they deserve, but I have found a few interesting matters which help my story, and Mary BJ herself had already studied and made use of them.

Mary BJ's work consists of extensive extracts, or whole letters, covering a period of a hundred and fifty years, with her connecting narrative, and a very comprehensive index of persons and topics. It comprises more than 800 pages of photocopied handwritten text, photographs, portraits and family trees.

## THE JOHNSONS

Mary Cowper Johnson's parents were William Cowper Johnson (WCJ) (1813–93; *Figure 3*) and Marianne Patteson (1812–94; *Figure 4*). WCJ's father, the Revd John Johnson (1769–1833; *Figure 5*), was the first in the Johnson line known to have been a clergyman, while his father, also John, was a tanner in Ludham with a flourishing business.[7] the Revd John Johnson's mother was Catharine Donne from a veryinteresting family whose relationship to the seventeenth-century divine John Donne (1573–1631) seems most likely but has not been proved.

There were many clergymen in the Donne family also, including Catharine's own father, the Revd Roger Donne, and here we come to one of the most interesting connections of the Powys family: William Cowper the poet (*Figure 6*). Roger Donne's sister, Anne, also married to a clergyman, was the mother of William Cowper. In 1790, at the age of 21, the younger John Johnson sought out his mother's famous cousin, nearly forty years his senior, and so started a friendship that

*Figure 3    Revd William Cowper Johnson (1813–93),*
*(photo by F. Treble, Norwich).*
On back, 'To my dearest Charley & Mary/ on my birthday Aug 18 1885/ W. Cowper Johnson aged 72'. (by courtesy of Louise de Bruin)

*Figure 4    Marianne Johnson, née Patteson, pencil drawing by T. P. Downs, 1844 (image size 14 by 14 in. on paper 20 by 16½ in.).*

*Figure 5    Revd John Johnson, by John Jackson (1778–1831), copied by
Gertrude M. Powys (image size 13 by 10 in.). (by courtesy of Rose Dyer)*
*Figure 6    (below) William Cowper, miniature by William Blake based on
Romney's portrait, 1801.(photo SPM collection)*
*Figure 7    Maria Johnson née Livius, by John Jackson, copied by Gertrude
M. Powys (image size 13 by 10 in.). (by courtesy of Rose Dyer)*

grew so strong that Johnson looked after the poet for the last five mad years of his life (he died in 1800); Johnson acquired the soubriquet 'Johnny of Norfolk'.

In 1808 the Revd John Johnson married Maria Dorothea Livius (1788–1864; *Figure 7*). He was Rector of Yaxham and Welborne from 1800 till his death in 1833, when he was succeeded by Maria's brother, Henry Livius; we shall hear more about Yaxham, which is 15 miles west of Norwich and just

13

outside East Dereham (*Figures 8, 9, 10*). However, there was no rectory for him to live in and he had to find curacies elsewhere nearer London until he was able to embark on his own project to build a rectory.

The death of Maria Dorothea's father George Livius in 1816

*Figure 8    Yaxham Church, East Dereham, Norfolk, 1999.*

*Figure 9    Yaxham Church from the east, postcard, early 20th c.*

brought money to her and her husband, enabling him to embark on a scheme to build his imposing rectory at Yaxham. The rectory he built in 1820–22 was a large and very attractive house, with ample accommodation for pupils (*Figure 11*); it was designed by an architect of some distinction, Robert Lugar, who may have had some early association with John Nash in South Wales, but was practicing in London from about 1799; a lot of his work was indeed in Wales and also in lowland Scotland. No other example of Lugar's architectural work in or near East Anglia is listed by Colvin,[8] though he was appointed county surveyor of Essex in 1812, so it would be interesting to know how Johnson came to commission such a good architect, described as a 'skilled practitioner of the picturesque'.

The Revd John Johnson had two other sons, John Barham Johnson and Henry Vaughan Johnson, born in 1818 and 1820 respectively.

*Figure 10    Memorial stones of Johnsons and Pattesons
in Yaxham churchyard, 1999.*
*From l. to r. with MI number given by Garland (see note 9):*
*A84 Henrietta Cowper Johnson, d. Dec 18 1934, aged 78 [Aunt Etta]*
*A85 Maria Theodora Johnson, d. May 17 1924, aged 78 [Aunt Dora]*
*A76 Eleanor Gertrude Johnson, d. Apr 12 1804, aged 16*
*A77 Maria Dorothy, relict of John Johnson, d. 1864, aged 75*
*A78 Eleanor, wife of William Patteson, d. Sept 3 1864, aged 64*
*A79 William Frederick Patteson, d. Nov 14 1881, aged 84*

*Figure 11    Yaxham Rectory, East Dereham, Norfolk*
*(1820–22, archt Robert Lugar), postcard, early 20th c.*

From his three sons stemmed a prolific brood of Cowper Johnsons, Barham Johnsons and Vaughan Johnsons, who, with their Donne cousins, intermarried with some regularity; once, when this was commented on, the reply was that 'we hardly met anyone else'. The name Cowper was in honour and memory of the poet, leading to a long trail of Cowpers amongst the Johnsons and in the Powys family as well.

In 1840 William Cowper Johnson married Marianne Patteson. The alliance of the Johnson family with the Pattesons had consequences of the greatest importance for the Powyses: for it is through the medium of the friendship of Marianne's brother John with WCJ and his curacy under the Revd Littleton Charles Powys at Stalbridge that ultimately Mary Cowper Johnson met the Revd Charles Francis Powys.

John Patteson (1814–1902, *Figure 12*) entered Corpus Christi College, Cambridge in 1832, a year before WCJ; even a gap of a single year can separate undergraduates but the friendship of these two young men at Cambridge is recorded.[9] Whether or not there were earlier contacts between the Patteson and Johnson families I cannot tell, but there is evidence that Pattesons and Donnes were in contact in the late eighteenth century (LDDJ, 21).

WCJ was for four years Curate at Yaxham and Welborne before he became Rector of Yaxham in 1843, because there was some concern over the propriety of offering him the living owned by the family. Once that was sorted out, he became Rector and remained there for almost 40 years, till 1880, and Yaxham Rectory was the only family home for the Cowper Johnsons until the youngest daughter was 24.

There were seven children in all, apart from a first baby who died within a few weeks of birth, and premature twins who died at birth, all in 1841. The first surviving child was Catharine Cowper, 'Aunt Kate' to the Montacute Powyses; second was the younger William Cowper Johnson (1844–1916), always known as 'Cowper', also a clergyman; then Maria Theodora, 'Aunt Dora'; Eleanor Gertrude (who died of TB when she was 16); Mary Cowper; Annie Elizabeth; and finally Henrietta Cowper, 'Aunt Etta'. The aunts Kate, Dora and Etta, especially the last two, were important and much-loved figures in the lives of the Montacute Powyses, and when they no longer lived at Yaxham, they lived in Norwich, especially in The Close. Kate married a cousin but had no children, and Annie married the Revd Cecil Blyth and had four children.

In 1880, WJC moved to Northwold (*Figures 13–17*), some 20 miles south-west of Yaxham, and remained Rector till his death in 1893, and he handed over Yaxham to his son, who was Rector there from 1880 till his death in 1916.

In *Autobiography*, John Cowper Powys recalls his visit to his various grandparents; his paternal

*Figure 12    Revd John Patteson (from LDDJ).*

17

grandfather had died early in the year that JCP was born, 1872, but his Powys grandmother Amelia was living in Weymouth till 1890. His account of visits to his mother's parents at Yaxham (i.e. before 1880) is much shorter; he starts, 'We had other relatives to visit ... who lived in a very different part of the country from Weymouth ...' (20). Of Northwold he has incredibly little to say, even though the children

*Figure 13    Northwold Rectory and Church, Norfolk, postcard, early 20th c.*

*Figure 14    Northwold Rectory, as it is now with tall range removed, 1999.*

visited it every summer, as is recorded by Littleton Powys in a whole chapter devoted to Northwold in *The Joy of It.*; Northwold was, Littleton says, 'my boyhood's Earthly Paradise' (78). Nevertheless, there is no doubt that Northwold made a great impression on JCP as well as on Littleton. Together they re-visited Northwold in the

*Figure 15    Northwold Church, Norfolk, from south-east, 1999.*

summer of 1929, as is recorded in JCP's *Diary* for that year[11] as well as by Littleton.

It is instructive to see what Catharine Bodham Johnson, Mary BJ's predecessor as family historian, thought were the chief characteristics of the various branches of the family (*Figure 18*).

Figure 19 (page ??) shows the family of WCJ and Marianne just before the First World War; this includes the husbands of two of

*Figure 16    Memorial wall tablet to Revd William Cowper Johnson sen., Northwold Church, 1999.*

*Figure 17    Memorial wall tablet to Revd John Johnson (d.1833) and his
daughter Catharine Anne (d.1833), Northwold Church, 1999.*

WCJ's daughters, the Revd C. F. Powys and the Revd Cecil Blyth,
Emily Barham Johnson who married her cousin Cowper, and one
young man, Reginald Blyth. This photograph is a remarkable picture,
because it shows all the children of WCJ gathered together, perhaps,
as Mary BJ commented (LDDJ, 696), for the first time in forty years.
This and the splendid frontispiece photograph were taken on June
21st 1910.[12] Mary Cowper Powys, seated on the left, though younger
than Kate and Dora (also seated), looks so much more aged than these
sisters; after all, they had had no children and she had borne eleven.

*Powys and Johnson*

At the same time as John Patteson met WCJ at Corpus both of them
would also have known the Revd Littleton Charles Powys (LCP)
(1790–1872), who was a Fellow of Corpus from 1814 to 1837; he
resigned his Fellowship in 1837 and immediately took John Patteson

*Figure 18    'The Chief Characteristics of the following Branches of the
Family, according to the judgment of Catharine Bodham Johnson',
holograph pasted into commonplace book of Eleanor Powys (85%).*

chief characteristics of the following
branches of the family, according to the judgment
of Catharine Bodham Johnson

W. B. Donne } had wit - humour - love of writing & poetry
C. S. Donne  } were faithful in friendship - good raconteurs
uncle Bodvay } but apt to embellish their stories - unpractical -
&c.              } unwilling to face unpleasant facts - book-lovers
                  even tempered & generous.

Johnsons.
Northwold   } had love of order & punctuality - no love of
Taxham      } money but careful of it - staunch in their
Welborne    } friendships - deeply religious - generous.
              had charm & much given to hospitality —
              were all over. Sensitive & easily hurt.

Pattesons    a contrast to above - gentle & quiet and
             apparently yielding but stubborn in some
             things - "The meek shall inherit the earth might
             be said of them —

Livius's     were lovable - somewhat autocratic - but
             self-sacrificing - hasty tempered - but to
             be trusted absolutely - honest & fearless -
             The Livius religion which was that of the
             Moravian Church was rather narrow -

The Donnes } drew              Johnsons } were
Johnsons    } &                 &        } musical
&           } painted           Livius   }
Livius      }

I do not think any of them had much
business capacity, but they looked on money as a
trust & were careful of it - but they were generous
& to my mind all utterly lovable.
                                    C. B. J

21

to be his curate,[13] and LCP's wife Amelia Powys in her notebook about her children refers to his great exertions in putting out a fire in Stalbridge church;[14] he stayed till 1844. What earlier contact there might have been between this Powys and WCJ is not at all clear; Mary BJ claims that when WCJ was at school at Sherborne (this was from 1827 to 1833) he had got to know LCP as Rector of Stalbridge, and that when WCJ had gone to a crammer in Thrapston, Northants, before going up to Cambridge (this would be in the summer of 1833) he had ridden over to see 'old Littleton Powys' whom he had known as a boy.[15] I am afraid there is some confusion here, for which we must blame the host of Littletons in the Powys family, a name which derives from the seventeenth-century marriage of an earlier Powys to Anne Littleton, daughter of Sir Adam Littleton, Chief Justice of North Wales.

This confusion needs to be addressed, as it has a bearing on the significance we must attach to John Patteson as a very important, even if not the original, point of contact. Figure 20 (page 30), which I will look at in more detail later, shows two collateral Powyses who are not relevant to the Corpus connection. The Revd Littleton Charles Powys was a Fellow of Corpus till 1837. His father was the Revd Littleton Powys who died in 1825, and was a younger brother of Thomas Powys, 1st Lord Lilford, who had a son, also Littleton Powys; this Littleton Powys was also the Revd as well as being Hon. and died in 1842. Now, the two Revd Littleton Powyses were successively Rectors of Titchmarsh, Northamptonshire, the elder Littleton Powys, grandfather of C. F. Powys, till 1805, and the Hon. Revd Littleton Powys from 1805 till 1842. Just to confuse matters a little more, the Hon. Revd Littleton Powys was Curate at Titchmarsh for two years till 1805 under the Rectorship of the older Revd Littleton Powys.

We can see then that when WCJ was at Sherborne School between 1827 and 1833 LCP was still several years away from the Rectorship of Stalbridge, while LCP's father had died two years before WCJ went to Sherborne. In 1833, when he is said to have ridden over to see the 'old Littleton Powys' this was clearly the much younger man from the senior branch of the family, not a direct ancestor of C. F. Powys. The

*Figure 19   The Cowper Johnsons, a family gathering at No 9 The Close, Norwich, June 21st 1910.
standing, l. to r.: Revd C. F. Powys, Annie (Mrs Blyth), Reginald Blyth, Revd Cecil Blyth, Henrietta Johnson ('Etta'),
Emily Barham Johnson (Mrs William Cowper Johnson), Revd William Cowper Johnson
seated, l. to r.: Mary Cowper Powys, Theodora Johnson ('Dora'), Catharine (Mrs Mowbray Donne, 'Kate')*

reason for his going to Sherborne was primarily the high reputation of its headmaster, Dr Lyon.

Accordingly, it is clear that we owe the meeting and marriage of Mary Cowper Johnson and Charles Francis Powys primarily to the meeting of WCJ and John Patteson and the curacy of John Patteson under LCP. One curious reflection on the chanciness of things is that if LCP had been able and had wanted to resign his Fellowship earlier he might not have met and invited John Patteson to be curate. In 1838 LCP married Amelia Knight, née Moilliet, who had been widowed in 1829; she was living at Impington Hall, 3 miles from Cambridge. I know of no information about how they met, but one might wonder whether LCP could have met Amelia some years earlier but had had to wait until a College living became available before resigning which enabled him to marry, like his contemporary Revd Thomas Greene, also a Fellow of Corpus: Greene was engaged for 17 years to John Patteson's aunt Elizabeth ('Aunt Greene') before he could be presented to the living of Fulmodestone, Norfolk in 1835.

Now we need to look at what brought Charles Francis Powys (CFP) to Norfolk. WCJ, as did many clergymen, took pupils in their homes, which were often large enough to accommodate them. There are references to 'Mr. Powys', that is CFP, in letters of 1860 between several of the young daughters; one says 'We have had such jolly games of Croquet lately, we generally play after dinner with the four gent. [i.e., their father's pupils]. Mr Blyth is quite an expert hand at it, but Mr Powys pokes too much.' (LDDJ, 449) If we remember that WCJ's Cambridge friend John Patteson had served as Curate under CFP's father LCP for seven years, and that WCJ had married the same friend's sister during that time, it is not difficult to imagine the correspondence between them which would place CFP in WCJ's household as a pupil. He was admitted to Corpus in 1862, following in his father's footsteps; he did not coincide with any other member of the Johnson or Patteson families, but when he came up to Cambridge to take his Master's degree in 1869, having been ordained in 1867, he stayed with the Johnsons for a week.

Mrs Johnson, Marianne, wrote to Cowper, then travelling in India, that

Mr Powys helped your Father ... gave a very nice sermon upon the Holy Spirit ... such a simple earnest Gospel sermon—he is very hearty in his work & is anxious to be a useful Clergyman ... his manner is solemn & devout ... & reminded me so much in manner of your Uncle John Patteson [Marianne's brother] ... He is grown a very strong looking man—he seemed to be so pleased to be with us & quite enjoyed the family party, after being so much alone in lodgings—he has lost his shyness very much ... (LDDJ, 547–8)

He does indeed appear to have enjoyed the family party and formed a strong attachment to one of them, because it was Mary Cowper Johnson, then aged 21, whom he asked to marry him in 1871; interestingly, her older sisters Kate and Dora, then 28 and 25, were unmarried. CFP had written to Mary's father, as was the custom, to seek his permission and asked him to pass his proposal on to her, but she was away from home, and WCJ wanted to give her CFP's letter himself, but CFP insisted that his letter should be sent on immediately, which WCJ did on June 19th, with his own letter which is worth quoting from briefly:

My dearest Child You will be I am sure pleased to receive such a proof of the esteem of a high-minded and good man as is contained in the enclosed note to you from Charles Powys. It is quite natural that you should be at the same time surprised and that you should wish for our parental advice ... [He then explains the delay in forwarding CFP's letter.] You know how much we regard Powys. If you think you could love him as a wife ought to love a husband, don't break the poor fellow's heart.' [16]

Mary's response was extraordinarily modest and self-effacing, greatly in contrast with the spiritedness of earlier letters. [17]

## The Patteson family [18]

The Pattesons were a family of considerable wealth and civic dignity, though, as with any family, their fortunes waxed and waned. The

Pattesons moved from Birmingham to Norwich in 1721 and built a house in Market Place, where the second Henry Sparke Patteson established a wholesale ironmongery and banking activities; in 1739 he was Sheriff.

Henry Sparke Patteson's younger son John Patteson (1727–1774), brother of Henry Sparke Patteson III, built himself a substantial house in Surrey Street in the southern part of the city, which later became the headquarters of the Norwich Union Fire Office. This house, No 9 Surrey Street, is one of the largest Georgian houses in Norwich; it was erected in 1764 to the designs of Robert Mylne and was extended in 1790 by John Soane:[19] only the best architects were good enough for the Pattesons! John Patteson established a wool-stapling business and was Mayor in 1766.

The next John Patteson (1755–1833), son of Henry Sparke Patteson III, was sent to Germany in 1768 to further his education, and made a long journey again on the Continent in 1778–9, visiting Germany, Switzerland and Northern Italy, attending amongst other things the King of Sardinia's stag hunt. He returned to a position of affluence and comfort, owning the Surrey Street house, estates in Colney and Bawburgh ('Babur'), and other country property.

In 1781 he married Elizabeth Staniforth of Attercliffe, who is described as the heiress of Robert Staniforth of Manchester and of the Revd Cox Macro of Norton Hall, Suffolk. Thus, she brought a substantial dowry and the ownership of Little Haugh Hall, Norton, 6 miles east of Bury St Edmunds, a house with an interior of the early eighteenth century which sends Pevsner into transports of delight.[20]

John Patteson became a very prosperous landowner; he was an Alderman, Sheriff in 1785, Mayor in 1788. In 1793 he purchased a brewery and added others to form the nucleus of Pockthorpe Brewery in Norwich. In 1802 he was MP for the pocket borough of Minehead, then in 1806–12 MP by election for Norwich. But then the Pattesons fell on hard times in the 1820s, a period of severe recession, and John retired to Mangreen Hall outside Norwich with his wife and two daughters; he died there in 1832, and his wife in 1838.

John Patteson's eldest daughter was Elizabeth, whom we shall meet as the wife of Thomas Greene, Fellow of Corpus. His eldest son was John Staniforth Patteson, who married Anne Elizabeth Tasker; they were the parents of Marianne Patteson who married WJC in 1840, of John Patteson, the Stalbridge Curate, and of Henry Staniforth Patteson the *Memoir* of whom has provided so much information on this family. Both sons went to Paston Grammar School (now Paston Sixth Form College) at North Walsham. Anne Tasker was the daughter of William Tasker who was a diamond merchant of Rotterdam; no doubt she helped to repair the family fortunes.

John Staniforth Patteson (1782–1832) was Mayor of Norwich in 1823; in 1824 he established the Triennal Musical Festivals. His family spent some weeks each year at Cromer and Lowestoft. Some years later, letters refer to Cowper Johnson children spending time at both places, and Mary Cowper Johnson refers to the Festival. In 1831 John Staniforth Patteson and his family moved to a country house at Cringleford, just west of Norwich, which becomes the Patteson base for many years and a frequent place of visit for the Cowper Johnsons, but he died the next year at the early age of 49. His son John was determined to go into the church, while the younger Henry Staniforth Patteson (1816–1898) trained for and entered the brewery, in which his father had been a partner.

In *A Glastonbury Romance* we hear that the beer at the Northwold Arms is 'Patteson's best ale and brewed in Norwich' (11). H. S. Patteson married in 1850. He was Sheriff in 1858, Mayor in 1862, Deputy Lieutenant of the county in 1859. John's clerical appointments, as well as his curacy at Stalbridge, included 12 years at Christ Church, Spitalfields in London, before he became Rector of Thorpe near Lowestoft in 1867 till 1896; like both William Cowper Johnsons, he was an Honorary Canon of Norwich.

A letter of H. S. Patteson to his mother in December 1835 refers to 'Walter, John [i.e. Patteson], and Johnson always drinking tea together on a Sunday, and then read some lecture, a chapter of the Bible, upon which they comment, and finish with a prayer.'[21] 'Johnson' is the elder William Cowper Johnson, who married John's sister Marianne in 1840. John Patteson himself married in 1846 Elizabeth Hoare who was the niece of Mrs Elizabeth Fry, the prison reformer, of

Joseph John Gurney, quaker philanthropist and writer, and of Samuel Gurney of the banking firm Overend, Gurney & Co.

Catharine Bodham Johnson (*Figure 18*) didn't think that any of the branches of the family had much business sense, but I think there must have been a great deal amongst the Pattesons, even if not in the other Johnson relations.

*Other families: Livius, Barham, Vaughan, Donne*

The parents of Maria Dorothea, John Johnson's wife, were from two families with inherited wealth. Her father, George Livius came from a family which, according to a letter written by his father, Peter Lewis Livius (1688–?1771), originated in Germany.[22] Peter Livius himself was born in Hamburg, but he went to Lisbon in 1709, married Susannah Humphrey from Waterford in Ireland, and their seven children were born there. The youngest, George, was taken by his mother to England shortly after birth because his feet were a little turned; he was educated in England, then returned to Lisbon, but evidently settled in England after making his fortune in India, serving in the East India Company. As a result of his conversion to the Moravian church in the 1780s George Livius (1743–1816) came to Bedford, home to one of the two greatest Moravian settlements in England, and in 1785 married Mary Foster-Barham who came from a strongly Moravian family.

John Cowper Powys referred to 'my great-grandfather' who came from Hamburg when he gave thanks for the Bronze Plaque of the Hamburg Academy of Arts.[23] Clearly this was a reference to the Hamburg-born Peter Livius of two generations earlier, but it would have spoiled the effect somewhat if JCP had had to say 'great-great-great-grandfather'. In Bedford the Liviuses belonged to the Moravian Church.

Maria Dorothea's mother was Mary Barham or Foster-Barham (1762–1837), whose father came from a long line of Fosters originating in Northumberland;[24] three generations had lived in Jamaica and owned sugar plantations, and Mary's father, originally Joseph Foster, had been adopted by his mother's second husband, Henry Barham, inheriting his estates and adding his name. Mary Barham's mother

28

came from a Welsh family, Vaughan of Trecoon or Trecwm, Pembrokeshire. Thus, we can account for the names Barham and Vaughan, as well as Cowper, in the descendants of the Revd John Johnson.

One of the most interesting members of the Donne family was William Bodham Donne (1807–82). He had a very wide literary circle; he was Librarian of the London Library and examiner of plays in the Lord Chancellor's Office. The letters between Donne and his friends were edited and published in 1905 by his granddaughter Catharine Bodham Johnson;[25] it contains a brief account of the Donne family, including the reference to the tradition that the Norfolk Donnes came originally from Wales, and were a branch of the family of Dwns of Picton and Cwdweli Castles, Pembrokeshire. So, here is yet another remote Welsh strain to join the distant and much-diluted Powysian one.

## THE CAMBRIDGE CONNECTION

When I started to look at the published history of Corpus Christi College,[26] I realised that the Powyses were not the only family of interest to us with a tradition of going to that college. The earliest Powys at Corpus was the Revd Littleton Charles Powys, but the rather selective chart which I have compiled (*Figure 20*), shows a clutch of other related families with members at Corpus: Johnson, Patteson, and Greene.[27]

The Greenes are a little remote perhaps, but there are references in Johnson letters to 'Aunt Greene'; Aunt Greene was Elizabeth the sister of John Staniforth Patteson, the maternal grandfather of Mary Cowper Johnson. This Patteson and some others of his family went to Trinity and Caius, but his brother-in-law, the Revd Thomas Greene, and LCP were exact contemporaries at Corpus; they were of the same age, admitted at the same time, and they were elected Fellows in the same year, 1814. In 1822 there were just seven Fellows of the College, so they could not avoid knowing each other well.

The Revd Thomas Greene was related to earlier Greenes at Corpus: Charles admitted 1764, Thomas (1727), another Thomas (1674) who was Master of Corpus 1698–1716, so there was a strong family continuity there. However, one of the most tantalising questions to ask is what brought LCP to Corpus in 1809, the date of his admission; and how was he elected a Fellow at the tender age of 24? His father Littleton and his uncle Thomas were at Emmanuel and King's respectively, also Cambridge colleges; before that, Powyses had been at Oxford. LCP remained a Fellow till his resignation in 1837. so that he

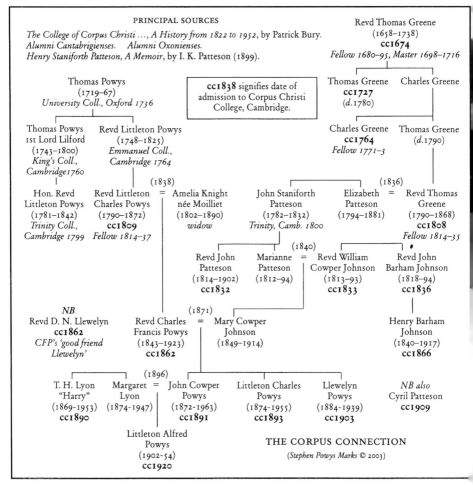

PRINCIPAL SOURCES

*The College of Corpus Christi ..., A History from 1822 to 1952*, by Patrick Bury.
*Alumni Cantabrigienses. Alumni Oxonienses.*
*Henry Staniforth Patteson, A Memoir*, by I. K. Patteson (1899).

cc1838 signifies date of admission to Corpus Christi College, Cambridge.

Revd Thomas Greene
(1658–1738)
cc1674
*Fellow 1680–95, Master 1698–1716*

Thomas Powys
(1719–67)
*University Coll., Oxford 1736*

Thomas Powys
1st Lord Lilford
(1743–1800)
*King's Coll., Cambridge 1760*

Revd Littleton Powys
(1748–1825)
*Emmanuel Coll., Cambridge 1764*

(1838)

Thomas Greene    Charles Greene
cc1727
(d.1780)

Charles Greene    Thomas Greene
cc1764         (d.1790)
*Fellow 1771–3*

(1836)

Hon. Revd
Littleton Powys
(1781–1842)
*Trinity Coll., Cambridge 1799*

Revd Littleton
Charles Powys
(1790–1872)
cc1809
*Fellow 1814–37*

Amelia Knight
née Moilliet
(1802–1890)
*widow*

John Staniforth
Patteson
(1782–1832)
*Trinity, Camb. 1800*

Elizabeth
Patteson
(1794–1881)

Revd Thomas
Greene
(1790–1868)
cc1808
*Fellow 1814–35*

(1840)

Revd John
Patteson
(1814–1902)
cc1832

Marianne
Patteson
(1812–94)

Revd William
Cowper Johnson
(1813–93)
cc1833

Revd John
Barham Johnson
(1818–94)
cc1836

*NB*
Revd D. N. Llewelyn
cc1862
*CFP's 'good friend
Llewelyn'*

(1871)

Revd Charles
Francis Powys
(1843–1923)
cc1862

Mary Cowper
Johnson
(1849–1914)

Henry Barham
Johnson
(1840–1917)
cc1866

(1896)

T. H. Lyon
"Harry"
(1869-1953)
cc1890

Margaret
Lyon
(1874-1947)

John Cowper
Powys
(1872-1963)
cc1891

Littleton Charles
Powys
(1874-1955)
cc1893

Llewelyn
Powys
(1884-1939)
cc1903

*NB also*
Cyril Patteson
cc1909

Littleton Alfred
Powys
(1902-54)
cc1920

THE CORPUS CONNECTION
*(Stephen Powys Marks © 2003)*

*Figure 20    The Corpus Connection set out as a genealogy.*

could marry a young widow, Amelia Knight née Moilliet, and become Rector of Stalbridge.

What is particularly interesting in the early-nineteenth-century period is that one generation after LCP, John Patteson was admitted in 1832, not long before LCP's resignation. LCP, installed at Stalbridge, promptly took on John Patteson as Curate; Patteson held this position from 1837 till 1844. A contemporary of John Patteson at Corpus was William Cowper Johnson, admitted in 1833; his father, the Revd John Johnson, had been at Caius (1787). WCJ in due course married John Patteson's sister Marianne. Marianne and WCJ became the parents of Mary Cowper Johnson, five other girls, and William Cowper Johnson Jnr. WCJ was followed at Corpus by his brother John Barham (1836) and John's son Henry Barham Johnson (1866), who was the father of Mary BJ. The youngest brother of WCJ went to Trinity (1839).

Thus we see that Greene's Patteson nephew-by-marriage became the Curate of his colleague-as-Fellow Powys, and the Patteson and Johnson families were linked by marriage through acquaintance at Corpus.

Because LCP married late at the age of 47; when his son CFP went up to Corpus he was two generations behind his father, being admitted in 1862, but the connection with the Johnson family, no doubt maintained through the Patteson acquaintance, led, as we have seen, to CFP meeting Mary Cowper Johnson, and to their betrothal and marriage in 1871.

Thus, four generations of Powyses were at Corpus, running from the first Littleton Charles to Littleton Alfred; two of John Cowper's brothers, another Littleton Charles and Llewelyn, were also at Corpus, but in addition a contemporary of John Cowper, admitted in 1891, was T. H. Lyon, Harry Lyon (1890). Through their friendship JCP met Margaret Lyon whom he married in 1896, another fruit of college acquaintance.

A further interesting Corpus connection concerns Llewelyn Powys. One of Llewelyn's godfathers was the Revd D. N. Llewelyn; this man was at Corpus at the same time as CFP, and was Rector of Llansannor, near Cowbridge in South Wales, from 1870 to 1887. In a letter to his son Llewelyn, CFP refers to the 'death of my good friend Llewelyn';[28] D. N. Llewelyn was listed in CFP's mother's address book.[29] It is clear that the only specifically Welsh name which CFP and Mary bestowed on any of their children was due to the friendship between college contemporaries.

Today there is a strong physical reminder of the family's association with Corpus in the very attractive watercolour of the college by Richard Bankes Harraden (*Figure 21*) which is now in my possession, having been at Montacute Vicarage and then in A. R. Powys's hands before being passed on to me by his younger daughter Eleanor Walton after the death of his son Oliver Powys in 1996. It appears to have been painted in the 1820s probably in preparation for the publication of a book of engravings of Cambridge colleges.[30] I am sure it belonged to the Revd L. C. Powys: perhaps it was presented to him when he resigned his Fellowship or he could himself have bought it from the artist.

*Figure 21    Corpus Christi College, Cambridge, water colour by R. B. Harraden, ?1820s (image size, 13 ½ by 22 in).*

## T. F. POWYS IN SUFFOLK

My last section is devoted to Theodore Francis Powys in Suffolk. I shall set out very briefly Theodore's schooling and farming experiences in this county. Both have been explored in some detail by Lawrence Mitchell.[31] He examines very thoroughly the influence of the ten years spent in one or other occupation, especially the farming experience, on Theodore's understanding of the country, farming practice and landscape, and on his writing; I need not explore this myself. This also involves the Wilkinson family which led to the close association of Louis Wilkinson with several of the Powyses.

### Schooling and the Wilkinson family

In short, Mitchell deduces from various contemporary documents and from later, often passing, references that Theodore went to Dorset Grammar School in 1886, probably in September, then to Sherborne Prep in January 1888, leaving there in April 1889; then he stayed at home a bit more than a year. He went to Eaton House School, Aldeburgh, on the Suffolk coast (*Figure 22*), during the summer term 1890, and spent three and a half terms there, the summer term of 1891 being his last. Its Headmaster was the Revd Walter George Wilkinson (1829– 1906, *Figure 23*), father of Louis Wilkinson. He moved his school to Aldeburgh in 1869, having previously been in Lowestoft, shortly after his marraige in 1867 to Charlotte Elizabeth Emra (1842– 1931).

*Figure 22    Eaton House, formerly Eaton House School, Aldeburgh, Suffolk, 1999.*

I would like to explore the background to the decision to send Theodore so far from home at the age of 14. First of all, of course, it was not very far from his

33

Johnson grandparents' home at Northwold and from Yaxham where his uncle Cowper was now Rector; it would, however, have been quite a cross-country journey even by the more extensive rail system then in being. It should also be remembered that these grandparents were both nearly eighty.

According to Louis Wilkinson, Theodore was sent to his father's school because 'his mother and mine were friends in girlhood'.[32] Mitchell has pointed out that this does not work chronologically: there was a difference of seven years between Charlotte Wilkinson (*b.*1842) and Mary Cowper Johnson (*b.*1849); it is most unlikely that they could have been girlhood friends, but there is no doubt they were acquainted, as we shall see below. It is worth looking at evidence of early contacts between the Wilkinson family and the Pattesons and Johnsons.

On August 29th 1830 John Patteson wrote to his sister Marianne from North Walsham where he was at Paston Grammar School or Free School. Patteson refers to sending a letter with 'Anne Wilkinson going to Norwich', and to a 'Willm Wilkinson'; another, written not later than 1832, refers to various unspecified Wilkinsons.[36] These are not direct ancestors of the schoolmaster, Revd Walter George Wilkinson. His grandfather, Watts Wilkinson Snr had an elder brother who had two sons, Robert and John; Robert had a wife Anne Jennings, and John had several children, one of whom could have been William.[37] At any rate, the Revd W. G. Wilkinson and his father did have cousins who could well have been the Wilkinsons referred to by John Patteson. We

*Figure 23*
*Revd Walter George Wilkinson.*
*(by courtesy of Chris Wilkinson)*

can safely say that there was an acquaintance or friendship between the Patteson and Wilkinson families long before Theodore's education came to be considered.

A little later, in 1844, WCJ had a pupil 'Mr Wilkinson' to be confirmed and then to be ordained to a curacy at Bicester (LDDJ, 373); Mitchell refers to Walter G. Wilkinson, then 15, reading the lesson for William Cowper Johnson in 1844. Clearly 'Mr Wilkinson' the pupil to be ordained as a curate was not Walter G. Wilkinson, as the latter was born in 1829.

A little later still, there are further references to Walter G. Wilkinson in letters; a few of these are quoted by Mitchell. In 1868 we read that 'Guy Symonds is with with Mr Wilkinson at Lowestoft now' (LDDJ, 497). In 1869, Theodora Johnson writes to her brother Cowper (in India): 'Guy is very happy with the Wilkinsons. We do not see much of them they are so engaged with all the boys. Mr Wilkinson more upright & stiff than ever if such a thing is possible.' (LDDJ, 510) (What does that tell us about Mr Wilkinson?) In September 1869 a Johnson cousin, Henry, went to Mr Wilkinson at Happisburgh for coaching, and in 1869 also Marianne Johnson writes to Cowper: 'We heard from Mrs Wilkinson ... they are going to leave Lowestoft and have engaged a larger house at Alborough ... with a playground. They have now 18 boys, so they are prospering at present. She has just got a little daughter.' (LDDJ, 566) This was Christabel, who died of tuberculosis in 1895.

Finally, there is Mary Cowper Johnson's own comment to her brother, also in 1869: 'Fancy Mrs Wilk. having an infant, only think of it with hooked nose and screwed mouth!' (LDDJ, 567) Mitchell is fairly sure that Mary Cowper Johnson and Mrs Wilkinson had not met before the latter's marriage in 1867, and discounts Louis Wilkinson's explanation of girlhood friendship, but I do not think we should judge Mary's feelings for Mrs Wilkinson too precisely by her rather snide remark about the infant; it looks more like cheerful banter to a beloved brother. Certainly, there were regular contacts between Johnsons and Wilkinsons at this time, and there was evident satisfaction about Guy Symond's education. The previous references indicate that there were earlier contacts between the Wilkinson family and the Johnsons and Pattesons, themselves united by marriage in 1840.

We should not be surprised that when late in the century the problem of Theodore's education was being considered by his parents the Revd W. G. Wilkinson's school should have been suggested.

## Farming

Louis Wilkinson explained Theodore's coming to farm in Suffolk thus: 'A few years later he decided to become a farmer, and again his mother wrote to mine, asking if she knew of any farm where he could learn the business.'[35] The 'few years' is wrong, for he came to Suffolk, as we shall see, in March 1892, less than a year after finishing at Eaton House School at the age of 15, but it is perfectly correct that Louis Wilkinson's mother could help.

It was arranged that Theodore should go to a farm at Rendham, two miles outside Saxmundham, owned by the husband of Louis's mother's sister, Arthur McDougall. McDougall's two sons had been contemporaries of Theodore at Eaton House School. McDougall was a considerable property owner in' the neighbourhood, including property in Sweffling, which is less than a miles from Rendham, near White House Farm. Theodore records in a diary that he arrived at Rendham on March 1st 1892; there is a slightly fictionalised account of life at Rendham in Theodore's autobiographical sketch 'This is Thyself.[36]

Thus, Theodore served a sort of apprenticeship in farming at Rendham for two years from March 1892. He then went to the

Figure 24    The White House, Sweffling, Suffolk, front, 1999.

extreme north of Norfolk to Warham, almost on the coast near Wells-next-the-Sea for about a year, returning to Suffolk to his own farm in Sweffling. This was White House Farm (*Figure 24*); he began in October 1895 and gave up in 1901, returning to live in Dorset. Mitchell sets out the Norfolk connections which led to the choice of Warham on the initiative of Mary Cowper Powys. Mitchell points out that Theodore did his farming at a very bad time, with dropping prices of land. Contrary to what is sometimes asserted Theodore did not buy his farm, but was a tenant and paid £376 16s 2p for the lease. He employed five, sometime six, farm labourers; of the £2,000 advanced by his father, he spent just over £1,600.

Among Theodore's visitors at White House Farm were Louis Wilkinson himself and A. R. Powys, who made a faint pencil sketch (*Figure 25*).[37]

*Figure 25    The White House, Sweffling, Suffolk, pencil sketch
by A. R. Powys, in sketchbook dated July 16th 1895.*

NOTES

ILLUSTRATIONS  Modern photographs are by Stephen Powys Marks, taken on the visit of 1999; other images are of objects in his collection unless otherwise acknowledged.
*PSN* signifies *The Powys Society Newsletter.*

1 Andrew Rogers, 'Spring in East Anglia', *PSN* 37(1999), 24–6.
2 Stephen Powys Marks, 'An Earlier Diarist: Caroline Girle—Mrs Philip Lybbe Powys', *PSN* 43 (2001), 32–41.
3 Stephen Powys Marks, 'The Corpus Connection', *PSN* 32 (1997), 35–6.
4 Mary Barham Johnson, ed., *Letters and Diaries of the Norfolk Families of Donne and Johnson, 1766–1917* (1987), photocopied manuscript of 764 numbered pages plus numerous pedigrees, photographs and other illustrations, in 3 volumes (referred to as LDDJ).
5 These papers were inherited by Mary BJ's niece Margaret Sharman, and on her death in 2001 passed to her son and daughter.
6 These papers consist of perhaps 200 letters to and from Mary Cowper Johnson (i.e. before her marriage) or Mary Cowper Powys (after her marriage) and to and from her father William Cowper Johnson and her mother Marianne, including letters from the 1830s onwards. The material inherited also includes a very small number of pockect diaries and mementos of C. F. Powys's elder brother Littleton Albert Powys kept by his mother Amelia (see note 17).
7 Margaret Sharman, 'The Tanner "In a Large Way"' [John Johnson], *PSN* 40 (2000), 42–6.
8 Howard Colvin, *A Biographical Dictionary of British Architects 1600–1840*, 3rd edition (New Haven and London: Yale University Press, 1995), 625–6.
9 Tom Garland, *The Monumental Inscriptions of the Church and Churchyard of St Peter, Yaxham, Norfolk* (Mid-Norfolk Family History Society, 1998).
10 I. K. Patteson, *Henry Staniforth Patteson, A Memoir* (1899), with pedigree, 62.
11 John Cowper Powys, *The Diaries for 1929*, ed. Anthony Head (London: Cecil Woolf, 1998), 58–63.
12 At least three photographs were taken on this occasion, the two reproduced in this volume and another seated version which was reproduced in 'The Powys Mother', page 63 (see note 15), and is slightly different from figure 19. The original of figure 19 has a letter D on the back, and that of the frontispiece the letter A; both are dated as given here, not 1913 or 1914 as stated by Mary BJ. The copy of the frontispiece photograph reproduced on page 6 has the following identification:
   'Photograph of the brothers and sisters of the Misses Cowper Johnson when they lived at 9 The Close about 1910: left to right, 1 Mrs Wm Cowper Johnson (Emily B.J), 2 Reggie Blyth (nephew), 3 Rev. C Blyth, 4 Aunt Annie Blyth, 5 Aunt Etta CJ, 6 Rev W Cowper Johnson, 7 Aunt Kate–Mrs Mowbray Donne, 8 Mrs Powys–Aunt Mary, 9 Uncle Charles Powys, 10 Aunt Dora C.J.'
13 I have one of his letters home from Stalbridge.
14 Amelia Powys, 'Recollections of Little Children', *PSN* 25 (1995), 36–43; see p. 37.
15 Mary Barham Johnson, 'The Powys Mother', *The Powys Review* 8 (1981), 57–64; see page 60.      16 SPM collection.

[17] Quoted in Stephen Powys Marks, 'Mary Cowper Johnson', *PSN* 24 (1995), 4–8; see p. 6.

[18] Much of the historical information in this section is taken from the *Memoir* of H. S. Patteson: see note 10. The name Patteson has no 'r'.

[19] Nikolaus Pevsner and Bill Wilson, *The Buildings of England: Norfolk 1: Norwich and North-East*, 2nd edition (London: Penguin Books,1997), 308.

[20] Nikolaus Pevsner, *The Buildings of England: Suffolk*, 2nd edition (Harmondsworth: Penguin Books, 1974), 380.

[21] Patteson, *Memoirs*, 50.

[22] Stephen Powys Marks, 'John Cowper Powys's "great-grandfather from Hamburg"', with Livius genealogy, *PSN* 37(199), 14–17.

[23] 'JCP Honoured', *PSN* 36 (1999), 38–9.

[24] A. H. Foster-Barham, *Fosters & Foster-Barhams: Genealogy of the Descendants of Roger Foster of Edrestone* (London: Adam and Charles Black, 1897).

[25] Catharine B. Johnson, *William B. Donne and his Friends* (London: Methuen & Co., 1905), with Donne pedigree.

[26] Patrick Bury, *The College of Corpus Christi and the Blessed Virgin Mary: A history from 1822 to 1952* (Cambridge, 1952).

[27] *Alumni Cantabrigienses*: Greene, Johnson, Patteson, Powys. *Alumni Oxonienses* also contains a very large number of Powys entries.

[28] Letter dated August 5th 1909 (SPM collection).          [29] SPM collection.

[30] Richard Harraden (1756–1838) and his son Richard Bankes Harraden (1778–1862) produced several sets of views of Cambridge, the earliest in 1799. The son published *Illustrations of the University of Cambridge* in 1830, comprising 54 views, 24 of which had appeared in earlier works. *(DNB)*

[31] J. Lawrence Mitchell, 'The Education of T. F. Powys', *The Powys Review* 19 (1986), 3–19; and, 'One foot in the furrow: T. F. Powys in East Anglia', *The Powys Review* 23 (1989), 3–24.

[32] Louis Wilkinson, 'Some Memories of T. F. Powys', in *Theodore: Essays on T. F. Powys*, ed. Father Brocard Sewell (Aylesford, Kent: St Albert's Press, 1964), 10. Louis Marlow [Wilkinson], *Seven Friends* (London: Richards Press, 1953), 90.

[33] SPM collection.

[34] I am indebted to Roland Wilkinson for explaining the intricacies of the Wilkinson family.

[35] Wilkinson, 'Some Memories of T. F. Powys', 10.

[36] T. F. Powys, 'This is Thyself', Introduced and annotated by J. Lawrence Mitchell, edited by Belinda Humfrey, *The Powys Review* 20 (1987), 5–26.

[37] SPM collection.

OTHER SOURCES

A Commonplace book given to Eleanor Powys, sister of Revd L. C. Powys, in 1820, with extensive genealogical and historical material inserted by G. M. Powys and another, including numerous pedigrees (SPM collection).

B *Victoria County History of Northamptonshire, Genealogical Volume: Northamptonshire Families*, ed. Oswald Barron (1906); pages 255–67 deal with the families of Powys Lord Lilford and Powys at Montacute.

C Helen Belgion, *Titchmarsh Past and Present* (Titchmarch, Northants, 1979).

D Stephen Powys Marks, 'What's in a name?', *PSN* 28 (1996), 18–23, with pedigree.

SUSAN RANDS

# The Powys-Fox Connection

In *Autobiography* John Cowper Powys tells us that 'his father's eyes used to burn with a fire that was at once secretive and blazing like the fire in the eyes of a long discrowned king when he told us how we were descended from the ancient Welsh Princes of Powysland';[1] this greatly impressed John Cowper and during his long life he became increasingly interested in lordship and race, in genes, genealogy and inherited characteristics of all kinds. Most of the characters of the great Wessex novels are relatively humble but even in these there are 'magnates'; Lord Carfax in *Wolf Solent,* The Marquis of P in *A Glastonbury Romance* and Mr. Comber, the newspaper proprietor in *Maiden Castle,* wield their influence with more effect than effort. However, the heroes of the two great Welsh novels of his old age are princes, and the hosts of characters are the crowds of people who constitute their courts and those of their enemies, and the scribes who keep the records, Rhisiart in *Owen Glendower* and the Henog in *Porius.* The more important the characters, particularly in *Porius,* the more we are told of their lineage; 'race' is inescapably significant in determining character and aptitudes.

Had his father spoken with the same fire of more immediate relations and ancestors, might John Cowper have written of them? That he knew something of them is shown in a letter to Louis Wilkinson of 2 May 1956:

> I saw 'The Bird Man' — who introduced 'The Little Owl' into the British Isles — once when I was with my father fishing, but he didn't see us and we went on to the church called Achurch where the Birdman's father has a monument with a long poem by Matthew Prior ... and where our uncle Littleton has a monument. It must have been the Birdman's son Stephen

with whom Lulu and Alyse once had tea in London and who became the lord after the death of, I think, his brother.[2]

'The Birdman' was of course Thomas Littleton Powys, fourth Baron Lilford, an eminent ornithologist,[3] and John Cowper was quite right about his son John, in fact the second son, the first having died young, being the fifth Baron Lilford, and his younger brother, Stephen being the sixth.[4]

That John Cowper was interested in monuments and heraldic symbols frequently appears; an early example is the use he made of the carving above the porch of Stoke-sub-Hamdon church in *Wood and Stone*; a more obscure but very typical example occurs in the description of Gypsy May's caravan in *Weymouth Sands*:

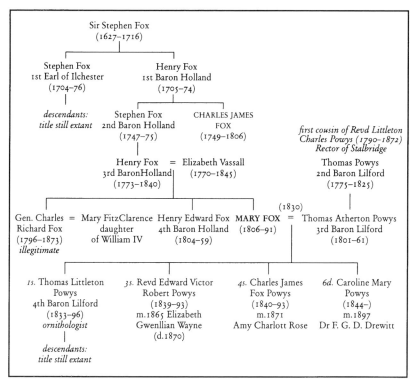

*Outline family tree of the Fox and Powys families.*

*Lady Mary Fox*
*engraved by M. I. Danforth from a painting by C. R. Leslie.*

Two supercilious china dogs, looking as if they had been stolen from the drive gates of the Earl of Ilchester, and as if nothing short of an Earl, or at least a Baron, would cause them to drop a fraction of their contempt for the generality of mankind, stood at either end of the dresser's lowest shelf, just above the stove.[5]

Two such dogs do indeed grace the gate post of the back drive that goes from Evershot to Melbury Park, the seat of the Earl of Ilchester in Dorset and it is surprising that they are *dogs,* for the Ilchester arms, and most of the monuments and ornaments about the Park and church are foxes, the family name being Fox-Strangways. This is a humorous and peripheral use of heraldic beasts; a much more integral use is made in *Maiden Castle* of the lions, or whatever they may be, on the gate-posts of Stalbridge Park, next to the rectory where the grandfather, Littleton Charles, of the Montacute Powyses, and his family, lived for so many years, and where their father grew up.[6]

Littleton Charles was a first cousin of the second Baron Lilford, their fathers being brothers. One of the second baron's grandsons, Edward Victor Robert Powys, third son of the third baron, was the rector of Thorpe Achurch, the parish mentioned in John Cowper's' letter, and in which stood Lilford Hall, the family seat. I first met Edward Powys in circumstances that surprised me, in the prefatory note to John Drinkwater's biography of *Charles James Fox*, published in 1928;[7] Edward Powys had allowed Drinkwater 'free use' of a number of his 'great grand-uncle's' letters and 'the manuscript diaries of Mrs Fox', the wife of Charles James Fox. Drinkwater quotes many interesting extracts from these which subsequent biographers seem to have overlooked. The papers must have come to Edward from his mother Mary, neé Fox, although why they came to him rather than to any other of his three brothers and his six sisters is a mystery.

Mary Fox was the only daughter of Charles James's nephew, the third Baron Holland and his famous wife Elizabeth who had entertained at Holland House all the leading politicians, writers and artists of their day. Orphaned as a baby, Henry, third Lord Holland had become the protégé of his famous uncle, and hence the recipient of these papers; he must have left them to Mary who entrusted them to her third son, who was thus the keeper of most valuable historical evidence.

Born in 1839 Edward Victor Robert Powys was a godson of Queen Victoria. His father, the third Baron Lilford, had been Lord-in-waiting to William IV as well as to Queen Victoria. This must have come about through his brother-in-law, General Sir Charles Richard Fox, the illegitimate elder brother of Lilford's wife, Mary. General Fox had the same parents as Mary but was born before they were married, as his mother had been unable to get divorced from her first husband in time. His illegitimacy seems to have been no bar to his happiness and preferment; he married Mary FitzClarence, his second choice from the illegitimate daughters of the long and happy union of William IV and the actress Dorothy Jordan. As Aide-de-camp to the King, and equerry to the widowed Queen Adelaide, he was much at court, and wrote to his younger brother, the fourth and last baron Holland, an interesting account of the king's final days and death bed.[8] He must have brought his brother-in-law into royal circles with him. Lilford, however, was dismissed three years after the king's death

*General Charles Richard Fox, by C. Landseer.*

44

but not before he had had time to make Queen Victoria a god-mother of his third son.

It is not apparent that Edward Powys derived any benefit from being the Queen's godson. He graduated from Queens' College, Cambridge in 1864, was ordained deacon in 1865, the year he married Elizabeth Gwenllian Wayne, only daughter and heir of William Watkyn Wayne of Plas Newydd, S. Wales.[9] Edward's first curacy was Danby Wiske, in Yorkshire, his second Southwold in Suffolk (1867–69); he was then vicar of St Nicholas, Warwick (1869–71) and of Thorpe Achurch, the family living, from 1872 to 1877. His four children Mervyn 1866, Helen 1867, George 1868 and Edward 1870 were born in quick succession; their mother died only two weeks after the birth of Edward, and only he and Mervyn survived to adulthood. Between leaving Achurch in 1877 and the date of his last living in Kemsing, Kent (1888–89) there is a curious gap in the career of E.V.R. Powys in which we hear of him in a another surprising capacity.[10]

In 1881 or 1882 he advertised in *The Times* for a travelling companion. The successful applicant was the young Alfred Harmsworth then aged seventeen, who became the great newspaper magnate Lord Northcliffe. As a youth he had just suffered the opprobium of getting the family maid with child, and had then had pneumonia; he needed a change to escape disgrace and to recover from illness. Evidently he and Powys 'set off from Boundary Road in a hansom cab waved good-bye from the windows by the assembled family. Alfred and his friend jingled down the road to Victoria and the boat train, and a leisurely tour of France that kept him out of the way for months.'[11] No record seems to exist of where they went, what they did or indeed of when they returned.

Alfred was, apparently, and photographs confirm it, a very good-looking youth, 'a picture of radiant health, buoyant, athletic looking, and easy and graceful in all his movements. His manners, too, were very delightful. As for the rest he seemed to be merely a careless onlooker on life. Nothing appeared to concern or ruffle or greatly interest him; but he had observant eyes, with a rather soft and caressing expression but also full of enquiry. They were eyes that warded off enquiry from the other side. He was friendly but

45

aloof ... .'[12] Soon after his return from the continent his journalistic
and publishing career gathered speed to such an extent that he could
afford to marry. Edward Powys conducted the service at Hampstead
Parish church, and 'remembered it as a very pretty wedding, made by
the youth and good looks of the bride and groom.'[13]

At some time Edward Powys became a member like his elder
brother, 'The Bird Man', of the Oriental Club in Hanover Square, and
belonged to it until the end of his long life. It had been founded in
1824, 'as a refuge for East India Company servants from the loneliness and unfamiliarity of home'. The company was dissolved and
from then on most members were the heads of the great merchant
houses of Calcutta, Bombay, Madras, Rangoon, Colombo; many
became the directors of banks or shipping companies; 'the general
belief was that affairs of tea and rubber plantations were largely
decided in comfortable corners of the Oriental's smoking room ... as
the club grew older in an ever deepening patina of dark mahogany,
dark carpets, huge dark pictures and a great deal of buff-coloured
paint.'[14] For E. V. R. Powys it seems to have been a home from home.
In the summary of his will *The Times* gives his address as Rutland
Court which is only a mile and a half from Hanover Square. Powys left
legacies to five of the club's servants. The bulk of his assets he left to
his son Mervyn, or his sons, or the current baron Lilford; but none of
these were to inherit if they became members of the Roman Catholic
Church. He originally intended to leave his 'large silver gilt cup with
cover and the case containing gold knife and fork and spoon (being
christening gifts to me from her Majesty Queen Victoria)' to Mervyn
but revokes this without saying who is to be the beneficiary instead.
To his two sons Mervyn and Edward he left 'such of his theological
and historical books as they may choose and the remainder of such
books to the rector and church wardens of Thorpe Achurch for the
use of successive rectors'.[15]

It appears that the sixth Lord Ilchester and his mother were
'assiduous in gathering Holland House papers that had descended to
the Powys family'.[16] Edward Powys had been invited to lunch at
Holland House and promised to bequeath General Fox's papers to
the Ilchesters. Many of these were letters from his younger brother

Henry, fourth Lord Holland, his father the third Lord Holland and his aunt Caroline Fox which had been given to Powys by General Fox's widow, his second wife, Katherine Moberly. The Ilchesters also received letters from Edward's youngest sister, Caroline Drewitt who had used them in her account of the 'Bird Man'.[17] She told Lady Ilchester that Charles Fox's illegitimate daughters, Miss Marston and Miss Willoughby, used to visit Lilford Hall in her childhood and Miss Willoughby in particular was much liked by her parents because she used to bring presents for the children.

At the time of his death Edward Powys still had Fox papers and possessions in his hands for in his will he bequeaths his Gold Seal, 'A Fox seated on a cushion with a bloodstone having the device of a hand holding an ear with the word "Remember" engraved thereon which formerly belonged to the Right Honourable Charles James Fox and my large brass mounted oak chest with brass plate inscribed with the name of the Earl of Ilchester including several volumes of the Fox MSS usually contained therein and also the large fan which belonged formerly to Elizabeth Vassall third Lady Holland to the person who at the time of my death shall be the Trustee of the Settlement under which the Earl of Ilchester will be tenant for life of (inter alia) the Mansion House known as Holland Park.'[18] Although Holland House was destroyed by a bomb in 1940 many of the papers therein had already been removed to Melbury. We can be grateful to Edward Powys for what he kept so safely and hope that his mother's diary may yet come to light.

It is time to return to this lady. Her mother, Elizabeth Vassall Holland, was probably the most remarkable hostess of the first half of the nineteenth century only rivalled by the third Lady Lansdowne. When she died Lord Greville wrote, 'all who had been accustomed to live at Holland House and continued to be her habituées will lament over the fall of that curtain on that long drama and the final extinction of the flickering remnant of social light that illuminated and adorned England and even Europe for half a century. The world never had seen and never will see again anything like Holland House. [...] Lady Holland contrived to assemble around her to the last a great society comprising every body that was conspicuous, remarkable and agreeable ... She cared very little for her children but she sometimes pretended to care for them.'[19] Growing up in such a household may have been interesting but it could not have been comfortable. It is unfortunate that most of the diaries that Mary kept seem to have been lost. She was a great favourite with her younger brother Henry who, in his journal, frequently refers to her beauty and virtue and says that he 'never saw a man worthy of such a high-minded, noble girl,' 'so amiable, so sensible, so clever with such an admirable understanding and such a noble perfect heart that she is the pride and pleasure of my existence'.[20]

When Mary was seventeen she was presented at court by Lady Lansdowne who was also kind to John Cowper's 'ideal woman', Lady Charlotte Guest, when she wanted to give a party. Mary had stayed at Bowood, the Lansdowne's country seat near Calne in Wiltshire, at least once when she was younger, for her brother remembers her after staying there, 'overflowing in gratitude to Lady Lansdowne and not yet aware that that excessive warmth and empressement of manner disguises the coldest heart and the least affectionate feelings.'[21] Most

*Hon. Henry Edward Fox, later 4th Lord Holland, by C. R. Leslie.*

accounts of Louisa Lansdowne are favourable so the harsh judgment of Lord Holland is intriguing; was he more perceptive than others or had he a particular grudge and, if the latter, what could it have been? Or did he simply misjudge Louisa whose endless social duties often put her under great strain? To Mary she must have seemed easier company, at least, than her own mother.

Sydney Smith (1771–1845), the eminent Divine and wit, describes Mary in Paris when she was eighteen, 'a bright, good, amiable little thing, rather too precise but a perfectly amiable little soul [...] always surrounded by Beaux, one of whom was Prince Frederick of Prussia'.[22] However, a letter from Lady Granville to her sister describes Mary's predicament a year or two later in relation to her mother: 'she is so tied by the leg, watched by the eye, so regulated, so tamed, so not to say this, not to do that, not to go there, not to stay here, to cut this man, to avoid that girl that she has lost all effect in society ... her very beaury suffers from it. She has no spirits, no expression, no conversation. Yet she is not low, she is not grave, she is not foolish. She sits by the side of our ladies and answers very prettily when spoken to. I never saw so many advantages thrown away.'[23] Two years later Lady Holland, also, was writing to her son in flattering terms about Mary:

> Mary is really a very surprizing German scholar I am told, & from her correspondence with her masters & the facility with which she translates, it really appears to be so. She is a very excellent person, so steady & well judging, & full of every right & honourable feeling. She is become quite a comfort to us all; & I begin to dread that encreasing, so as to make it a pang whenever she marries. Yet one cannot be so selfish, with all her beauty, modesty, innocence & charms, to wish to keep her from the comforts of a family of her own; but it will now be a cruel loss to us, dear girl.[24]

In April 1830 Mary accepted Thomas Powys, third Baron Lilford; as described by Sydney Smith he sounds very like a character in one of John Cowper Powys's novels: 'He is like an Apothecary in no great practice. I could not, were I a damsel, marry him. He is a quiz, not slightly or superficially but his heart beats and his blood circulates quizzically; it is an incurable case. He would make all London awkward before London could make him like other people and put him at his ease.'²⁵ According to his mother-in-law 'he never swerved from the most devoted love' for Mary and 'the whole decision and choice has been her own doing'.²⁶ They were married by special license in the library of Holland Park on 24 May 1830 and went to live at Lilford Hall, a handsome Jacobean mansion in its own extensive park on the bank of the river Nene in Northamptonshire. There they brought up four sons and six daughters all born in the first thirteen years of their marriage. The first child was a daughter called Adelaide, after the queen, the second a son, Thomas Littleton; Lord Holland noted in his journal for June 1833: 'assisted at the christening of my grandson, T. Powys'.²⁷

In 1859 when Mary's dearly loved brother Henry, fourth and last Lord Holland died, her friend Harriet Mundy of Markeaton wrote to commiserate. Lord Lilford's reply, written from Lilford Hall and dated 4 January 1860, survives:

My dear Mrs Mundy,
    We both feel deeply your and Mundy's kindness in your inquiries after poor dear Mary.
    She has indeed suffered sadly from this severe shock which though not wholly unexpected (and for a time we had some faint hopes) yet when it did come was to her quite overwhelming. Yet I think the constant uncertainty of the telegraphic messages and the delay in their transmission was almost more trying to her nerves than the fatal news when at last it did come.
    She is now I am thankful to say much more composed and at times cheerful, surrounded as we are by married and unmarried sons and daughters and the kindness and real sympathy of those who knew the mutual strong affection which subsisted so long between Henry and herself has much soothed and fortified her.
    She feels most severely however the extinction of the name

which she has long so long and so dearly prized.
Yours most sincerely
Lilford

This kind, conscientious husband died the following year.[28]
Mary outlived him by thirty years. Her will is surprisingly brief. She
left money to her servants, to the Minister and churchwardens of
St Marylebone, in London, and of Thorpe Achurch and Pilton at
Lilford for the benefit of the poor, and one hundred pounds to each of
her grand-daughters, Rachel Burroughs and Florence Crighton: to
her youngest daughter Caroline, unmarried at the time of her death,
she left one thousand pounds and all her household effects; everything else, valued at £12,946 11d. was to be shared between this
daughter and Mary's youngest son, Charles James Fox, a Colonel in
the sixty-ninth regiment.[29] He married Amy Charlotte Rose of
Woolston Heath, and died aged fifty-three without issue only two
years after his mother. His name was the last to perpetuate the Powys
connection with England's greatest Republican and John Cowper's
favourite of all our Politicians.[30]

*[notes overleaf]*

*Lilford Hall, the south or entrance front.*

51

## NOTES

1 John Cowper Powys, *Autobiography* (London: Pan Books, Picador, 1982), 26.
2 John Cowper Powys, *Letters of John Cowper Powys to Louis Wilkinson, 1935–1956* (London: Village Press, 1974), 363–4.
3 Susan Rands, 'Fourth Lord Lilford' *The Powys Newsletter* 34 (1998), 31–35.
4 Oswald Barron, ed., *Victoria County History of Northamptonshire Geneological Volume* (London: Archibald Constable and Company, 1906), 266.
5 John Cowper Powys, *Weymouth Sands* (London: Pan Books, Picador, 1980), 139.
6 Susan Rands, 'The Gateposts of Stalbridge Park' *The Powys Review* 25 (1990), 54–5.
7 John Drinkwater, *Charles James Fox* (London: Ernest Benn, 1928).
8 Abraham D. Kriegal, ed., *The Holland House Diaries 1831–1840: The Diary of Henry Richard Vassall Fox, Third Lord Holland, with Extracts from the Diary of Dr. John Allen* (London: Routledge and Kegan Paul, 1977).
9 Barron, 1906, 265.
10 J. A. Venn, *Alumni Cantabrigienses*, Pt 2, Vol. 5 (Cambridge UP, 1940), 178.
11 Paul Ferris, *The House of Northcliffe: The Harmsworths of Fleet Street* (London: Weidenfeld and Nicolson, 1971), 24–5.
12 Aaron Watson, *A Newspaper Man's Memories* (London: Allen and Unwin, 1930).
13 Ferris, 1971, 32.
14 Denis Mostyn Forrest, *The Oriental: The Life Story of a West End Club*, 2nd edition (London: Batsford, 1979), 235, 149.
15 Public Records Office: Will of E. V. R. Powys.
16 Dr Christopher Wright of the British Library, Letter to Susan Rands, 15 October 2001.
17 Caroline Mary Powys Drewitt, *Lord Lilford Thomas Littleton, Fourth Baron F. Z. S. President of the British Ornithologists' Union: A Memoir by his Sister* (London: Smith, Elder & Co., 1900), *passim.*
18 Public Records Office: Will of Mary, third Lady Lilford.
19 Roger Fulford, ed., *The Greville Memoirs* (London: Batsford, 1963), 211–12.
20 Ilchester, Giles Stephen Holland Fox-Strangways, ed., *The Journal of Henry Edward Fox, the 4th Lord Holland* (London: T. Butterworth, 1923), 94, 189.
21 *Ibid.*, 50.
22 Sydney Smith, *Letters,* ed. Nowell C. Smith (Oxford: Clarendon Press, 1953), 155–6.
23 Quoted by Ilchester, *Letters of Elizabeth, Lady Holland to Her Son, 1821–1845* (London: John Murray, 1946), 40.
24 *Ibid.*, 50.
25 Sydney Smith, *op. cit.*, Letter to Lady Grey, 16 August 1829.
26 *Lady Holland to Her Son, op. cit.*, 109.
27 *The Holland House Diaries, op. cit.*, 224.
28 Letter of Lord Lilford to Harriet Mundy (Private Collection).
29 Public Records Office: Will of Mary, third Lady Lilford.
30 John Cowper Powys, *Letters to Louis Wilkinson, op. cit.*, 361.

BARBARA OZIEBLO

# The Poet Gamel Woolsey:
# The Creation of a Mythical Middle-Earth

The model for Llewelyn Powys's Dittany Stone, Gamel Woolsey (1895–1968), would have been, if we are to believe the narrator of the 'imaginary autobiography' *Love and Death*, seductive and mischievous like Nimue, who trapped Merlin in his own dream of love, but gave him nothing in return.[1] The accounts we have of Woolsey, however, do not allow us to picture her as a Lady of the Lake, luring gallant knights to their doom. On the whole, we are told that she was languid and dreamy, and preferred to sit in the sun with a cat on her lap, the *New Yorker* on the ground at her feet covered by a pile of science-fiction magazines. That, at least, is the image that her husband, Gerald Brenan has left us with. Others that knew her, such as John Whitworth, stress her sense of humour and her liveliness;[2] but all affirm that she had early created a private world for herself, a legendary 'middle earth' in which she preferred to dwell. As Powys says of Dittany, 'our real world was her shadow-world and our shadow-world was her actual world' (48).

The poems Woolsey published in the collection *Middle Earth* (1931),[3] reveal this private, sorrowful and yet tentatively hopeful life she had fashioned, the last quatrain of the title poem summing up her attitude to life:

> It is not heaven, it is not hell,
> This world between them where I dwell.
> With secret pain, with open mirth,
> I go my way on middle earth. (12)

Woolsey took the title of *Middle Earth* from the popular ballad 'Clerk Saunders', in which the insouciant cocks crow airily on 'merry middle-earth' even when maid Margaret's lover has been killed by one of her brothers, when she had been found lying in his arms. Lines 77 and 78 are reproduced on the title page of the 1931 volume (but omitted in Kenneth Hopkins's edition):

> O cocks are crowing on merry middle-earth,
> I wot the wild fowls are boding day.[4]

By the time Woolsey published *Middle Earth* she had survived a number of bouts with TB, an unhappy marriage, three miscarriages or abortions, and had abruptly ended a passionate love affair with Llewelyn Powys by marrying Gerald Brenan — not to mention her father's death when she was an adolescent, and her mother's drinking. It is a disturbing collection of poems that attests the author's developing gift and her extreme sensitivity, and makes one wonder why she did not write and publish more. I hope that this essay will throw light on Gamel Woolsey's experiences and poetic ambition and also suggest answers to this question that perplexes her biographer, and surely her readers too.

'All that the child remembers now', the opening poem of *Middle Earth* — the only collection of her poetry that Woolsey saw published — glosses all the stories that moulded her imagination. The white geese on her counterpane, London Bridge, Banbury Cross, Brer Rabbit, all the princes and princesses of fairyland come together in an impersonal, passive pageant in her memory. She recognizes that her bed 'was close to fairyland' (2); but it is only the Unicorns and other fabulous creatures that approach 'Out of the mythical unknown/ By some strange cord of fancy led' (3). Tellingly, these creatures that guard her sleep contrast with Dah, the non-stereotypical mammy whose stories of Brer Rabbit are 'alien to the English blood' (7) and who 'does not care, her task is done,/ Another child is put to bed' (3). But it is not the African tales alone that the child finds alien; her imagination is only stirred when masculine deeds of daring are required. So she envisages herself riding with her father's men to the hunt and is transformed into the 'Youngest Son' who wears magic shoes and scales the 'glassy tower' (8) to rescue the imprisoned Princess. She begs for a place on the prow of Osiris' ship, and is now

Roland, now Oliver on the bloodied fields of Roncesvalles (10).
Roland and Oliver, of course, die on the battlefield in a vain act of
courage which centuries of readers have applauded; the courage with
which Woolsey struggled to fulfill the role 'Of Woman, and of Wife'
— as Emily Dickinson had starkly put it (Poem 732) — while at the
same time working to realize her literary ambitions, has never been
recognized. Neither has her small, but accomplished, *oeuvre*. In her
second novel, *Patterns on the Sand* — still to be published — Woolsey
draws a realistic and harrowing picture of what it meant to be a young
woman in her native Charleston in the early twentieth century.[5] All
that her protagonist can do is wait for something to happen, and all
that can happen to a young woman is for a man to fall in love with her.
In *One Way of Love*,[6] written roughly at the same time as Woolsey was
preparing the manuscript for *Middle Earth*, Mariana too waits for love
to assuage her loneliness, and she 'had a curious fear that if she were
not to find a lover she would be lonely in another world as well as in
this' (36).

Woolsey, like her heroine Mariana, however, did not find happiness
in love. She had met Llewelyn Powys in that legendary Greenwich
Village cul-de-sac, Patchin Place, which has been home to so many
literary figures. Powys and his wife, Alyse Gregory, had left New York
for England in 1925, where they had settled on the White Nose in
Dorset, but they were back for a few months at the end of 1927, in
rooms at No 5. Powys was to write a series of articles for the *New York
Herald Tribune* and Gregory, starved of the literary companionship
and stimulus she had been used to when working for *The Dial*, must
have looked forward to seeing her old friends again, and to visiting her
parents. She knew that Betty, Powys's previous flame, was in Europe,
and surely did not suspect that her husband would find another love in
New York. She would meet Gamel Woolsey on the stairs, but paid
little attention to her; one day Woolsey left a poem, 'Spring in
England', in their letter box.[7] Woolsey was at this time trying to end
her marriage with Rex Hunter, who, if *One Way of Love* is indeed the
autobiographical novel that Gerald Brenan claimed it to be — and it
does coincide with what we know of Woolsey's life — considered her
a piece of property for his use and pleasure. Alan, Mariana's husband

in the novel, 'did not like to go about with a wife. It made him, he felt, a less romantic figure' (131). Woolsey, as Mariana in the novel, had been deeply hurt by Alan/Hunter's refusal to be pleased at the child she had conceived, and yet felt a delicious 'feeling of freedom' (229) when she left him. According to Richard Perceval Graves, the real Hunter was not willing to allow his wife to leave him easily, and Woolsey was 'enduring a long and final series of visits' from him at the time she met Llewelyn Powys.[8]

The love between Powys and Woolsey has been well documented through their letters, published in 1973 by Malcolm Elwin and in 1983 by Kenneth Hopkins, and, of course, in Gregory's diaries, published as *The Cry of the Gull*.[9] Just as the situation between the three was becoming unsustainable for Woolsey, she met Gerald Brenan, who appeared to her as a rescuing knight and who was delighted to play that role; he was, as he himself put it, looking for a wife (he had recently heard that Juliana, an Andalusian serving girl with whom he had had a passionate affair in Yegen, in the Spanish Alpujarras, had given birth to his daughter).[10] After a couple of outings, Woolsey, quite taken by this talkative young man who carried about him the aura of poet and writer connected to the Bloomsbury circle (he had not yet published anything of note), showed him her poems and the manuscript of her novel. He did not care much for the poems; according to his biographer, Jonathan Gathorne-Hardy, 'Gamel's skill as a poet came too close to Gerald's most precious ambition', although Gathorne-Hardy considers that 'the worst of her poems are better than the best of Gerald's' — a somewhat backhanded compliment.[11] The unfinished novel, however, captured Brenan's imagination, and he fell in love with its author. In the diaries he kept throughout his life and on which he would later base *Personal Record*, he expatiated on the wonders of Woolsey's talent, on her 'exquisite sensibility ... the integrity and straightforwardness of her mind and character ... the quality and precision [of her writing] ... the surprising beauty of the images.'[12] In *Personal Record* he dwelt more on the novel's faults, of which he was, he says, immediately aware; all the same, he did what he could to find a publisher for the manuscript. Gathorne-Hardy's interpretation of the working of a gentleman's mind leads him to comment that 'The writer's key to a woman's heart (or bed) is not dancing but the promise to get her novel or poems published' (255) and, at this time, Brenan was willing to try such a ploy. He sent the manuscript to David (Bunny) Garnett of the Nonesuch Press, but his friend was not overly enthusiastic; he preferred Woolsey's poems, although he did praise the scenes in the novel 'where she writes about going to bed', which he considered had a 'trustful[,] unforced, natural quality'.[13] Brenan, too, always the vicarious lover, had remarked on these moments, as would most people; Frances Partridge, who was 'enthralled' by the novel, enjoyed the 'descriptions of love-making' most, and thought they were 'the best, without a moments' doubt, that I have ever read in modern literature'.[14]

In spite of Brenan's good intentions, it seems that the Powys connection proved more useful for it was Victor Gollancz, the recently established radical publisher, who had brought out a number of novels by Louis Wilkinson, Llewelyn Powys's friend, that accepted the manuscript.[15] But it was not a lucky choice: Gollancz had *One Way of Love* typeset and the proofs dispatched to Woolsey before he realized that the content of the novel might bring him trouble, and stopped publication. In those years immediately after the obscenity trials involving *Lady Chatterley's Lover* and *The Well of Loneliness* publishers probably did well to be careful; late in 1931 Gollancz had been forced to withdraw Rosalind Wade's *Children, Be Happy!* following a libel case involving sexual explicitness.[16] This made him wary, even though (at least to our twenty-first century sensibilities — or lack of them) we find nothing in the least offensive in Woolsey's novel. But David Garnett would admit that he had come 'to the conclusion that it was very likely to be seized';[17] the more sophisticated Virginia Woolf was quite scathing, however, both of Woolsey's novel and Gollancz's decision: 'Well then the indecent novel by Mrs Gerald Brenan has come our way, and for half a sniff I don't see much to it — trembling like an aspen, she says that men co-co-copulate with women. That's a fact. Did you know it?' she wrote to Clive Bell on 29 February 1932.[18]

Gollancz's defection was a blow to Woolsey; she would not return to her novel again till almost the end of her life when she had a copy of the proofs bound; she gave this copy the elegiac title, *Innocence*, and, underneath, placed the following lines from William Blake's 'To the Accuser Who is the God of this World':

Truly, my Satan, thou art but a Dunce,
And dost not know the Garment from the Man
Every Harlot was a Virgin once
Nor canst thou ever change Kate into Nan.

This copy of *Innocence/One Way of Love* is in the British Library, sent there by Gerald Brenan not three weeks after Woolsey's death, with a letter to the Chief Librarian (5 February 1968) explaining that: 'As my wife was a close friend of all the Powys family as well as of Arthur Waley and Bertrand Russell, this autobiographical novel, which reflects her temperament, ... has an interest which its merits do not justify' [*sic*].[19] Presumably, Brenan had forgotten his initial enthusiastic response to his wife's novel, which was eventually published by Virago, in 1987, under the original title, and without Blake's bitter, accusatory lines.

The relationship between Woolsey and Brenan was complicated from the start by jealousies and rivalries; she would never completely free herself from the hold Llewelyn Powys had over her, and neither would he forget his obsessive love for Carrington. Although both were presumably pleased with the literary successes of the other, Gathorne-Hardy, who is on the whole sympathetic toward Woolsey, shows how complex such pleasure must have been. He offers a perceptive insight into their relationship when he suggests that Brenan was 'slightly irritated [that Woolsey] got so much money': $850, for a science-fiction story, 'The Star of Double Darkness' published by the *Saturday Evening Post*, 18 June 1955.[20] Brenan's irritation in this case was possibly also caused by his annoyance that Woolsey spent her time reading and writing science-fiction stories, when she should have been doing more translating, which he believed she did well, and which could have brought her a steady income — or perhaps he was annoyed because she left the running of the house to the servants, or because she was not industriously typing his manuscripts for him, a chore she hated.

Woolsey's work as typist (the accepted thing for a wife to do) began early on in her relationship with Brenan; when they were in Yegen in 1933, Brenan, in an attempt to 'exorcise' Carrington, wrote a journal of his love for the painter, from 1925 to Carrington's death in 1932.[21] Woolsey typed it for him; admittedly, the affair had taken place before they met, but all the same, his need to relive it in minute detail — and his desire to share this with her — could hardly have made for gratifying work, even if typing had been her favorite pastime. Many years later, by which time her secretarial skills must surely have improved (she had typed *The Spanish Labyrinth* and *The Literature of the Spanish People* by then), after typing out Brenan's *A Life of One's Own* (1961), she wrote to Phyllis Playter: 'I've just finished typing Gerald's Autobiography. I'm such a poor inaccurate typist that I felt it a terrible task, but it is finished at last.'[22] And, on another occasion, in an undated letter to Annie Davis she wrote that she had recovered sufficiently from a trip to England and Paris 'to be able to work on Gerald's Prado article when we have a spare moment between the visits, which have been coming thick and fast lately.'[23] One cannot help wondering what such 'work' entailed; her typing was certainly not purely mechanical as she signalled anything she did not like for Brenan's attention, which he would then correct or change before Woolsey's typescript was sent to a professional typist.[24]

Alyse Gregory, who became a very close friend and with whom she maintained a life-long correspondence, was always aware of how much time Woolsey devoted to Brenan, and at what cost. Gregory considered Woolsey to have a great gift and was constantly urging her to write and publish more, as in this letter written in 1966, in which she begs her friend to gather all her poems and prepare them for publication:

> Surely Gerald would help you [find a publisher], you have thrown all your hours into helping him. Poetry is your true métier. You could include in a special section your translations as well ... Are you going to let the days drift by or use them entirely to the profit of Gerald? If you had them in the shape of a book they would be sure anyway of being preserved.[25]

Woolsey did work haphazardly on her poetry in the last years of her life; Brenan would later give her manuscripts to Kenneth Hopkins, who published most of them in *The Collected Poems of Gamel Woolsey*.

Woolsey had started writing poetry while still at school. At about fourteen she had been sent, together with her sister Marie, to the new school for girls that Miss Mary Vardrine McBee opened in Charleston, in 1909. The school, housed in a splendid columned building, built by Patrick Duncan in 1816, is still considered one of the finest examples of Regency architecture in the city; its then spacious grounds and elegant approach must have appealed to Woolsey (although the building has been preserved, the surrounding area has changed somewhat as modern school buildings have been added). The four and a half story flying staircase and surrounding stair hall must have been just as impressive then as now, and undoubtedly appealed to the adolescent Gamel Woolsey's whimsical imagination. Woolsey was clearly an active member of the school, both as a boarder and, after the death of her father, William Walton Woolsey, in 1910, as a day student, when her mother, Bessie Gammell Woolsey, left the Aiken plantation and returned to Charleston. Gamel, known then as Elizabeth, or Elsa, G. Woolsey, graduated from Ashley Hall in 1913. She had been instrumental in the creation of the school magazine, *Cerberus*, the first issue of which, bearing her name as Editor-in-Chief on the masthead, appeared in December 1912; the following year, having already graduated, she was demoted to Assistant Editor. Her earliest stories and poems appear in this magazine that published pieces written by the students, and a 'Society' section, with information on the social lives of students and alumnae. Thus in the December 1914 issue we learn that 'Elsa Woolsey and Marguerite Miller spent two months studying landscape painting at Woodstock, N.Y.,' and that, 'at the outbreak of the war we find a number of our Alumnae in Europe. One finds them among the sightseers that crowd the steamboat offices clamoring for passage home.' This was an annual expedition organized by the school, and in 1914, Gamel Woolsey had joined the group. In May 1920, *Cerberus* reports that Elsa Woolsey, with other alumnae, was taking art courses from

Mr. Alfred Hutty, of Woodstock. Hutty was a well-known painter, a member of the so-called 'Charleston Renaissance' of the early twenties, and it was through him that Woolsey was introduced to the Woodstock art colony in the Catskills where she would retreat in the summers to write, enjoying the position of 'our poetess' among the artists.[26]

Woolsey's interest in art, together with her poems and stories, also found a place in *Cerberus*, her signed drawing being selected to head the series 'Legends' that was published through several volumes. Although there is no way we can know for sure, it is not unlikely that Woolsey, given her interest in legends and mythology, devised and encouraged such a series. The drawing, signed 'E. G. W.', shows a castle on a hill, a forest, and a wall broken by a gateway leading to the mysterious world beyond.[27] It is also most likely that the name of the magazine, *Cerberus*, was suggested by Woolsey; the choice of the three-headed dog guarding the entrance to Hades must have seemed very sophisticated to the young girls that Woolsey was leading into this literary adventure. There may have been a teacher who stimulated this love of myth and legend, perhaps Miss McBee herself, or Louise Kingsley or Mabel E. Keiller who both taught English. Biography and Mythology formed a part of the Preparatory History course, but possibly Woolsey would have been too old to take that when she joined the school. And we do know that she had been an avid devourer of stories in her childhood, listening to Con, her favorite stepbrother, reading Homer in English and in Greek, and reading all she could lay her hands on, disregarding her mother and her mammy when they told her to 'Put the books away, put the books away' and go to bed.[28]

Woolsey's love of theatricals was also encouraged at Ashley Hall; Miss McBee, the school founder and principal, established a tradition of performing a Shakespeare play to be given as part of the graduation ceremonies (the school continued this tradition into the 1970s). Woolsey played Silvius, the Shepherd, in *As You Like It* in June 1911, and one of the Lords in *Much Ado About Nothing* in June 1912. In the school photograph of *As You Like It*, although hers was not a major part, and she is partly hidden behind another student, Woolsey's oval face and slightly stooped posture can be picked out easily. One of the myths frequently repeated about Gamel Woolsey is that she ran away from Charleston to pursue the career of an actress in New York;[29] I have not found any evidence to substantiate such a myth, except of course the well-known photograph which is used to endorse it, where she is in costume in a clearly histrionic pose.[30] Information garnered from *Cerberus* would rather point toward ambitions in the world of painting or writing, but I have seen no pictures, except for the *Cerberus* drawing. Woolsey, clearly, did not 'run away' to New York; she had family there, her stepbrother, John Woolsey, the famous *Ulysses* lawyer, and she must have had Woodstock friends there too, and, for a time at least, her mother was with her. She may have found Charleston social life stifling — she portrays it as such in *Patterns on the Sand* — although the city was beginning an artistic renaissance that would make it famous, at least in South Carolina, and Woolsey, who had 'come out' at the St Cecilia Ball in 1914, was in a position to know all the Charleston 'movers and shakers'. One of the founders of the Poetry Society was the poet Josephine S. Pinckney (1895–1957), who had graduated with Woolsey from Ashley Hall. The first meeting of the Society was held in October 1920, in the South Carolina Society Hall, almost directly opposite Woolsey's home on Meeting Street. The Poetry Society documents tell us that Woolsey's mother was a member in 1920–21, but not the following year; Woolsey's name is not on the list, according to the City Directory she was no longer living at Meeting Street in 1922.[31]

After graduating, Woolsey continued at Ashley Hall as a 'Special Student'; unfortunately, some of the Catalogues that list students are missing, but the 1916–17 Catalogue gives her name, and that of one other girl, as 'Special Students' in 1915–16. Whether this meant that Woolsey was continuing her art and literature studies, or was perhaps preparing for college, (the school had been founded with the goal of preparing young women for college and university entrance, there being no other such school in the area at the time) is impossible to tell. *Cerberus* is still published by Ashley Hall, run by a student board with a faculty advisor; the pieces published are selected by the board, but it is the English teachers who encourage students to send their pieces in. It seems this was the practice from the founding of the magazine.

Although the editorials of *Cerberus* are unsigned, the first one (December 1912) was in all probability written by Woolsey in her capacity of Editor-in-Chief. It exhorts the girls of Ashley Hall not to be 'sheep' and chides them for being 'humble followers of any girl who takes the lead ... willing to accept that girl's idea, whether it be good or bad.' And it ends 'Why not stop this game of "Follow the Leader"? Have your own ideas about things in this school, and express them, not someone else's. Be independent' (18).

A number of Woolsey's poems and stories were published in *Cerberus* and, as one would expect, reflect her reading. According to the 1909 school Catalogue, she would have read Sir Walter Scott's *The Lady of the Lake* and Lord Alfred Tennyson's *Idylls of the King*, both significant texts in her private 'middle earth' dwelling. Her short stories have a notably Conradian air in their subject matter, intensity, and in the use of a narrator; 'On Board the 'Orion', on friendship and death in a shipwreck, was possibly inspired by the Titanic, which had gone down the previous year. 'Le Bien-Heureux' deals with the happiness that the knowledge of the precise moment when he is to die brings a captain in a Huzzar regiment, and 'Narrow Light' is about a youth who sacrifices his life for what turns out to be a sail twisted about a cross bar floating in the stormy waters and only just visible from the lighthouse where he worked as an apprentice.[32]

The presence of death in these stories hardly surprises those familiar with Woolsey's work; the poems, however, do not dwell on death and, except for one, are much more optimistic than we would expect. Most are exercises on nature inspired by Wordsworth or Tennyson, that vary, with considerable skill, the traditional pentameters of English poetry, and create at times complicated, but always unobtrusive, rhyme schemes. The first poem, 'Before Dawn', is in the persona of a man condemned to die. The opening stanza, made up of four rhymed couplets, captures the regret and melancholy that characterize Woolsey's later poems in which, however, the direction of her gaze was to change. This poem projects the reader into a future that is being cut off, whereas in the later poems, Woolsey looks back with regret at what has gone, or at what never came to be, for example, in 'The Search for Demeter'. The rhyming scheme and the metrics of

'Before Dawn' become more intricate as the poem proceeds, thus spontaneously evoking an effect of doom and finality.

'The Wanderers', published in June the following year, is a romantic, self-congratulatory expression of the happiness that comes from enjoying freedom from restrictions, a mood that Woolsey would rarely capture in her mature poems. The traditional form, rhyme and metrics mark this poem as a class exercise — but a highly satisfactory one, indicating an already accomplished poet. A poem published in December 1913, titled 'The Trees' is also optimistic and laudatory, praising the 'one' who stands out from the mass, with their zeal, optimism and love of life. Other poems, such as 'The Night Wind' (December 1913) — in spite of its ambivalent use of the wind/wolf metaphor — exhort the reader to be awake to both 'hopes and fears'. Woolsey was clearly drawn to ballads, songs and roundels, popular forms that capture the great deeds of heroes and the romantic hopes of simple folks. Although she continued to use such models, these poems contrast with those published in 1931 in *Middle Earth*; the later poems are undoubtedly more skilfully executed and the mood is considerably more sombre, sad and weary. Woolsey had by then lost the youthful innocence that her early poems exude.

When *Middle Earth* was published, Brenan must have sent a copy to Carrington, possibly against Woolsey's wishes for she was far too sensitive not to realize that her companion's previous lover mocked her, and considered her boring. But Carrington admired the poems, and wrote to Woolsey to tell her that she particularly liked 'To a Dear Acquaintance', 'About the Sunrise', 'Indifference', 'The Useless Gift', and 'The Scarecrow'.[33] The bitterness at the passing of time and of love, the mournful tone and the despair that these poems capture must have spoken to Carrington, who had known her own disappointments and would have recognized the mood that Woolsey evoked in the lingering refrain of 'About the Sunrise': 'My dreams went by on horseback/ Laughing scornfully' (39), as also the futile hope in the twice-repeated line 'Come to me with kind indifference,/ And kiss my mouth' in the poem titled 'Indifference' (38).

Woolsey would surely have understood the irony of Carrington liking the poem 'The Useless Gift': Carrington's wedding gift to

Brenan and Woolsey had perhaps not been useless, but certainly, under the circumstances, unusable: she gave them a patchwork quilt she had made up of her discarded dresses, dresses she had worn during her affair with Brenan, when she had refused him again and again. She told Brenan that she had 'muttered spells' over the quilt, which he quite believed; 'It was the most lovely quilt I had ever seen — but the gift of a witch', he wrote in his private diary.[34]

Although the publication of *Middle Earth* passed almost unnoticed, Woolsey continued writing poetry, but only saw one other poem into print. This was 'The Search for Demeter',[35] a long poem in free verse, written after her mother's death, through which she expresses her feelings of guilt, regret and the ever more tenuous hope of forgiveness:

> How can we wash away
> our guilt? How can we find again
> the mistaken turning —
> go back and follow the unnoticed path
> that leads to another world,
> in another May? (146)

The poem is set in Italy, and invokes the mother-daughter dyad, the Greek Demeter and Persephone and the Roman Ceres and Koré. By using both Greek and Roman names for mother and daughter Woolsey stresses the universality of mother love and loss, and so can place herself in the position of the daughter who cannot find her mother:

> In our time we have all been Koré,
> each of us once, once only,
> has been loved. (144)

Woolsey's mother had died in 1951; she was shocked and grieved by this death she had been unable to foresee or attend, and mourned in silence. Given that Woolsey had not seen her mother since she had left the United States in 1929, it is easy to assume that they had not been close, but, after his wife's death, Brenan burned Mrs Woolsey's letters, so we know next to nothing of their relationship. However,

Woolsey did mention her mother when writing to Phyllis Playter, and in one undated letter tells how the worry caused by her mother's drinking had brought on her first attack of TB when she had been about seventeen.[36] In the same letter she gives an acute analysis of her mother's character, an analysis that, in many ways, she could have applied to herself. She believed that her mother had 'always tried to escape from life' and had retreated into ill health and inaction as a means of drawing attention. It is clear from this letter that Woolsey felt guilty not only at leaving her mother, but also at causing her pain by her behavior, that is, by not being the model daughter who marries and provides perfect grand-children. As the years went by, her feelings became so complex that she could not talk to Brenan of her mother, and he grew to resent her inability to share her intimate thoughts with him.[37] 'The Search for Demeter' allowed Woolsey to express all those emotions she had been repressing for so long. She sent a copy to Alyse Gregory, who must have been somewhat perplexed at her friend's use of modernist forms and themes, and made this clear. Woolsey replied that: 'I knew I ought not to give my poem to anyone without adding an introduction or notes.' She explains the Demeter and Persephone myth (with which Gregory must surely have been familiar) and describes the statues at Agrigento and Segesta, which reminded her of statues of the Madonna and Child. And then she wistfully confirms that: 'The poem is about my mother and her death, as you will have realized. But it does need notes — as much as *The Waste Land* — I'm afraid.'[38]

'The Search for Demeter' was published in *Botteghe Oscure*, in 1956. This avant-garde, multi-lingual literary journal was published in Rome, Italy by the Princess Caetani from 1948 to 1960. Marguerite Chapin, from New London, Connecticut, was studying music in Paris when Prince Caetani saw her, fell in love, and married her. She was a 'self-contained, slightly self-effacing' editor who was 'always eager for new works' and who accepted both known and unknown writers as long as she found their work invigorating and exciting. She wanted 'texts', not criticism and commentary, and was not interested in politics;[39] the authors she selected number over '650 of thirty-odd nationalities', and volume XVIII, in which Woolsey's poem appeared, included work, among others, by Muriel Spark, Theodore Roethke, George Steiner, María Zambrano, Jorge Guillén, Octavio Paz and five Philippine poets.[40] I have found no comment by Woolsey on her poem other than the letter to Alyse Gregory mentioned above, but this success must have confirmed her faith in herself as a poet. Jonathan Gathorne-Hardy tells us that even Gerald Brenan 'was able to praise [his wife's poem] unreservedly' (426).

Kenneth Hopkins would reprint 'The Search for Demeter' as a single volume in 1980 and he included it in the *Collected Poems* in 1984. Hopkins used a slightly different version from that published by *Botteghe Oscure*; among the papers bequeathed him by Brenan he had found four different versions and had settled on the third, which is slightly shorter and corrects the numbering of the sections (the *Botteghe Oscure* version had run sections v and vi into one, omitting the number vi).[41] Woolsey had made few changes in the extant manuscripts, except in the third section of the poem, where the version selected by Hopkins is, indeed, far superior to that originally printed. She replaced the first line 'In the middle years of my age' for the much more evocative 'In that arid time of my life', and added the line 'sifting through the rubbish of the past' before 'I found I had committed all the sins', thus creating a vivid picture of the waste land of those years and the sterility of her actions. She also eliminated the flattening repetition of 'committed', using 'enacted' and 'perpetuated', so giving the lines greater agility and energy.

The success of 'The Search for Demeter' spurred Woolsey on to polish previous poems and to write more, as Gregory was always urging her to do, and in 1959 she submitted all her work to T. S. Eliot, whom she admired immensely, for possible publication by Faber and Faber. The rejection, when it came in 1960, was a 'severe blow' after which, according to Brenan, she 'abandoned all thought of literary work', and would not hear of him paying for a private edition.[42] After her death, Brenan did eventually pay, at least in part, for the publication of Woolsey's poetry, thus in some way making up for her hours of typing his manuscripts and for his lack of faith in her talent while she was alive. Kenneth Hopkins, who had published *The Powys Brothers: A Biographical Appreciation* in 1967, had applied to Brenan for permission to publish Woolsey's poetry, which Brenan was happy to give, and to pay for, at least in part.[43] Hopkins, in his *The Powys Brothers*, only mentioned Woolsey once, including her name in a list of people with whom Llewelyn Powys had corresponded, but he was intrigued by her person and her poetry, and set out to publish her work and write her biography. Unfortunately, he died before he could finish his task; he did, however, between 1977 and 1980, publish a number of slim volumes of her poetry, which he then gathered together in *The Collected Poems of Gamel Woolsey* (1984), hoping to publish the *Complete Poems* once he had scoured the magazines and journals in which she might have published during the twenties, and to include her translations from the Spanish. In Hopkins's papers in the Harry Ransom Humanities Research Center there are some poems not included in the *Collected Poems*, among them 'Faith at Forty Second Street', which had appeared in the *New York Evening Post* supplement, the *Literary Review*, on 3 June 1922, and which, with its self-mocking flippancy, is reminiscent of the young Edna St Vincent Millay. The translations are from Spanish classical and contemporary poets, and include poems by Góngora, Quevedo, Pedro Espinosa, Antonio Machado, Luis Cernuda, Luis Rosales, Leopoldo Panero, Vicente Aleixandre, Rafael Alberti and Gerardo Diego.

Hopkins's publications of Woolsey's poems allowed Brenan to redeem himself as his wife's critic. On 29 August 1977, after the publication of *Twenty-Eight Sonnets*, he wrote Hopkins that the sonnets 'have delighted me ... I was surprised on reading a few of them to see how good they were, how pure and clear the language and how well they flowed.' A few days later (1 September) he wrote again:

I have been reading and rereading Gamel's sonnets with deep emotion. They seem to me much better than I thought them when I saw them in typescript. They are in the romantic tradition — and why not — but are much more beautifully and precisely phrased, in far purer language — than Rossetti's language. Eliot, when he refused to publish them for Faber, might have seen that they belong to the age they were written in and were not really a harking back to the last century.

On 8 February 1978(?), he wrote to Hopkins that he was 'enchanted' by, presumably, the poems in *The Last Leaf Falls* (1978), and admitted that 'I was blind not to recognize sufficiently what a true poet she was.' Not only had he not been able to recognize her gift, but, after years of companionship and marriage, when she was clearly close to death, he chose to repudiate her. Mrs Antoinette Moat had asked Woolsey for some of her poems for an anthology, and she selected six and must have asked Brenan to send them. Brenan did so, but with the following injunction: 'Please note that she writes under her maiden name of Gamel Woolsey and that her married name should not be mentioned.'[44]

The reasons, which I set out to explore in this piece, of why Gamel Woolsey's literary *oeuvre* is so exiguous, are clearly many, and although it seems to me that the evidence, more than once, points in the direction of her husband's negative attitude to her writing, it is only fair to insist that Woolsey's life before she met Brenan, in particular the TB she had contracted as a young woman and her troubling affair with Llewelyn Powys, had marked her deeply. In order to escape the memories she did not want to live with and the guilt she felt for having 'wasted most of my life' she frequently withdrew into a 'sort of trance — in[to] Limbo'.[45] Particularly in later life, she felt not only that she dwelled in a mythical 'middle earth' inaccessible to those around her, but that her own life lacked coherence and purpose. An undated letter (postmarked 9 January 1963) to Phyllis Playter, to whom she entrusted the intimate thoughts she did not share with Brenan, expresses this most cogently: 'I've sometimes had a feeling that we go in and out of parallel universes — sometimes we have a different past. Sometimes a different future — things aren't as fixed as we imagine. I'd like to think so because the past is both my castle and my prison.' The past, as castle and as prison, as experiences both lived through and imagined, gave her the material with which she created a legendary dwelling-place, her private 'middle earth', inhabited by love, regret, guilt, but never completely devoid of hope.

A selection of Gamel Woolsey's early poems
from *Cerberus*, the Ashley Hall school magazine.
(Published with permission of Margaret C. MacDonald,
Headmistress of the school.)

## Before Dawn

I do not wish to die; I have not tasted yet
Life's pleasure, or its pain, grief, or regret.
They tell me I shall die; I shall not see
Another sunrise brighten field and tree,
Another sunset with its golden light,
Another twilight deepen into night.
I do not wish to die — I shall have seen
Only life's dawn and night, no day between.

I see a light in the east that grows;
It brings with it death to one who waits.
I hear the dawn wind that softly blows;
It bears on its wings the will of the fates.
I hear the firing-squad, as the wind grows strong,
The relief of the guard, the stir of the curious waiting
     throng
Already assembled in the yard.

They were right. I shall never see again
The yellow fields of waving grain,
The glories of the Southern Cross,
Old live-oaks hung with Spanish moss,
Cherokee without blot or stain.

 In the cool dawn I watch the light
Grow in the sky.
This is the hour the fates decreed
That I should die.

(Cerberus I:1 December 1912)

## The Wanderers

The moon comes up — the glorious stars attend her,
The cool wind blows — it freshens with the dawn;
Happy are we who have the earth for dwelling,
Happy are we whose lantern is the dawn.

The sea lies there, the lovely dawn reflecting;
The tall palms here rise from the yellow sands;
Happy are we who have the dawn to light us,
Happy are we whose garden is all lands.

Who dwell in houses have their walls as boundaries,
They cannot see the stars for walls too high;
Happy are we whose dwelling is the wide earth,
Happy are we whose ceiling is the sky.

*(Cerberus* I:4 June 1913)

## The Trees

Far on the edge of some deserted mire
Where all the trees are dead and dull and same,
Stands one whose crest is like a living fire
With every leaf a point of brilliant flame.

So in the world where some are dull and lonely,
And some are touched with pride and some with
shame,
Stands one whose heart is of the morning only,
With every thought a living, glowing flame.

*(Cerberus* 2:1 December 1913)

## The Night Wind

The wind — the wolf that wanders in the wood,
Rustles the branches with his shaggy hide.
I hear his foot-steps in the falling rain,
I hear his breathing in the dark outside.

I hear his howling in the hungry sea,
And see his eyes gleam in the fire's spark,
Safe by my hearth, I hear him at the door,
And hear his eager panting in the dark.

On frozen nights when all is hushed and still,
When lights are dim and fires are burning low.
I hear his breathing at my frost-bound door,
And find his foot-prints in the fallen snow.

So he will wander when all times are past
Doomed through the long, forgotten, lonely years,
To wander in the night and dark and cold
To wake the heart of man to hopes and fears.
                    (*Cerberus* 2:1 December 1913 )

## To W. M.

Your eyes are the gray of a stormy sea,
    Your hair is the gold of the wind-swept sands,
And you hold the heart and the soul of me
    In the cup of your slender hands.

Your voice has the haunting melody
    Of the wind that breathes o'er the desert sands,
The soft melodious threnody
    Of the waves that break on the lonely strands.

You have changed the course of the world for me —
    No more I wander in lonely lands,
For you hold the heart and the soul of me
    In the cup of your slender hands.
                    (*Cerberus* 2:2 February 1914)

## Autumn

The sunlight falling on the grass
Turns the dry turf to cloth of gold;
With gilded hoofs the cattle pass,

The sunlight falling on the grass.
The sere leaves gleam like burnished brass
Across the open wind-swept wold;
The sunlight falling on the grass
Turns the dry turf to cloth of gold.

(Cerberus 2:4 June 1914)

## Song

I saw a ship through bright waves gliding;
　A ship, and she would come to me.
I saw a ship o'er dim gulfs riding;
　A ship, and she was bringing thee.

Oh, waves, make smooth a path before her,
　Dolphins to greet her, leap in air,
Oh, wild west wind, breathe softly o'er her,
　Fill her white sails, and bring her here.

She seems to come with treasure laden,
　She seems to come yet draws not near.
Come to me swift, the dream is fading,
　Ah, it is vanished in the air.

(Cerberus 3:4 June 1915)

## Gamel Woolsey, 'Faith at Forty Second Street'

(Literary Review supplement New York Evening Post, 3 June 1922, p. 703)

On a day that was lovely to live or die on
I sat and smiled at a library lion;
The beast was granite and grey and grim,
But he flicked a lash when I smiled at him.
If I had the faith of a Sainted Soul
I'd tickle his whiskers, and stroke his jowl,
I'd clutch a lock of his stony hair,
And I would lead him away from there.
His mate would follow, and we would go,
Walking stately, and staid, and slow,

73

Down the marble steps to the noisy street,
Through the gaping, hurrying crowd we'd meet
With a granite lion hand in hand
I'd smile at the folk when they'd stare and stand
But I'd pat my lions, and stroke their noses,
And perhaps I'd buy for them a wreath of roses;
I'd smooth their whiskers, their manes I'd deck,
I'd wind an arm round each stony neck.
And nights of silver, and days of blue
We'd go walking the Avenue.

## NOTES

I would like to thank the Beinecke Rare Book and Manuscript Library, Yale University, and the Harry Ransom Humanities Research Center (HRHRC) at the University of Texas at Austin for Research Fellowships which enabled me to consult their collections related to Gamel Woolsey; thanks also to Margaret Tenney, Archivist at Ashley Hall for information on Woolsey's school days, and to Margaret C. MacDonald, Headmistress of the school, for permission to reproduce some of Woolsey's poems published in *Cerberus*. Also, my thanks to Peter Carravetta for his comments on Woolsey's poetry.

1 Llewelyn Powys, *Love and Death: An Imaginary Autobiography* (1939) (London: Bodley Head, 1950), 114.
2 Interview with John Whitworth, Tangiers, 5 October 2002.
3 Gamel Woolsey, *Middle Earth: Thirty Six Poems* (New York: Simon &Schuster, 1931); quotations are from Kenneth Hopkins, ed., *The Collected Poems of Gamel Woolsey* (Norfolk: Warren House Press, 1984).
4 Arthur Quiller-Couch, ed. *The Oxford Book of Ballads*, 1910. <http:www.bartleby.com/243/27.html> (3-03-03).
5 Gamel Woolsey, *Patterns on the Sand*, unpublished typescript in the Kenneth Hopkins Collection in the HRHRC. See Barbara Ozieblo, 'Love and Disappointment: Gamel Woolsey's unpublished novel *Patterns on the Sand*', *Powys Notes* (Spring 2002), 5–11.
6 Gamel Woolsey, *One Way of Love* (London: Virago, 1987).
7 Alyse Gregory, 'Intimate Confession'. Llewelyn Powys Collection, HRHRC.
8 Richard Perceval Graves, *The Powys Brothers* (Oxford: Oxford University Press, 1984), 203.
9 Malcolm Elwin, ed., *So Wild a Thing: Llewelyn Powys Letters to Gamel Woolsey* (Penzance, Cornwall: The Ark Press, 1973); Kenneth Hopkins, ed., *The Letters of Gamel Woolsey to Llewelyn Powys, 1930–1939* (Norfolk: Warren House Press, 1983); Michael Adam, ed., *The Cry of a Gull: Extracts from Journals of Alyse Gregory* (London: The Ark Press, 1973).

10 Gerald Brenan, *Personal Record 1920–1972* (1974) (Cambridge: Cambridge University Press, 1979), 218.

11 Jonathan Gathorne-Hardy, *The Interior Castle: A Life of Gerald Brenan* (London: Sinclair Stenvenson, 1992), 254.

12 Gerald Brenan, Notebook 4, 1928–32. Gerald Brenan Collection, HRHRC.

13 David Garnett to Gerald Brenan, 18 March 1931 and August 1930. Gerald Brenan Collection, HRHRC.

14 Frances Partridge to Gamel Woolsey, undated. Gerald Brenan Papers, HRHRC.

15 Woolsey would have known Louis Wilkinson through Llewelyn Powys. See Kenneth Hopkins, 'Gamel Woolsey: A Poet from Aiken, South Carolina', *The South Carolina Review* (12:2 Spring 1980), 36.

16 The Bertram Rota Catalogue of used books (18 September 2002) contained the following entry: 'BANNED Books. Wade (Rosalind). 'Children, Be Happy!' Victor Gollancz Ltd., 1931. . . . *The author's first novel that was suppressed shortly after publication as a result of an action brought by a Miss Joyce Butterworth who claimed to have been libelled by an 'alleged very grave immorality' in this 'thinly veiled' portrait of life in a girls' private school in west London. It was estimated at the time that following the publisher's withdrawal of the book that there could not be more than 100 copies 'in the hands of the public'.* <www.bertramrota.co.uk/293-2.htm> (18-09-02). In fact, the novel was based on a German play by Christa Winsloe, *Madchen in Uniform* (1930), that had been made into a film by Leontine Sagan in 1931.

17 David Garnett to Gerald Brenan, 17 Feb 1932. Gerald Brenan Papers, HRHRC.

18 Virginia Woolf, *The Sickle and the Moon: The Letters of Virginia Woolf.* Vol. 5: 1932–1935, ed. Nigel Nicholson (London: The Hogarth Press, 1979), 27.

19 This letter is kept with the copy of *One Way of Love* in the British Library.

20 Gathorne-Hardy, 417; the story was reprinted in *The Powys Journal* VIII (1998), 145–55.

21 Gathorne-Hardy, 277.

22 Gamel Woolsey to Phyllis Playter, undated but postmarked 20 Feb 1961. Copies of Woolsey's letters to Playter are in the Kenneth Hopkins Collection, HRHRC.

23 Gamel Woolsey to Annie Davis, sent from Churriana, probably in the early 1960s. Kenneth Hopkins Collection, HRHRC.

24 Gathorne-Hardy, 379n.

25 Alyse Gregory to Gamel Woolsey, undated 1966. Gerald Brenan Collection, HRHRC.

26 Hervey White, MS of his unpublished autobiography, 240. University of Iowa Library, Special Collection. In *One Way of Love*, 'Edgewood', in the Catskills, figures prominently as a retreat where Mariana recovers, both physically and psychologically, from her marriage to Alan.

27 *Cerberus* (2:1, Dec. 1913), 15.

28 Gamel Woolsey, 'All that the child remembers now', Kenneth Hopkins, ed., *The Collected Poems of Gamel Woolsey*, 9.

29 Gerald Brenan to Kenneth Hopkins, 30 October 1977. Kenneth Hopkins Collection, HRHRC.

30 This photograph was probably taken at the Woodstock festivals, originated by Hervey White in 1916. In his autobiography, White indicates that 'Elsie Woolsey'

was to play the Queen of Sheba in his adaptation of Flaubert's *Temptation of Saint Anthony* (240). This would probably have been in 1916. There is no other mention of Woolsey, but she may well have taken part in other productions. The photograph in question is reproduced in Gathorne-Hardy, opposite page 436.

31 See *The Year Book of the Poetry Society of South Carolina, 1921* (Charleston, SC) 1921; Frank Durham, 'South Carolina's Poetry Society' *South Atlantic Quarterly* (LII:2, April 1953), 277–85; and Herbert P. Shippey, 'Josephine Pinckney'. James B. Meriwether, ed., *South Carolina Women Writers* (Spartanburg, S.C.: The Reprint Co., 1979), 83–95.

32 'On Board the 'Orion'' (I:3, April 1913); 'Le Bien-Heureux' (I:4, June 1913); 'Narrow Light' (3:4, June 1915).

33 Dora Carrington to Gamel Woolsey, 24 November 1931. Gerald Brenan Collection, HRHRC.

34 Gerald Brenan, Notebook 5. Gerald Brenan Collection, HRHRC.

35 Gamel Woolsey, *The Collected Poems of Gamel Woolsey*, 141–52.

36 Although Woolsey says she was 'about seventeen', Anne Waring Warren, in a letter to Lynne Rhodes (16 April 1979, Kenneth Hopkins Collection, HRHRC), gives the date of 1917 for Woolsey's illness which she ascribes to the unhealthy conditions on the return voyage from Europe (which took place in 1914 and not in 1917); I think it more likely that Woolsey contracted TB in 1917, when she would have been twenty-two, than in 1912, when she was a successful student at Ashley Hall.

37 Gerald Brenan to Alyse Gregory, 8 Oct 1946. Kenneth Hopkins Collection, HRHRC.

38 Gamel Woolsey to Alyse Gregory, undated. Kenneth Hopkins Collection, HRHRC.

39 Eugene Ferdinand Walter, 'Recollections of Princess Caetani', HRHRC leaflet for the exhibition on *Botteghe Oscure*, 1991.

40 Archibald MacLeish, Introduction. *Botteghe Oscure: Index, 1949–1960* (Middletown, CT: Wesleyan University Press), ix.

41 Kenneth Hopkins, notes on 'The Search for Demeter'. Kenneth Hopkins Collection, HRHRC.

42 Gerald Brenan, *Personal Record*, 369.

43 Gerald Brenan to Kenneth Hopkins, 17 march 1977. Kenneth Hopkins Collection, HRHRC.

44 Gerald Brenan to Mrs Antoinette Moat, 30 October 1967. Kenneth Hopkins Collection, HRHRC.

45 Gamel Woolsey to Phyllis Playter; undated but postmarked 16 December 1961.

JACQUELINE PELTIER

# Llewelyn and Alyse Gregory:
# A Correspondence with Dr Marie Stopes

The world has changed tremendously since the end of World War Two, and for most people living now it is sometimes difficult to imagine what it was like during the better part of the Powys's life, brought up during Victorian times and writing most of their books before 1950. I therefore thought it might prove valuable to give an indirect description of the way people lived, and loved, through the correspondence of two remarkable women, who played their part in the changing western world.

Alyse Gregory wrote about a dozen letters to Marie Stopes, between November 1939 and June 1947 which are presently held at The British Library, among the Stopes papers.[1] Of Marie's own letters, I have unfortunately only two. Although the letters from Alyse's pen seem most of the time a little cold, they nevertheless

*Alyse during the Suffrage Campaign in New Jersey, about 1910.*
*(by courtesy of Shelley Byinton)*

provide some interesting information about her and Marie's lives at that time, and will allow us a more general reflection on their achievements.

Alyse Gregory and Marie Stopes, almost exact contemporaries, had, at least superficially, a few things in common: they both supported the Suffragettes (Marie Stopes had joined the Women's Social and Political Union in 1912 and at about the same time Alyse was asked to organise the suffrage campaign in New Jersey), led active and successful professional lives, were writers, and both married in their late thirties. They took life seriously, and were not particularly endowed with any sense of humour. The most important common denominator is their indomitable courage when defending their beliefs. But they were in fact very different: Alyse was a discreet, introspective, open-minded, self-distrustful, ironic, intellectual woman, who shunned all forms of public attention, at least from the time she married Llewelyn. As for Marie Stopes, she was a compound of different contradictory characteristics: very energetic, intellectually gifted but stubborn, an egoist verging on the paranoid, who could nevertheless be generous; favouring eugenics and racial theories, she showed extreme intolerance towards abortion and all sexual 'deviations'. She showed an uncanny flair for using publicity for herself, her ideas and her literary output. She had a will of iron and never took 'no' for an answer. She had as much self-confidence as Alyse had little. Her prejudices were those of a conservative with radical feelings of both left and right. As one of her biographers remarked:

> At least she knew how to evoke violent responses from every stratum of society. Her achievements, today taken for granted, can only be understood against the background of opposition from the various churches, from all political parties, from women themselves, and the public at large.[2]

Alyse who had had an eventful life before she met Llewelyn and was a feminist at heart, shared Marie Stopes' ideas about the liberation of women from the curse of unwanted childbirth and venereal disease and also agreed that enlightenment concerning sex life, (what Alyse with delicacy called 'sexual dalliance'), was an absolute necessity for the general public. Her book of essays, *Wheels on Gravel*, (dedicated to Gamel Woolsey) is in a way a very feminist work, and well could John Cowper Powys write in the Preface:

The book constitutes a notable challenge to most of our masculine habits of thought; and the deepest things it contains, though perhaps not the liveliest, are allusions to the bitter tragedy of sex-jealousy and love's frustrations.[3]

She certainly must have admired the pioneer work Dr Stopes had done from 1918 onwards, for the 'facts of life' as even children know them now were not in the least common knowledge in those years. Even in the 1930s, problems of birth control and sexual education were still not popular issues.

But it was on the problem of marriage itself that they held opposing views. Marie Stopes aimed desperately at the married state and declared at some point after her second marriage: 'I am incurably romantic, being in favour of monogamic marriage.' and in *Married Love* she insists:

The happiness of a perfect marriage, which enhances the vitality of the private life, renders one not only capable of adding to the stream of the life-blood of the community of children, but by marriage one is also rendered a fitter and more perfect instrument for one's own particular work, the results of which should be shared by society as a whole...[4]

For Alyse, marriage was a subjection, the abandonment of a woman's freedom; it was, according to her, "self-immolation". Sex-instinct is "in its very essence, anarchic." The plight of woman at that time is described with sympathy:

Intimidated by the fear of pregnancy as well as by the prejudices still so prevalent as to the importance of chastity, she must, to gain her most valued experiences, be of either so strong a character as to defy the rulings of the society, or of so weak a one that she is overridden against her own wishes and self-respect.[5]

79

Marriage, in Alyse's eyes, endangers the love and desire the man had felt at the beginning for his mate:

Both men and women are born polygamous and yet have entrenched themselves within monogamy, and this conflict in nature results in untold misery both for men and for women.[6]

In fact Alyse held more revolutionary views than Marie, and would have much favoured a free relationship where love is stimulated by infidelity, rather than marriage, with its danger of becoming stale and "losing the stimulus of uncertainty".[7]

❖ ❖ ❖

Alyse and Llewelyn met Dr Marie Stopes at Max Gate, Dorchester, in August 1932, introduced by Hardy's widow, Florence, who at that time accepted visits more readily than had been the case during Thomas Hardy's lifetime. Marie Stopes had bought The Old Lighthouse at Portland Bill as a summer home,[8] and they met sometimes afterwards. About fifteen letters were also exchanged between Llewelyn and Marie Stopes up to 1939.

Although the name of Marie Stopes[9] and the clinics which bear her name are well-known, it seems necessary to dwell a little on her life, which was one of constant battle in favour of sexual knowledge for all, far ahead of her time. She had had a rigorous childhood, due to a rigid education, with a father interested in fossils and a mother very active in women's suffrage. Marie was gifted, highly competitive, worked hard and by 1905, after obtaining a PhD in Palæobotany from Munich, (the first woman to do so, with Honours) and London — she was the youngest Doctor of Science in Britain — she became an acknowledged specialist on the structure of coal[10] and the names she later gave to the four components of coal are still used today. She went to Japan in 1907 to work on plant fossils at the Botanical Institute in Tokyo and immediately made an expedition to Hokkaido to bring back samples of post-Carboniferous coal-balls. She remained there eighteen months. During those years she published several major papers on fossil plant study. When she came back, she was made Lecturer in Fossil Botany at Manchester University.

Even though by that time Marie Stopes had become an acknowledged scientist, on the personal level her life was far from satisfactory. At the age of 30, she was still a single woman, desperately yearning for a normal life, which for her went with the enviable state of marriage. Although a specialist of the male-female reproductive aspects of plant life, she still knew very little about human reproduction. In these post-Victorian times this was to be expected, when there was a complete ignorance, for both men and women, of the most simple sexual principles.

Her expectations of sexual experience came from books, which she read voraciously, Browning, Swinburne, for instance, and she later also read one book on sex, *Love's Coming of Age* (1896) by Edward Carpenter, which was to exert some influence on her, because of its mystical glorification of sex. Carpenter, a Cambridge mathematician and a Marxist, underlined the fact that the prime object of sex was not the procreation of children 'but *union*, the physical union as the allegory and expression of the real union'.[11] She met him and they discussed her *Married Love*, still in manuscript: 'He has made two or three useful suggestions, but mostly approves', she wrote.

So anxious was she to enter the married state that she made a disastrous first marriage in 1911 with Reginald Ruggles Gates, a fellow scientist and distinguished specialist in the then new field of genetics whom she met at a scientific congress in St Louis, Missouri. In 1914 Marie realised that her husband was impotent. Her life became intolerable, and she took the courageous decision to leave him, and to file a nullity suit against him. Not being able to find adequate legal help, she decided to take the case into her own hands and so read her way through English law and more or less every book on sex in English, French or German, as well as treatises on the physiology of reproduction, especially the works of the French Auguste Forel, *Sexual Ethics* and *The Sexual Question*, which had just been translated, and Havelock Ellis's *Man and Woman*, published in 1894. She finally obtained her divorce in 1916. Ruth Hall implies, nevertheless, that poor Reginald may have felt overawed by the energetic, demanding, successful Marie ... Anyhow the ignominy of the miserable experience she had undergone led Marie Stopes to the unavoidable conclusion that something positive had to be done to

help women out of a similar subjection, due to total ignorance. In
1913 she wrote with some exaltation to Aylmer Maude, the official
translator and biographer of Tolstoy, who was to prove a life-long
friend and admirer:

> What is there at present bigger than the women's movement
> that I *could* die for? And supposing I was anxious to die —
> what is there my death could really, materially benefit?[12]

She finally decided not to die, but soon found what she could
effectively do: she started to write what was going to be an explosive
book, *Married Love,* rated in 1935 by a group of American academics
the 16th in a list of the twenty-five most influential books of the
previous fifty years, after *Das Kapital* but ahead of *Mein Kampf* and
Einstein's *Relativity.* It was in fact the very first sex manual of its kind.

> Man, through prudery, through the custom of ignoring the
> woman's side of marriage and considering his own whim as
> marriage law, has largely lost the art of stirring a chaste partner
> to physical love.[13]

This book was immediately followed by *Wise Parenthood,* in which
she advocated

> the restrained and sacramental rhythmic performance of the
> marriage rite of physical union, throughout the whole married
> life, as an act of supreme value in itself, separate and distinct
> from its value as a basis for the procreation of children.[14]

In those years, the 1920s, she met with much acclaim but also had to
face strong opposition from various churches:

> In July 1920 the Lambeth Conference of Anglican bishops
> passed a resolution calling on all high-principled men and
> women to bring pressure to bear on national and local govern-
> ment to remove 'such incentives to vice as indecent literature,
> suggestive plays and films, the open or secret sale of contra-
> ceptives, and the continued existence of brothels'.[15]

But it was the Catholic Church which proved the most inveterate enemy. It was also argued — and even by some at the extreme right among Anglicans — that birth control was a class conspiracy against the poor, because by reducing their numbers, their voting strength was also reduced. It was also alleged that the poor were made victims of experiments. The Catholic Church also used its influence on the press, and *The Times* for instance refused to accept any advertisements concerning her. As late as 1955, *Family Doctor*, published by the British Medical Association, candidly admitted that the ban was 'dictated by our large Irish and Catholic readership'.

In 1918, she had married Humphrey Verdon Roe, a wealthy industrialist who shared her interest in birth control and would devote his life to helping her, and in 1924, at the age of 43, she bore him a son, Harry, the apple of her eye. During these years she published ten books on sex, marriage and birth control, as well as three stage plays, many pamphlets and articles. She also wrote poetry (not alas of the highest order) and even the scenario for a successful cinematic version of her ideas. Her friends included G. B. Shaw, Thomas Hardy and H. G. Wells. She was famous as a propagandist for birth-control, was a public lecturer much in demand, and with the help of her husband opened several birth control clinics around the country. Unfortunately, notwithstanding her initial passionate proclamations about the bliss of her marriage, six or seven years afterwards it crumbled, and one again wonders if Marie, with her overbearing behaviour, was not in effect crushing the men in her life.

By 1938, at the age of 58, she had fallen in love with a young poet, Keith Briant. Their liaison lasted until Keith Briant's marriage in 1943, and the book of poems she wrote, *Love Songs for Young Lovers*, is clearly inspired by her love for Briant, although she took pains to claim that

> Many of the most personally worded have no basis in any physical experience of my own, but came swiftly transmitted from the store-house of human emotion … Nowadays nothing is too personal for expression in prose, so surely there can be no good reason why the deep pools of the love experience of the human heart should be denied a poet because of the

particularity of the radiance that may flash from the surface ripples.[16]

In 1939 Marie Stopes who was used to sending her books for approval to many of her acquaintances, especially influential people, sent Llewelyn her book of poems. In a letter written from Switzerland in October 1939, Llewelyn answered, thanking her for sending him these poems. He compliments her for 'the splendid work you have done", "the pluck and independence of your character', but he also makes some critical comments on her style, her too vehement love of beauty and the frequent use of the word 'rosy':

> ... It seems to me a significant little word. ... I sometimes feel my enthusiasm and admiration a little daunted by this "rosy" quality. ... I have expressed the feeling before, and have received from you an ironic rebuke. What I really feel is that your nature has in it a *rift*. Perhaps you should have been either a poor neglected poet *or* a practical philanthropist, either a passionate alchemist *or* a nice successful socially ambitious woman.

He also shows a cautious reserve concerning her poetical stance, stressing the fact that he does not yet understand her character

> ... for well I know there is something in your being that is remarkable, but only having been privileged to see you in glimpses, I have never been able to SEE *for certain* the unadulterated gold.
> What I mean by the word 'rift' is the suspicion I have built up by straws and thistle-down that your good sense and practical vigour of mind saw through the humbug of the old conventions and took steps, and very practical steps, to modify its malicious intention to interfere with the force and natural happiness of human beings, but your mind has not rejected the values of these people as a poet should.[17]

The letter shows Llewelyn's gift for critical analysis, uttered here in a gentle tone that does not give offence. Marie was grateful for his observations, she wrote back, exclaiming 'so valuable and so cheering to a lonely writer to be read by one who too can write'. She had no hesitation in placing both of them on the same pedestal ...

But Llewelyn, by that time is far too ill to be able to pursue this correspondence. Alyse wrote a short note in his place on November 21, thanking Dr Stopes for her latest letter. On Saturday, 2nd December, Llewelyn died.

Marie Stopes sent Alyse a cablegram and then a letter in which she no doubt expressed her condolences, probably full of hope and the banal re-assurance in the after-life one writes in these circumstances. Alyse answered:

No I am afraid I cannot share your belief in so promising a conclusion to our earthly life. Before the final majesty of a corpse my mind returns once more to a belief in annihilation, which belief to me gives a tragic dignity to the like of man that it otherwise would not have. My husband remained true to his life and philosophy and died without fear saying that he had had a happy life and now longed to be 'crisp ash'.

And at the end of the letter she adds:

Though we do not share a belief in the immortality of the soul, I think we both believe in those human values of tolerance, fearlessness and personal integrity here on earth. (Dec. 11, 1939)

The two women will exchange a few letters from then on during the war, most of the time perfunctory and noncommittal at least on Alyse's part, for she seemed to share Llewelyn's ambivalent feelings towards Marie Stopes.

In the spring of 1940 Alyse had decided to publish a volume of Llewelyn's letters. On the 7th of March, 1940, Marie who was very careful with her correspondence and kept copies of all the letters she sent and received, wrote to Alyse:

I have heard that you are collecting with a view to publishing, Llewelyn Powys's letters to various people. I have some, and as you know one of his last literary letters was to me. I shall be glad to let you have these for publication if you will let me know.

I think his letters should form a most interesting volume which people who care for literature and for him will like to have.

On March 11, Alyse answered that 'Yes, I should be glad to have any letters you have from my husband.' Concurring with Marie's views she adds:

Yes, I do hope they will be of interest to lovers of literature, and will illuminate his work and show the many different sides of his character, which was however so integrated a one.

In the next letter (April 27) she thanks Marie Stopes for having taken the trouble to copy the letters herself, instead of sending them to her to copy, but admits to some puzzlement about one passage in Llewelyn's last October 1939 letter. Alyse feels it necessary to warn her:

I have already copied enough letters for several volumes so I fear in the end there will have to be a very drastic elimination.

and in *The Letters of Llewelyn Powys*, selected and edited by Louis Wilkinson[18], only the last letter Llewelyn wrote to Marie Stopes was chosen.

One minor point shows that the two women attached the same importance to keeping their maiden names. In the April 27 letter mentioned above, Alyse remarks on the fact that she is spoken of as

<u>Miss</u> Gregory and not <u>Mrs</u> Gregory. I always hate it that the Miss goes with one's father's name and the Mrs with one's husband — and the word Mrs has always been to me an objectionable one even if I had not always since my marriage kept my own name for professional reasons.

which is something Marie had decided long ago for herself. In 1911, at the time of her first — unfortunate — marriage with Dr Reginald Ruggles Gates she made it clear:

In the first place, notwithstanding my marriage, my legal name is Marie C. Stopes. As I have been for some time, and still am entitled to the courtesy of the title of 'Doctor', the situation is relieved of any difficulty regarding the application of either 'Mrs' or 'Miss' to that name.[19]

Three days later, on April 30, Alyse thanked Dr Stopes for sending her 'your article on Havelock Ellis[20] which had interested me very much when I read it in the Literary Guide and of which I am now glad to have this copy.' As mentioned previously his works had been one of the great influences in Marie Stopes' own development.

Marie's letter also included some cuttings from the October 1939 letter for Alyse to decipher, leading Alyse to write :

The sentence itself is a little confused — my husband wrote letters carelessly, quick from the tip of his pen and from his thoughts which were quicker ...

On June 7 1943, Marie Stopes wrote an *Open Letter to the Bishop of St Albans,* after he had called for parliamentary action to ban the sale of contraceptives to all but married people, and only on production of a medical certificate. She had no hesitation in upbraiding him in the most virulent words:

One notes with revulsion the inherent cruelty in your effort to force women against their wills by coercive ignorance to bear children they do not feel physically fit or do not want to bear. It is without doubt the most blasphemous form of slave driving, for we should be made in God's image and begotten in love.[21]

This *Letter*, which was only published by the Rationalist press, elicited from Alyse the first letter in which she shows a warm appraisal and true respect for Marie's unyielding courage. It seems to have touched something in her so deep that she even underlines some words, something she was not prone to do:

I do admire you so much for that article of yours in *The Free Thinker* written with so much audacity, vigour and logic — the

87

letter to the Bishop of St Albans — what a bold and coura-
geous and <u>compassionate</u> pen you have! And I think *The Free
Thinker* should be congratulated on printing such a letter and
I doubt if any other paper would have taken it.

  If I were the Bishop of St Albans I would shiver in my shoes
to have such an indictment appear with my post. I suppose he
will just blink his eyes and take an extra helping of marmalade
with his toast, clear his throat six times and then say what a
dangerous woman you are. And dangerous you are to all the
iniquities <u>he</u> upholds. I think women every where should
thank you for that letter and for all the wonderful good which
you do. (July 5, 1943)

And she adds, after her signature:

  It is a powerful, irrefutable and eloquent letter.

  In the next letter, July 30, 1943, Alyse praises a 'moving poem'
Marie has sent her:

  I think you transcend so great a tragedy in a wonderful way, a
  way that helps others to face the worst with courage and
  poetic understanding. It really came as a shock to me for I did
  not know that you had lost this gallant and beautiful son. I
  liked particularly the stanza beginning
  'In a wild moment
  all was wrenched in twain'

and she even goes so far as to write with what seems like genuine
sympathy on her part:

  … there are many striking and beautiful lines. Yes I wish my
  husband could have seen it.

She ends her letter with

  And I do thank you so much for this imaginative and courageous and very moving poem.

  The war meanwhile was raging and Dr Stopes let her Old Lighthouse to three young naval lieutenants, but even at Norbury Park in

Surrey, her usual place of residence, she didn't feel safe from German bombs, for a few fell in the park and she even told a British officer she thought Goering was deliberately attacking her home. In the summer of 1944 she asked Alyse if it would be possible to find her a house in East Chaldon. Alyse answered her, August 5, 1944, and it is the only instance where she calls her 'Dear Mary Stopes' (instead of the usual 'Dear Dr Stopes'), maybe in order to attenuate her lack of enthusiasm, stressing the fact that the village was already full of people bombed out. She was probably not too keen on having Marie so near Chydyok, and kept her at arm's length. Honesty compelled her to add:

> This part of the coast was a centre to some extent for air raids before the invasion, but since then, it has been comparatively quiet. It is a shame your beautiful lighthouse was taken from you.

Theodore had fled East Chaldon for Mappowder in 1940 and several German bombs did fall over this area dangerously situated too near the Isle of Portland and its naval base. Weymouth too greatly suffered from bombardments.

*The Old Lighthouse at Portland Bill as a summer house.*
*(by courtesy of Louise de Bruin)*

Alyse also mentions that:

The Letters have sold very well and a biography is being written about Llewelyn by Malcolm Elwin, who has written a number of standard works on 19th century writers.[22] (August 5, 1944)

Exactly one year separates this letter from the following, 4 August 1945: it is the end of the war and Alyse congratulates Marie Stopes who has now recovered the possession of her lighthouse and has invited Alyse to visit her:

It is charming of you to give me so generous an invitation to come and see you. I have not been to Weymouth for almost a year and seldom leave the downs but I shall certainly try to arrange one day to come and see you when every thing is propitious, and will give you plenty of warning ahead. Your return to Portland gives me a lovely feeling that the war really is over.

In 1946, *The Life of Llewelyn Powys* was published by John Lane The Bodley Head. On June 4, 1947 Marie Stopes wrote to Alyse:

I have had Elwin's Life of Llewelyn by me for some time, but extreme burdens & duties prevented me finishing it, I now have. I did not like to write to you until I had read it all. It makes me grieve than ever that so bright and strong a personality should have been betrayed by miserable little things like germs. It also made me appreciate him more than ever as a writer when I read his kindly profoundly helpful letter on being a poet. Has the young disciple turned into a real poet?
　　But most of all I want to know what you think of the book —does it please you? Or leave you resigned? or make you rage at parts of it? Elwin might have had your original approval — one would have expected Louis Wilkinson ...(the rest of the letter is missing).

This letter is a good example of Marie's orderly and direct way of dealing with matters in her life. It is written with gusto and style, and we feel that her praise of Llewelyn as a writer is sincere. She appreciates his talent, but also his generosity towards other writers.

An interesting reference concerns 'the young disciple', who was none other than Kenneth Hopkins. In the Epilogue to *Advice To a Young Poet*, Hopkins remembers:

> One day, fifteen years ago, Llewelyn Powys gave me a copy of *Impassioned Clay*, the longest and finest of his philosophical essays, inscribing it with a quotation taken from the body of the book: "By day and by night, no sight that we see, but has its own poetical burden." I had never read anything like this before, and I read on and on, when I returned home, amazed and uplifted.[23]

She also manifests an undisguised curiosity about Alyse's judgment of Malcolm Elwin's biography and at the same time shows her regard for Alyse's opinion. As we know, Elwin was extremely discreet concerning some aspects of Llewelyn's life, particularly about Gamel Woolsey who in the biography is just 'a friend'. But Marie probably knew of the affair.

It exposes another typical instance of Marie Stopes' directness, sometimes verging on the insensitive. Her way of referring to Llewelyn's death as caused by 'miserable little things' is blunt, but it certainly underlines her dread of germs which lasted all her life, as did her love for healthy people with a robust constitution and her preoccupation with eugenics. She, not unreasonably in those days before antibiotics, took drastic measures herself never to catch any germs from people around her, either from flu or from other infections such as VD.

In the very last letter of this exchange, June 6, 1947, Alyse answers with a non committal letter:

> How kind of you to write such a friendly and understanding letter! I think Malcolm wrote a competent, honest, and interesting biography — and he did it con amore. It is difficult for one closely connected with some one to get any true perspective on his life for we judge those we love so subjec-

tively. Mr E. is a scrupulous biographer and I think that is the thing of most importance.

Alyse would never of course have confided to Marie Stopes her own torturing thoughts about her past life with Llewelyn, she was too reticent and reserved a woman.[24] But in her diary she wrote:

M.E's biography of L. has come. It is an honest book and a generous one — a good piece of research, but who can resurrect the living man? He said L. liked to walk because of the rythmical [sic] movement, etc. He liked to walk because his senses were all alert. In the city every sight engaged him and in the country every sight delighted him. He never walked just for exercise, or 'the rythmical movement'. Everyone that writes of him presents him refracted through his own temperament, only his own words speak. Nowhere in these pages is L. to be found.[25]

She later comes back to the biography and adds:

What strangers write about a man is pure fantasy, and what those near him write is a subjective dream. His words alone speak, but so differently to each that it is as if they were by a magician's trick turned from pennies to golden sovereigns and back again [...] One critic says L. is a writer of mild country essays to be classed with Miss Mitford, another that he is a powerful thinker, another that he is a prig, another that he is a lecher and a sadist. It is all a whirling falsehood. Each seeks self-justification, no one judges with detachment. [...] I never return to reading L. without finding wisdom afresh in his words.[26]

Alyse who certainly was not a conceited woman but who lived in relative solitude, does however in the same letter confide to Marie that:

I have an autobiography (written up to the time I met my husband) coming out sometime during this coming year in the USA. I have not yet tried to place it in this country.

Her autobiography *The Day is Gone*,[27] although well written and tolerably honest, is in fact a disappointing book for readers seeking the 'real' Alyse and she was well aware that she had not had the courage to go to the depths of self-analysis. Many a time in her diaries she reiterates her knowledge that she had failed, a feeling which she describes in one typical arch sentence:

It is somewhat of a feat, however, to have escaped altogether out of a book written entirely about a subject that never appears.[28]

Finally, she also informs Marie that she will be away 'through most of August as I am going to Switzerland'. This was to recovers Llewelyn's ashes.

While in Switzerland, Alyse wrote in her journal:

When Lisaly said "There are Lulu's ashes", I felt as if I had been living in a thin upper air of falsehood, for all the tragedy of those days returned — and there in that little box was all my life. Even after the death of the one we love the struggle to possess our own lives, our own souls, continues. This palpable earth with firm, round, succulent apples bearing down the branches before my eyes, and purple grapes ripening over my head is but an outward semblance. The truth is hidden and lost within us.[29]

Their correspondence seems to have stopped at that point, at least to our knowledge, and it is not very plausible that the two women even met. Alyse cherished her solitude too much to sacrifice it to social calls. As to Marie, she was witnessing a new political and social era, alien to her, and her only son, whom she had loved with such (s)motherly love, was making his escape through a marriage she judged 'a betrayal'. But both Alyse and Marie were all their lives stalwart in the belief that 'A married woman's body and soul should be essentially her own.'[30]

*[notes overleaf]*

NOTES

1 Stopes Papers, Part 3, Literary and Publishing, n° 58501, Vol. LV (3). I wish to thank Leslie Booth, who, aware of my interest in Alyse Gregory, had copies made and sent to me when he came across these Letters.
2 *Marie Stopes, a biography*, by Ruth Hall (London: André Deutsch, 1977). I am much indebted to Ruth Hall's biography for all the data and facts evoked in this paper. There is a more recent readily available biography, *Marie Stopes & The Sexual Revolution*, by June Rose (London: Faber & Faber, 1992).
3 *Wheels on Gravel* (London: John Lane The Bodley Head, 1938).
4 *Married Love*, by A. C. Fifield, 1918, 106.
5 *Wheels on Gravel*, 67.
6 *Ibid.*, 64.
7 *Ibid.*, 67.
8 In 1930 Marie had become the first curator of Portland Museum, housed in two thatched cottages, nestling above Church Ope Cove. One of these cottages had inspired Thomas Hardy for *The Well-Beloved*.
9 She was voted 'Woman of the Millennium' by *The Guardian* readers in 1999.
10 See for instance 'The Four Visible Ingredients in Banded Bituminous Coal: Studies in the Composition of Coal', *Proceedings of the Royal Society*, London, vol. 90, 1919.
11 *Marie Stopes, a biography*, 90.
12 *Marie Stopes, a biography*, 110.
13 Marie Stopes, *Married Love*, 104.
14 *Wise Parenthood*, by A. C. Fifield, 1918, 148.
15 *Marie Stopes, a biography*, 156.
16 *Marie Stopes, a biography*, 285.
17 *The Letters of Llewelyn Powys* (London: John Lane The Bodley Head, 1943), 314.
18 With an Introduction by Alyse Gregory (London: John Lane The Bodley Head, 1943).
19 Ruth Hall, *Marie Stopes, a biography*, 93.
20 Marie Stopes, obituary of Havelock Ellis in *Literary Guide*, September 1939.
21 *Marie Stopes, a biography*, 291. Although Ruth Hall thought the letter, 'in view of its rather extreme expression', was not published, it <u>was</u> apparently, by the Rationalist Press, to which Llewelyn subscribed.
22 Malcolm Elwin was the author of *Savage Landor*, *Old Gods Falling*, *De Quincey*, *Victorian Wallflowers*, *Thackeray: A Personality* and *Charles Reade: A Biography*.
23 *Advice to a Young Poet*, ed. by R. L. Blackmore (Fairleigh Dickinson University Press, 1969).
24 For more details about Alyse Gregory see *Alyse Gregory, A Woman at her Window*, by J. Peltier, Powys Heritage Series (London: Cecil Woolf, 1999).
25 Alyse Gregory, December 1946, Diaries (unpublished).
26 Alyse Gregory, January 25, 1947, Diaries (unpublished).
27 Alyse Gregory, *The Day Is Gone* (New York: E. P. Dutton & Co., 1948).
28 Alyse Gregory, August 19, 1948, Diaries (unpublished).
29 Alyse Gregory, September 1947, Diaries (unpublished).
30 Marie Stopes, *Married Love*, 71.

MELVON L. ANKENY

# Gladys Brown Ficke and *The Final Beauty*

In 1936, two years after John Cowper Powys and Phyllis Playter departed America and Phudd Bottom for Dorset and then Wales, their friend and neighbour, the poet Arthur Davison Ficke revealed that his wife, Gladys Brown Ficke, had written a novel with two of the main characters based on John and Phyllis. In a letter to Lloyd Emerson Siberell he wrote

> I have spent most of the last 48 hours reading a remarkable novel, written by my wife. She has worked on it for two years, and I have not seen it before. Jack is the central figure—and it is by far the best portrait of him that has yet been put down on paper. If it ever gets into print, you will howl with delight— you will simply howl! And so will Jack. But the chances of a publisher wanting it are not very good. It is much too fine a piece of work to have a large sale. Still, one always hopes. She hasn't tried it on anyone yet; in fact, there is a good deal of work she still has to do in revision. Do you think that the title, "THE BIRD IN THE ICE-BOX" sounds cheap? I can't make up my mind. (The BIRD is of course not Jack—but his girl-friend. It's an extraordinary novel.)[1]

In 1927 John visited the Fickes in Santa Fe. Arthur was now married to his second wife, Gladys Brown, and was recuperating from a bout with pulmonary tuberculosis. In a letter to Phyllis, John reported the Fickes' plan to return east in the spring and their purchase of Upstate New York property (which they would later name Hardhack), a decision which would later influence John and Phyllis's own move to Phudd Bottom in 1930.

They have bought to live on when he's cured a farm of 300

acres ext where Edna St Vincent and Mr Boissevain live about 30 miles from Albany in our very favourite country — Ficke is a bit nervous as to whether he'll like the complete isolation & long snow-covered winters — but his wife is fixed & resolute to do it. ... He and his horse-taming Gladys seem so serenely happy together after five years of association that its pleasing to see. ...[2]

The eventual discovery of Phudd Bottom by John and Phyllis was due largely to the Fickes living nearby. John's diary records that 'It was in Arthur's car that with the T.T. [Phyllis, the Tiny Thin, The Tao] I saw first our little house at Hillsdale.'[3] And the financial arrangements which made the purchase possible were brokered by Ficke by means of a loan repaid by the sale of a manuscript. In a letter to Lloyd Emerson Siberell, Arthur whimsically wrote:

I do not remember which book it was [*Wolf Solent*], or what price was paid: all I recall is that some such thing as you recount did actually happen, in the early days of J. C. Powys' Columbia County reign. As I remember, he mentioned to me that somebody would like to buy the m.s. of some one of his books; and he wanted to know if he could ask $100.00 for it — and I proceeded to perform an Indian dance of fury, and told him he was a Goddamfool and needed a guardian, and that our price was $2,000.00, and that I would handle the matter for him. Which I did, and got him some very large sum. Since which day, John has always regarded me with eyes in which a kind of solemn terror and awe were visible — as if he thought I were allied with the Devil and could produce rabbits from goldfish-bowls. This episode, and the fact that I could drive an automobile, are probably the whole basis of the great respect which John has always had for me! [4]

The use of the dismissive 'his girl-friend' in Arthur's letter to Siberell about Gladys's novel ('The BIRD is of course not Jack—but his girl-friend.') was characteristic of the relationship of Arthur and Gladys Ficke with Phyllis Playter. John's diaries of the Upstate years (1930–34) record Phyllis's continuing distresses whenever she was in personal contact with the Fickes. In a series of entries in 1930 John wrote:

> They are simple where the T.T. is very subtle and they have no more idea of what she is like than they have of the Holy Ghost.[5]

> I know that they do not set themselves to find out what she is really like. She speaks and no one listens.[6]

> Then she was taken by Gladys for a drive which to her was like the Inquisition.[7]

> Arthur drove back at midnight. He spoke benevolently to me but in some subtle way and with a kind of metallic hardness they made the T.T. feel a wicked 'draught'. When we got home and she had changed her dress to do her packing I found her crying (out by the tree on the road) and it was because of their hard egoism directed towards the child Hilary [Masters] and Warwick [Powys] and towards herself but making a pet of me. I do not like such behaviour and I cannot allow it for the T.T. is a twig in my soul and Warwick is of my clan ...[8]

> She spoke of how strange it was that Gladys and Arthur completely disregard her personality.[9]

> [And he records over a year later] But the presence of Gladys troubled and agitated her—as it always does—The T.T. suffers in her soul from Arthur & Gladys.[10]

John also recorded in his diary his brother Llewelyn's opinion of the Fickes:

> Lulu finds Arthur benevolent but rather hard to illuminate and exhausting to talk to. He thinks Gladys is ... but I care not to report his rather harsh and hasty verdict. He does not at all get Gladys's better qualities — her garden — her horse — her quietness. He does not like her.[11]

The Fickes were considered good friends by John and as neighbors they lived within walking distance of Phudd Bottom. They were generous in chauffeuring John and Phyllis on various errands and visits. But even John felt a certain sense of 'forelock tugging' in reference to the occupants of Hardhack which he sometimes equated with Montacute House and the remembered relationship of vicarage to manor house:

> Gladys came. She is to take us up to Montacute House to see the Squire this afternoon. My feelings are exactly of that same sort — but I am older foxier & very much fiercer & craftier than I was in those days.[12]

And some disagreement was inevitable due to Arthur and Gladys' continuing and undoubtedly well-meaning attempts to act on behalf of John and Phyllis.

> [The] most agitating clash has occurred between Arthur and us over the question of Mr. Keedick [John's lecture agent]. To cool my mind I have just walked to the Iron Bridge. The night is cool and wild and blowing. He thinks I am a fool. He wants to be my Ambassador Plenipotentiary. What does he know? How can he know?[13] [And later.] Arthur and Gladys came to discuss the Keedick affair and as I dodged and dived and squirmed and coiled and slithered … — and Arthur and Gladys *laid down the Law* what did the T.T. do but burst out. Arthur really began, he got angry himself with her as well as irritated with me and was unpardonably sarcastic and then the T.T. got really angry and even said 'Yes I am angry!'[14]

The ongoing currents of discord and slight domestic dramas between the two households were obvious material for discussion and fertile ground for storytelling and fictionalization.

> And also in addition to the Kitchen Stove having gone out, Gladys came and began teaching her how to manage the little Black and how to 'rub his nose in the stuff'. Lo and Behold, the T.T. did stand up to Gladys and actually told her not to come into her house and to interfere. It was nearly a scene … but not exactly a scene for the T.T. became disarmingly frank about her manias and weaknesses. Gladys laughed, but laughed very

awkwardly while her fingers tapped her skin. 'It is funny,' she said. But she will never interfere again; in my opinion![15]

And adding richness to the personal observations and experiences of Gladys, the publication of *Autobiography* in 1934 provided primary documentation of John's fetishes and ritualized behaviour.

## THE NOVEL

Gladys Brown's unpublished novel, titled *The Final Beauty* (the earlier title *The Bird in the Ice-box* having been discarded) is part of the Arthur Davison Ficke Papers at Yale University in the Yale Collection of American Literature, Beinecke Rare Book and Manuscript Library. The title page bears the name of a literary agency suggesting that there was at least some attempt at publication and the manuscript shows evidence of re-writing and re-working. Some recognizable events and characterizations in the work are based on occurrences and personalities known to Gladys, woven together in fanciful ways in a story about innocence, love, renunciation, and the good of the common man. The novel is set in three different locales: rural Pennsylvania, New York City, and rural Connecticut.

The major characters of the novel are Nathalia Bradford (based on Phyllis Playter), Daxton Sillis (based on John Cowper Powys), and Edward Lucas (whose character seems suggested by Evans Rodgers). Evans Rodgers is mentioned in John Cowper Powys's diaries as a newspaper writer (and hopeful novel writer) who was a visitor to Phudd Bottom in 1931 and 1933. Rodgers was an admirer of John's writings and wrote an article based on his visits to Phudd Bottom which was to be published in the June 1934 issue of the Cincinnati publication, *The Outrider: A Journal for the Civilized Minority*. The publication ceased with the May 1934 issue. Later he revised the article, calling it 'The Cult of Powys' and added a 'Second Movement' where he expounded on what he understood Powys's message or philosophy of life to be. The revised article (submitted from New Orleans, where he was then working at the *New Orleans Item*) was to be published in Lloyd Emerson Siberell's *Imprimatur* but it too ceased before publication. Phyllis Playter does not, of course, appear in the

Rodgers article in much the same way that she is absent from the pages of John's *Autobiography*. A copy of the unpublished article is in the Siberell Papers at OSUL. Nothing additional is known of Rodgers.

The early portions of the novel contain some informed impressions of Phyllis Playter's early life. Very little is recorded about Phyllis's life before she met John and what there is describes a lonely existence. In conversation she talked of life as a solitary child, a private education in Boston until she was eighteen when she moved to join her parents in Kansas City, her depression and melancholy when she attempted to write, and her secretarial work in Kansas City.[16] She also loved music and art, dancing and the theatre.[17] Perhaps some of Gladys's impressions were gained from Phyllis herself and from friends of hers who visited both Phudd Bottom and Hardhack. The name of the character based on Phyllis is Nathalia — and was perhaps suggested by the visit of her close friend, Nataly Ort, in 1931. John refers to 'Mrs. O.' as Natalia in several diary entries and she and Phyllis did visit Gladys. Discussing their visit the

conversation veered at last to the difficulty which the T.T. has in coping with Gladys and also her double personality, so that, as she says, she is always the *opposite of everything she is*! It touched me to remark Natalia's devotion to the T.T. & her blind admiration & puzzled respect for her — without really comprehending her ... but being sincere in her respect.[18]

Gladys was familiar with the bohemian New York — Greenwich Village ambience and the milieu of Ficke, Millay, and the circle of Powys friends and family, including Dreiser, Rex Hunter, and the artist, Reginald Marsh. Some of the settings in the New York City portion of her novel reflect this. Romany Marie's restaurant complete with artwork from struggling artists plays a prominent part and some drunken parties and partygoers in other scenes are undoubtedly modelled from observation. But the final section of the novel, which is set in rural Connecticut, offers the most intriguing characterizations of people and events.

The novel opens with 18-year-old Nathalia Bradford and her stern all important father who has renounced his dream of returning in financial triumph to England to reclaim the ancestral Bradford Manor in Dorset. He has purchased an 80-acre estate in Pennsylvania where 'the elms are quite as fine as those in Dorset'.

Nathalia is described as

> undersized, pale faced, stoop shouldered, and her head, loaded at the back with a great knot of hair in an outmoded fashion, seemed too heavy for her long neck. Her eyes were very large and beautiful, almost Oriental in the long sweep of dark brow, her nose was small and slightly aquiline. … Everything about her suggested fragility: her voice low pitched and without resonance, her way of moving with sudden hesitations, hands lifted in doubt, her gentle manners — her restraint might have been nothing but timidity. She lacked the animation and assurance so much affected and admired by Americans.

Nathalia's American mother had died soon after her birth and she had led a rather protected, friendless, and aloof existence, studying music, educated by English tutors and subjected to their 'carping discipline and dictatorial arrogance'. It was Mr. Bradford's aim to preserve 'a strictly English atmosphere in his home' so that he and his daughter would be prepared for their eventual remove to Dorset.

The family settles in the somewhat battered Dutch mansion of Richmond Bide, watched over by seven great elms and sans running water and indoor bathrooms. But Nathalia soon discovers the joy of being allowed to walk alone in the fields and woodlands and adopts her special place, 'the spinney' where a grove of birch trees offers refuge from the ancient elms. She reflects on her solitary life as a child, insulated from friendship with 'vulgar, dirty, ignorant, profane and American' children and forced to invent a melancholy imaginary world.

> All her life she had had one-sided half sorrowful friendships with imaginary people. Cracks in the walls of the old Trenton house, steps in the stairs, pieces of furniture, articles of clothing — all were people whose needs and desires, jealousies and joys she understood. She had acquired what was forbid-

den; companionship with kindred spirits. They consoled her for her isolation from the street-urchins.

Soon there is a momentous occurrence in Nathalia's life with the introduction of a new tutor, beautiful and young Cornelia Willan, who has been engaged to instruct her in the English Classics. Nathalia is enthralled with Miss Willan and her revelation that one's emotional nature can be cultivated through the study of poetry. In a voice 'as soft as love itself, and her eyes were suddenly soft and gentle', Miss Willan's words mesmerize her

> If you love something — or someone — no matter how much, if you can't express it it's a hidden thing. It's gold in the ground. Let the great poets teach you how to mine it. <u>Speak out your love</u>.

The lessons in poetry soon develop into attempts to free Nathalia's spirit with a change to 'duck skirts, silk shirts and white pumps' and a trip to the hairdressers and bobbed hair. Slight embraces and kisses from Cornelia (who is now 'Nell') encourage Nathalia's emotional attachment to her. Mr. Bradford is not enthralled by the changes and scornfully pronounces 'You look masculine. I am no feminist and never have been.'

The next tutoring session finds the two girls in the 'glazed and glittering heat' of the spinney where they are soon lying naked as Nell reads from Shakespeare's Sonnets and divulges the secret that

> His lover was a boy ... Yes, it's one of those darling secrets — when boys are lovers, and when girls are lovers. Do you know, I think it's nicer to love a girl than a boy.

The seduction scene is interrupted by the imminent arrival of Mr. Bradford who has become suspicious of the 'peculiar' relationship of student and teacher. Clothes are rapidly retrieved in some disarray and *Paradise Lost* again becomes the subject of attention although Nell whispers, 'It was regained.'

The only suggestion of any kind of lesbian experience for Phyllis resides in some elliptical entries in the diaries. John makes an intriguing entry:

The T.T. had a complicated Bad Dream including a grown up Dorothy Reed the little girl she used to play those Corinthian Games with in Boston; Games that stimulate my fancy — it is Petrushka's Temptation to think of them![19]

It's not known what John meant by 'Corinthian Games' although there is a sexual connotation in some meanings of Corinthian — as in being licentious — and a tangential suggestion of homosexuality. In an earlier entry he tantalizingly records that

Helen Morgan came to tea — & gave the T.T. a wrist-watch so prettily. I got a thrill from watching her caress the T.T.'s hand & white arm sheathed like an Arum Lily stalk by her new sleeves — calyx-like. I was enchanted by hearing these refined & aristocratic young girls play and rally and tease and float on the waves of their nervous interest in each other.[20]

In the novel Nell leaves to teach at a girls' school in Connecticut. Nathalia is left with her desire for a college education thwarted by her father's lack of money and settles for the compromise of learning to type as a means of accomplishing something practical. She soon forms a friendship with Ed Lucas, whom she had first noticed from the shelter of the spinney; 'a young man with bright taffy-colored hair' who is 'a big strapping fellow in a faded blue shirt and overalls'. He is planning to leave his family's farm for New York to follow his dream of writing for a newspaper. He is suspicious of Nathalia's acquaintance with Nell Willan but they reach an agreement that 'It's natural for fellows and girls to like each other.' Nathalia is afraid to run away to the city but the idealistic Ed encourages her.

If everybody don't make the best they can of themselves they're wasting their talents. They're wasting life force. I read once how life can evolve to a great perfection. I believe that. But if you don't work for it you're working against it. It can't come by itself. Every last one of us has got to cultivate our own gardens — I mean ourselves – and if we don't, why then we're really holding up the — the final beauty.

Nathalia does leave with Ed for New York City and her upset father

agrees to pay for her room at the Y.W.C.A. Ed introduces her to
Greenwich Village and Faustina's Bohemia, a basement restaurant
(based on Romany Marie's). The Great Depression makes employ-
ment difficult for Ed but Faustina introduces him to Dick Waterbury
who works at *The Postal* [New York Post?]. Through this contact he
is introduced to some of Waterbury's amoral friends.

Nathalia visits Nell in the apartment she shares with an intimate
friend and is referred to a stenographer's bureau run by one of her
lesbian friends. Nell also explains to the innocent Nathalia the 'ABC
of sex education' by means of a book with diagrams.

> Nevertheless as Nathalia looked at them she was afflicted with
> appalling sensations; and her wonder deepened into horror.
> ...She at last knew the unknown something that had always
> eluded her. ...this tremendous ... incredible ... Monstrosity!

Enter Daxton Sillis.

Troubled by her perceptions of other human beings and their
sexuality, Nathalia begins to 'think New York is horrible. Everybody
gets unnatural here.' Yet 'despite her disgust ... her eyes kept noticing
men and her brain kept flinging up reminders of a certain part that she
had never seen except in diagram. Awful to think of.' But as she goes
to attend a concert of Efrem Khalov, a conductor whom she had long
idolized, she makes a chance acquaintance. Told there is standing
room only, she is befriended by a man who offers to show her a place
where she can sit in the Family Circle.

> He was tall and gaunt, forty-five years old or more, quite
> elderly, and his shoulders stooped. He had a grizzled mop of
> hair and heavy overhanging brows that made his eyes look
> sunken, though they were not sunken and his cheeks had a
> healthy weather-beaten glow. His nose was an eagle's beak and
> his mouth, wide as a clown's, curved up at the corners ... .

And his accent is that of an Englishman.

Driven to tears by the final selection on the programme which
gives her an intimation of 'having heard a faint echo of what would be
God's omniscient song. That would be the final beauty, what life

intends.....' Nathalia is comforted with a Powysian response.

'You have felt the only kind of ecstasy that is worthy of respect. I had supposed that the female organism was incapable of it — or, I should say, an unlikely resort for it. But I have seen it lodge in you and tear at your vitals!' He pronounced these words with a kind of demonic fervor as if he rejoiced in the bloody havoc he imagined.

He tells Nathalia that he is terrified of women and their 'redoubtable, unassailable composure' and that his 'male audacity is undone by their superior knowingness'. But she is different in her wistful timidity and when she was

pierced to the very bowels by the lance of beauty I was captivated! The magnificent Bach Passacaglia shattered you and I soared up to the peaks of daring courage on its wings: I took charge of you! Now, little Missy, I have returned you to your nest, safe and sound from the flight in high regions. May you be forever delicate and timid as a bird.

Nathalia agrees to attend a gallery opening in the Village on Saturday night 'and after asking her name and giving his, Daxton Sillis, he went away flourishing his hat and grinning like a clown.'
The descriptions of Daxton at the gallery opening in conversation seem particularly apt:

Gaunt, angular and electric [he] was standing bent over with his hands grasping his knees while he talked vehemently. He had a beaked nose and a big mouth; his shabby tweed coat bulged at the pockets and his unpressed trousers were worn pale at the knees. He was so wrapped up in what he said that one was persuaded of his integrity.

Daxton Sillis, although an American of New England background, was sent to England as a small boy to be educated by his missionary parents who were serving in India. He has the quintessential accent of the cultured Englishman and also has ties to Dorset. He is engaged in writing about music and the graphic arts in his belief that in their sublimity they are the antithesis of the 'utter loathsomeness of the human race.'

After a somewhat shocking party at a painter's home with others of the Village bohemian set, Daxton apologetically escorts Nathalia home. In the taxi he holds her hands, kisses both them and his own and

> she felt a kind of mystical, unbodily marriage celebrated. And it was marriage enough for two who eschewed the gross, corporeal being; but Nathalia knew not yet the meaning of her own elemental happiness.

Daxton confides his fondness of 'lovely thin hands and knees' which give him 'a delicious pleasure'. He is rewarded by Nathalia pulling up her skirt

> to display her knees, thin, showing the bones and sleek in silk stockings. 'Oh —' he sighed and laid his hand across them. 'Oh, my dear — what a delight — what a rapture! I am infinitely consoled for every mortal iniquity.'

But on the way to his hotel, Daxton deplores his behaviour:

> enamored of a little girl, a child with the knees of a greyhound. Old enough to be her father, great beast! great monstrous slathering ape! filled with rapture and a lust to touch her knees. How long would it take the greyhound to become a bitch? Aye, that would fix you, old demon! When woman breasts and rumps come you'd scuttle for your very life.

Ed Lucas had attended the same gallery opening as Nathalia and in a later scene at the Y.W.C.A. they argue about her new friends and he grabs her roughly in a passionate kiss. This is interrupted by the matron and leaves a shamed Nathalia thinking of 'Ed's hot and sinister kisses. But can the marriage ceremony make less distasteful the acts of marriage? ... Can one never get away from this thing?'

At the end of a traumatic visit to an artists' ball, Nathalia finally meets Daxton again. She confides to him that she wishes to help him, be like him and live in his way.

Will you take me, Daxton? Let me be with you. Let me help you, surely I can. I am a good typist now, I can work for you, and I can help you in many ways.

Daxton confesses some of his 'manias!' (underlined in true JCP fashion) and they spend the night together with only the caressing and kissing of Nathalia's knees as the physical expression of their love. At Daxton's urging, they decide to

go at once courageously into the green hills and valleys and find our home. ... A little cottage with vines and the shadow of a hill and the murmur of a brook's voice, with all the stirring life that these things unfold —

Nathalia and Daxton, with his walking stick, discover in the rolling hills of Connecticut, near the village of Merrilton, the cottage they are seeking.

Like a Don Quixote in flapping tweed he charged forward, sword in hand, and she, the doubting Sancho, trailed along seeing no castle in the air. He knocked at the door. When it opened he was standing with hat, stick and bundle of rubbers clasped against his stomach and somehow he managed to bow.

She was wholly reconciled to escape with Daxton; and now in retrospect the little cottage snuggled in the hills seemed truly the refuge for a pair of idealists.

Prior to moving to Connecticut, Daxton and Nathalia have an interview with her father. Mr. Bradford is intrigued and intimidated by Daxton's English manner and assents to their living together. Nathalia explains

that we don't want to marry as most people do; we want to live together and share whatever fortunes or misfortunes may come to us, but we aren't——we aren't lovers in the usual sense of the word.

In the village of Merrilton, they are known as Mr. And Mrs. Sillis, and neither of them corrects the mistake.

I am very glad, my dear, [Daxton says] that you've not corrected the natives when they address you as Mrs. Sillis; for these people, I fear, are quite as primitive as persons of a similar class in England; and they might — I don't say they would — but they <u>might</u> exhibit signs of moral outrage did they know the true state of affairs.

The portrayal of their neighbours is unflattering and bleak. The Chipworths and the Chidleys are somewhat mean and grasping and Harry Chipworth remains a constant sexual threat to Nathalia. If the novel had achieved publication, one wonders how actual neighbors, the Kricks and the Steitz, and Miss McNeill who came in to cook and clean, would have reacted.

Mrs. Chipworth scrubbed for the indecent pair and salved her conscience by putting aside for Christmas the very high pay she received. ... It was understood far and wide that Mr. Sillis was a fool, he'd pay anything asked, always providing his 'little whore' — the men whispered this and guffawed — was not at hand to correct him. With excellent wit they spoke of him as 'Mr. Silly.'

The use of Mr. Silly falls into John's tradition of calling himself a zany, a ninny, and of his Sherborne nickname 'Moony', or his references to 'John Loony'.

During Evans Rodgers first visit in 1931, he stayed at the Steitz home and also visited with the Fickes. An undercurrent of local suspicion was indicated in John's diary.

I found Mr Rodgers just arrived for tea. He told us that Mrs Steitz had displayed curiosity about us.[21] [And later] We were all at breakfast at noon when Gladys came back from Hudson. She came in saying 'Let us talk Dirt' & we discussed what Mr Rodgers had said about the Suspicions of Mrs Steitz with regard to our Relations. ...[22]

In the novel Gladys captures many of the daily domestic routines and concerns at Phudd Bottom which are familiar to readers of John's

published diaries. Preparing high tea at 5 o'clock and the difficulties of
a bland vegetarian diet as adequate sustenance for Nathalia (Phyllis)
are represented. 'She grew more wan and pale as the months passed.'
In the diaries, John records this same difficulty:

> The T.T. I found very upset for she felt so exhausted & hungry
> for she cannot cook enough for herself alone. It is very
> serious. Ailinon! Ailinon! She wished we were both dead. ...[23]

Nathalia's (Phyllis) love of gardening is also described in the novel.

> She flew about, happily doing things: digging garden plots in
> front of the house, planting seeds in flower-pots, old sauce-
> pans, broken glasses, tomato cans, anything that would hold
> soil; and these cluttered every sunny window-sill in the house.

Later in some wintry scenes — Daxton (John) is seen in his
sheepskin coat going for eggs, milk and the post. There is also an
amusing sequence of Daxton attempting to take out the ashes and
trying to light fires — much as constantly recorded in the diaries.

Scenes of physical intimacy in the cottage consist of the moments
of saying goodnight when Daxton would 'caress her, kiss her cheeks
and neck, her hands and at last her knees'. Or as Nathalia later refers
to it 'the moment for love-making'. She then retires to her bedroom
and Daxton to his nightly ritual in a scene reminiscent of *Autobiography*:

> He approached it with failing confidence for he was not
> always successful. Sometimes, especially if the sky were
> bright, the fold of hills out at which he looked would refuse to
> merge and melt into the familiar lane that seemed to hold the
> alchemy of magic. Terrible, vile, obscene thoughts paraded
> across his vision. It was not a new experience, for these filthy
> images had hovered around him throughout his life; and his
> ritual had not always driven them away. Now they were more
> powerful and more alluring. His imagination was excited by
> the nearness of his girl. He knew that his pulses throbbed with
> excitement; the forbidden pleasure held him spellbound as

surely as the divine joy of infinitude had ever held him in bodiless trance. Instead of feeling the beauty of life he thought of its wickedness and thought of it with cringing pleasure. Of every dirty thing he had ever heard and every bawdy book he had ever read and every lewd picture he had ever seen—with pleasure! With pulsating joy and lust! He would be consumed with a grotesque and horrible delight.

The imagery of the bird begins to appear more and more in the novel. Daxton now refers to Nathalia as 'my little greybird' instead of the previous greyhound. And he gives a pure white cat to Nathalia. They name 'him' Samson (perhaps a joke regarding their sexual innocence) although they soon discover that Samson is very female and soon begins to add her/his progeny to the household.

Daxton tells of his early years in an Anglo-Catholic school in England, which he attended from the age of eight. Gladys includes a convincing scene in this section where Daxton is bullied by some of the other boys. They give him a sandwich of 'goat's milk cheese' which is really chopped suet and then reveal to him that it is 'Fat! Fat! Fat' — and he is revolted by it and runs out vomiting as he runs to the privy. It resonates with scenes of bullying in *Autobiography*. There is a scene of homosexual seduction by a father confessor figure, Father Eaton, although it seems improbable that it was suggested by any occurrence in John's background. [It could be right out of the current files of the Catholic church scandals in America and other countries.] But it is given as Daxton's reason for renouncing 'both Christianity and lust'.

A sense of the close companionship and working relationship of John and Phyllis is seen in various scenes of the novel.

Ah, they were happy, these two, fated for each other. Daxton kept telling her so in words and in action. She never entered the room without his looking up with eyes that focused slowly away from his work to smile at her ... a formidable sense of his goodness and love. With all her heart she returned the love and tried to emulate his nature.

At night they wooed and parted unwed like the first two mortals. In the fall the long worked-over manuscript was at last finished.

Nathalia's work diligently typing Daxton's manuscript is similarly detailed in the diaries. 'The typing paper has come to an end so that the T.T. can have a holiday.' And 'she also started Typing again which I was opposed to but she did it in the morning. ...'²⁴

Daxton's book, *Therapy of Art*, is released in February and sells well even though it is in the midst of the Great Depression — astute businessmen who are purchasing contemporary landscapes — thinking that the book will lead people to nature and to nature painting, are promoting it.

It was his belief that man could find repose for his spirit only in the negation of worldly, competitive ambitions, which, as products of a half civilized civilization, he judged to have been developed partly through accident and partly through man's misunderstanding of his own nature and needs. ... The most malleable material: the highest type of cultivated and sensitized persons: and the simplest of the peasantry who had not yet developed the refinement of cruelty known in the great centres of business and industry. ... The artists, he believed, were the ones who had reached the heights, cold there, and lonely, and his directions were primarily to guide them down into the true garden of Eden. ... His system, his <u>Secret</u> he called it. ... It was to discover the sound and color and form of beauty and to allow this God-created magnificence to be the source of happiness.

Nathalia reads an article by Ed Lucas in *The Postal* and she responds with a letter concerning the value of 'solitude'. At his response 'her heart rejoiced for a second and then sank leaden like a shot bird'.

Daxton continually visits his sacred shrine, a mountain laurel, bringing small offerings of mould and moss, spraying his urine at its base, invoking its protection to 'recast decay, transmute despair.'

In dark brown corduroy he was the color of dead and rain-soaked leaves, soon to be earth; out of blue cuffs, too long and protruding beyond his coat sleeves, his thin, white wrists and blue-veined hands came like the buds of an exotic lily; woolen stockings hung rumpled below his knickerbockers, making his legs like the shapeless stems of trees; and the green bandana handkerchief that hung from one pocket could have been a cluster of living leaves. He was camouflaged for the forest. ... He dreamed his own rhapsodic dream.

Daxton worries that 'this life is unnatural' for Nathalia and that she should 'be transplanted to a happier soil'. And as in the diary, they discuss whether they should have a child: 'It is possible that my way is not that of any woman. Nathalia, do you long to have a child?' which terrifies Daxton 'of the thing that might be asked of him ...'.

The original title of the novel, *The Bird in the Ice-Box*, comes from the following scene in the novel. A phoebe bird is brought to the steps of the cottage by Samson — and preserved in the icebox:

She put it in the icebox, the splendid white sepulcher lately acquired and shut it in. But before going to bed that night Nathalia, driven by nervous incredulity, opened the gates again and inspected the symbol of herself. Alas, it had not revived.

The bird is sent to the taxidermist and Nathalia muses, 'Greybird, he calls me. I'm the bird in the icebox.'

The diaries record a similar incident at Phudd Bottom:

The Mees has been killing a lot of birds of late. One the T.T. has sent to be stuffed but she cannot resist anger & even hate towards the Mees. She tries to shut her up thus struggling against Nature. What can be done?[25] [and later] Mr. Johnson brought the Mail — our Stuffed Bird after 3 months — from Rowland's the taxidermist.[26]

In the final scenes of the novel, Ed Lucas arranges for a visit to the cottage with the excuse of interviewing and writing an article on Daxton for *The Postal*. He tells his editor of his personal relationship with Sillis and 'Mrs. Sillis'. 'I swear I can get you a story nobody else can.' He also remembers the 'girl who once had slipped like an affectionate wood nymph into his embrace'. Ed had experienced some difficult times in New York but had re-dedicated himself to his idealistic pursuit of the 'Final Beauty'.

To have doubted one's own first principles is the mark of a civilized man. Well, he had doubted his first principles but now he was returning to them. Unless one worked for it — the Final Beauty — one worked against it. ... Every beauty that he could imagine of art and science and industry, of nature in its wild and cultivated phases, the life of creatures, sport, love and the raising of lovely, healthy children was a part of the Final Beauty. He imagined men somehow getting together to produce out of the endless wealth of the world enough and more than enough for their physical needs so that their aesthetic and spiritual necessities could at last be attended to.

Anticipating his visit, Nathalia thinks again of

the bird in the icebox. She would come out and sit on a dead twig and look alive. Her dear old friend would think she was alive. He would come and talk politely and make foolish notes about Daxton and then he would go away again and everything would be the same as before.

Ed is met at the train by Harry Chipworth —

A country man approached him and showing two rows of strong green teeth said: 'Friend of Miss. Bradford's?'
[On the way] Their eyes met for a quick mutual examination. 'Mrs. Sillis,' said Edward, 'is an old friend of mine.'
'She told me,' said the man grinning.
'I used to know her when she was Miss. Bradford.'
Again their eyes met. The countryman said nothing; and Edward Lucas felt sure that he had won in a little contest of insinuation.

In the interactions of Daxton with his guest, Gladys captures some of the qualities which must have made John Cowper Powys the remarkable platform performer that he was reputed to be. As *Autobiography* states, he had an inveterate tendency to be ... *a philosophic actor.* ... I have always been an actor in ideas — a charlatan if you will and I am prepared to justify it; for is not Nature herself the nursing mother of all Mimes and Mummers, of all Pierrots, Petrushkas, and Punchinellos?[27]

And perhaps Gladys had also experienced a Powys lecture!

Hilariously poking fun at himself, like a clown, he told the story of the goat's milk cheese ... and with every manner of exaggeration made the young man shout with laughter. Ah, he could be a buffoon.

Nathalia listened — observing to herself coolly 'Daxton was the eloquent one.'

With his agile fingers pressed ten in a row against the table's edge he glared his fierce endearing earnestness. ...

Daxton, the genial host, the sophisticate in raveled tweeds, the sage or clown or court entertainer, whatever he chose to be if he wished to choose, shuffled his wits for a new play. Seduce, allure, bewitch, wheedle, cajole, call upon the Muses, the Mystics, and the Myomancers but never the cohorts of controversy.

He then brings up the subject of *King Lear*:

Daxton began to act, literally to act <u>King Lear</u>. He was the vain, misguided King, contemptible, pitiful and mad; and with a twist of his face he was sly Regan; and his rugged brow smoothed and he was true Cordelia. 'Let it be so; thy truth then be thy dower.' He was knight and courtier and servant; and supremely he was the Fool whose lines he chanted and sang, though he had no singing voice, and sometimes squawked like a parrot. ...

The little hill-house became a castle, a mountain crag, a storm-tossed forest where a mad-man talked to a wisely raving fool. ...

Daxton was neither fool nor madman though he raved; and the two listeners were caught in the magical spell of King Lear, probably never before delivered with such sound and fury.

Not all of it by any means; and yet, leaping from one chosen place to another he played the play. At last he was the beaten, cheerless, lonely King. ...

Edward sat speechless, staring at the man who had worked a magic before his eyes; and Daxton turned away with a sigh.

'Everywhere there is beastliness and filth,' he muttered, 'but every man can delight in the beauty that lies at the edge of the cesspool, aye, is in it if he have vision to see.'

But Ed Lucas is aware of the figure of Nathalia

so meekly positive, he thought, a useful zero – standing beside her man's figure, making it larger. Once she had a denomination of her own — small or large, who could say? — but plus something. Where was her music and her brave resolution to advance whatever gifts she had? [He was also] conscious at the same time of the almost hungry look on her saddened face, and of the unadorning curve of hair over her blue-veined temples, and of the dress that hung too long, too straight, too flat, the dress certainly of an old maid. The starved spinster of Daxton Sillis, he thought; and hatred for this philosophy of retirement into the good and beautiful — a cowardly retreat with lies and deception and frauds and deliberate blindness to the common fate of man for golden rule — stifled him with heavy indignation.

In the novel's denouement, Nathalia revolts against the cerebral 'love-making' of Daxton and thinks of Ed Lucas lying in the spare room. As she returns downstairs, Ed comes out of his room, they embrace and Nathalia admits she loves him. But she is firm in her commitment to Daxton and her renunciation of life. 'I shall have to stay here until I'm dead all the way through.' Ed is determined that she must 'choose life!' And it is then that Daxton comes downstairs.

'I heard your whispers, not what you said. But I knew – aye, I knew. This afternoon I felt in my bones that Edward was my enemy. ...'

'Listen to me!' He turned swiftly and hurled his fiercest

115

glare at them. 'No one can be my enemy! Do you understand? No one can be my enemy!'

He leaned over Nathalia's cowering figure, touched her shoulder with his sensitive fingers. 'Little greybird — fly away — fly away —'

She covered her tear-stained face; with that gesture she gave him up; and he turned back to the moon-flooded doorway.

His chin lifted, he said: 'Do you think I would cage a bird?' His wide open eyes stared into the shadowed distance. The heavy carving of his face was like stone in the pale blue sheen of light.

Now his spirit fled out into the quiet woods. Like a wounded animal he wanted to be alone and crouched close to the ground; he sniffed the odor of it on the faint breeze and dreamed of a timeless content that lay under the shelter of his altar, deep, deep , in the earth.

THE END

Arthur Davison Ficke died 30 November 1945 and Gladys Brown Ficke 14 May 1973. In 1950 his papers were given to Yale University by Gladys Brown Ficke. The collection also includes Gladys's papers and along with *The Final Beauty* is her manuscript *of Arthur Davison Ficke: A Biography*. The finding aid to the Ficke collection can be found in the Yale University Library, Finding Aid Database at http://webtext.library.yale.edu/finddocs/fadsear.htm.

AFTERWORD

The sexual aspect of Daxton and Nathalia's relationship in the novel is quite likely based on Gladys's perceptions and knowledge of Arthur's conversations with John. Discussions of John's sexual predilections are coloured by his enigmatic statements of being 'happy in my way' as compared to 'Lulu's way' with references to Tantric or Tibetan practices:

not in Lulu's manner but in my own Tibetan manner I made

love to the T.T.[28] [or] I was so thrilled to see her that my
pleasure passed the limit practiced by the Late Dalai Lama ...
& attained the level always spoken of by Lulu — when he
writes 'I was Happy'.[29]

An extraordinary exchange of letters offers some information on
the topic but ultimately it comes down to the question of who was
telling the 'truth' and whose 'truth' was it? Arthur, in a letter to the
'Most Incredible of all Possible Jacks' asked John directly about his
sexual practices:

And speaking of perversions — I want to ask you something
which you are by no means obliged to answer. You remember
that once, when you were posing for a portrait, I was trying to
keep you awake by talking to you. And in the course of our
talk, you hinted something so incredible that I asked you if I
had your permission to ask you a direct question about the
matter. You readily said that I might. So I said in the most
scientific and unequivocal words I could think of: "Do you
really mean to try to convey to me the idea that you have never
in your whole life had a normal orgasm inside the body of a
woman?" "Never in my whole life", you replied, with fiendish
glee as you saw me completely flabbergasted. Well, I am still
flabbergasted — so much so that I now repeat the identical
question I asked you then. And do you dare give me the same
answer now? Do you not repent of attempting so to deceive
me? What do you say, old Monster of Phudd? Do you wish me
to go to my grave still wondering what possible motive you
could have had for lying to me on that occasion?[30]

John's reply to 'Arthur Darling' answered the question in his own
rhetorically gilded circumlocutious manner:

Let me rush to answer as Categorically Laconically and with
the nearest Approach to truth possible in a world wherein
truth is NOT one of the elements discoverable by Science
your most exciting question — I wd be prepared to swear
before Minos, Rhadamanthus and perhaps even Hitler, that

the only time I have ever committed fornication in my whole life — with or without the Licence of God and Holy Church — was on the occasion when with a sublime Deviation from my normal ways I begat my dear son Littleton Alfred just 33 years older [*sic*] than I am as I am 33 years younger than my Father on the 30th of August 190–. ... I can't do THAT piece of mathematics but 'twas 19 and something 1906 would make him 30 so wd it be 1903 but that looks an odd, uneven, UNNATURAL date for him to have been born on! ...

But it is as far as I can tell CERTAIN AND SURE that save for that one single serious and consequential and gravely responsible Lapse from my Natural Normal and Incurable ways tastes inclinations preferences and prejudices — I have never, so Help me God and my dear redeemer, ever committed the Notorious and often referred-to, ORTHODOX ACT OF COPULATION upon which the hinges of so many complications turn and must turn, and should turn; and only now and then — by the Grace of God — ARE DODGED! ...

Your old 'John 'Once-and-No-more!'"
IN ALL AFFECTION; WHATEVER HAPPENS TO EITHER OF US.[31] ĭ

WORKS CITED

Unless otherwise noted, all quotations are from the manuscript of *The Final Beauty* by Gladys Brown Ficke, the Arthur Davison Ficke Papers, Yale Collection of American Literature, Beinecke Rare Book and Manuscript Library. Permission was granted by the Yale Committee on Literary Property on behalf of Yale University, the owner of literary rights.

The quotations from John Cowper Powys's Diaries (JCP Diary) by date are from the following sources:
Powys, John Cowper, *The Diary of John Cowper Powys for 1929*, ed. Anthony Head (London: Cecil Woolf, 1998).
——, *The Diary of John Cowper Powys 1930*, ed. Frederick Davies (London: Greymitre Books, 1987).
——, *The Diary of John Cowper Powys 1931*, ed. Jeffrey Kwintner (London: Jeffrey Kwintner, 1990).

———, *Petrushka and the Dancer: The Diaries of John Cowper Powys 1929–1939*, ed. Morine Krissdóttir (Manchester: Carcanet Press, 1995).
The author's reading of the original diaries in the National Library of Wales.

Items listed as OSUL are from the Lloyd Emerson Siberell papers, Rare Books and Manuscripts, The Ohio State University Libraries.

NOTES

1  A. D. Ficke, letter to L. E. Siberell, 8 November, 1936. (OSUL)
2  J. C. Powys, letter to P. Playter, 1 August, 1927. (courtesy M. Krissdóttir)
3  JCP Diary, 12 February, 1930.
4  A. D. Ficke, letter to L. E. Siberell, 27 December, 1943. (OSUL)
5  JCP Diary, 15 June, 1930.
6  JCP Diary, 16 June, 1930.
7  JCP Diary, 3 August, 1930.
8  JCP Diary, 4 August, 1930.
9  JCP Diary, 29 November, 1930.
10  JCP Diary, 10 October, 1931.
11  JCP Diary, 21 August, 1930.
12  JCP Diary, 11 May, 1931.
13  JCP Diary, 13 September, 1930.
14  JCP Diary, 14 September, 1930.
15  JCP Diary, 14 December, 1930.
16  Humphrey, Belinda, ed., *Recollections of the Powys Brothers* (London: Peter Owen, 1980), 31, and Graves, Richard Perceval, *The Brothers Powys* (London: Routledge & Kegan Paul, 1983), 150–151.
17  Krissdottir, Morine. 'Phyllis through John's Diary', *The Powys Journal* 3 (1993), 32.
18  JCP Diary, 2 August, 1931.
19  JCP Diary, 2 May, 1931.
20  JCP Diary, 12 March, 1931.
21  JCP Diary, 9 August, 1931.
22  JCP Diary, 11 August, 1931.
23  JCP Diary, 9 July, 1932.
24  JCP Diary, 26 January, 1931 and 20 April, 1931.
25  JCP Diary, 5 October, 1933.
26  JCP Diary, 6 December, 1933.
27  Powys, John Cowper, *Autobiography* (New York: Simon and Schuster, 1934), 124.
28  JCP Diary, 16 April, 1934.
29  JCP Diary, 20 December, 1933.
30  A. D. Ficke, letter to J. C. Powys, 21 April, 1936. (OSUL)
31  J. C. Powys, letter to A. D. Ficke, 3 May, 1936. (OSUL)

J. LAWRENCE MITCHELL

# Theodore Powys and John Death *

*'He, under Whom I have my dominion and my power, is a dark star.' Who can escape Him?*

(*Unclay*)

While Theodore Powys was bedridden with flu on March 28, 1929, Sylvia Townsend Warner paid one of her frequent visits. She enjoyed reading to him and feeding him tidbits of information likely to provoke his morbid curiosity — on this occasion the initial instalment of a grave-digger's diary in the latest issue of *The Country-man*. After praising her contribution to *Kindness in a Corner* (1930), he asked: 'Do you think it would be proper for me to introduce Death into a story?' and began to share his 'first thoughts' for a work he had already entitled *Unclay* (Harman, 33; *Recollections*,133). The next day, Good Friday, Sylvia's text was Norman Ault's recently published *Seventeenth Century Lyrics* (1928) a copy of which had been pre-sented to Theodore by their publisher and friend Charles Prentice in November 1928. She noted in her diary that 'the poems Theo marked [were] nearly all about death' (STW Diary, Dorset County Museum; see also *Recollections*, 133) One of them, 'The Prayer' by Jeremy Taylor, from the festival hymns included in *The Golden Grove* (1655), is unequivocally the source of the novel title Theodore had men-tioned the day before. For in Theodore's copy, the relevant page number (285) has been written in pencil on the fly-leaf and the neologism 'unclay', has been underlined in the poem:

> My soul doth pant towards thee,
> My God, source of eternal life.

* A paper read at the Powys Society Conference, Millfield, 2002.

Flesh fights with me:
O, end the strife,
And part us, that in peace I may
Unclay
My wearied spirit, and take
My flight to thy eternal spring,
Where, for his sake
Who is my king,
I may wash all my tears away,
That day.

Of course, Theodore had long been familiar with Taylor's work. As early as April 26 1906, he told Louis Wilkinson: 'I have been reading Jeremy Taylor and recommend him to your notice; he is a cock of the right kind' (*Welsh Ambassadors*, 76 ). So he must have been re-reading Taylor's *The Rule and Exercises of Holy Dying* (1651) in preparation for *Unclay*. While outlining the plot of the novel for Sylvia, he also mentioned 'that sad Mr. Taylor', observing that 'It is a little terrible to be with him. One sees him in his pit of despair and feels that one has but to take a step to be in it toHo' (Harman 41–42). One other early trace of the genesis of *Unclay* is to be found at the back of Theodore's copy of *The Book of Common Prayer* (a present from his mother in 1895), where he scribbled a few pencil notes — unfortunately not dated: 'Unclay / Facey of Dodder / the small farmer / who loves Susie Dawe'.

That 'John Death' as protagonist is introduced only in Powys's *last* novel, the realistic allegory, *Unclay* (1929), cannot be deemed accidental. Powys had already reinvented God in his own image in *Mr. Weston's Good Wine* (1927) and now presented Death as a friendly forgetful fellow of uncertain occupation with whom the innocent clergyman, Mr Hayhoe, is quickly on first name terms. Could it be that, in thus confronting 'the last enemy' in fictional form and reducing him to a mere character in a novel, Powys completed his self-administered remedy and rid himself of his fear of death? Though the question cannot, of course, be answered definitively, it is the case that in later years he *was* capable of joking about his own death. He told his

wife, Violet, for example, that should he die from eating the mush-
rooms he liked to gather, she could keep as many cats as she liked after
she buried him (Scutt, 15). And he also liked to remind everyone that
there was no escaping John Death. Even in replying to brother John's
birthday letter in 1946, Theodore wrote: 'all I can think of and
consider now is Master John Death' (TFP to JCP, 22 December
1946). And sometimes John enters Theodore's world : 'Mrs Playter
[Phyllis's mother] comes next in line for Master J. Death being 83 and
next comes Brother John in his 78th year' (JCP to TFP, 19 December
1949; PR3 77),

I seek here to explore the roots of Theodore's obsession with
death, to register the significance of those moments when death
intruded upon his quiet life — notably the murder of his ELDER son,
Dicky — and, finally, to reconstruct the story of his own death from
documentary sources, especially family letters and diaries.

## I. ROOTS OF OBSESSION WITH DEATH

Although we know all too little about the early life of Theodore
Powys and less still about the forces that shaped his mental life, there
are tantalizing glimpses of evidence in his writings. 'Under The
Bondage of Fear' (1904), one of his first and most autobiographical
pieces, offers a picture of a sensitive and guilt-ridden child, here called
'Jake', exposed to a stern Old Testament God and to the terrors of
hellfire and damnation: 'As a babe, he lived ever in a vale of tears, and
growing older his terrors increased. Being very delicate and weakly,
and loving no noisy or rough games, he was despised of his brother'
(HRHRC ms). In church the boy is terrified by the 'harsh words' of
the priest whose references to 'deep and dark sins' convince him that
'he was defiled by them'. He finds some consolation in an 'old book'
[Pilgrim's Progress] but is haunted by nightmares in which demons
mock him or he is 'a martyr of the olden times and ... bound naked to
a stake' while those lighting the pyre repeat 'This is the righteous
judgement of God'. This brief account of the mental afflictions of
Theodore's fictional alter ego has the ring of truth to it and accords
well with what we know about Theodore himself. In fact, he was

troubled by nightmares his entire life (Theodora Scutt recalls how 'through two thick walls his cries would wake me' Scutt 244) and he suffered something akin to a nervous breakdown while quite young. Bunyan's allegory is, of course, recognized, along with the Bible, as a seminal influence upon his fiction; but no other account exists, to the best of my knowledge, of the psychological reasons for its importance to him, save that to be found in 'Under The Bondage Of Fear'. Young Jake's nightmare death at the stake which is equated with 'the righteous judgement of God' is, however, given gentler fictional shape in Theodore's published novels and stories as 'God's Gift'. There are a number of possible sources for this conceit, but Theodore may first have encountered it in *The Rule and Exercises of Holy Dying* (1651) where the emphasis is slightly different: 'and because eternal life is the gift of God, I have less reason to despair' (228). Nonetheless, the full significance of this singular vision of death can only be appreciated when we recognize that the phrase 'God's Gift' is also a gloss upon Powys's first name, Theodore, from Greek *theos* = 'God' + *doron* = 'gift'. The anglicized form of the Hebrew equivalent is 'Nathaniel', a name that occurs most notably in Theodore's sombre fable 'Darkness and Nathaniel'.

It was from his mother's side of the family that Theodore Powys seems to have inherited his melancholic, even morbid, predisposition. His mother, Mary Cowper Powys, was the daughter of a clergyman, the Reverend William Cowper Johnson of Yaxham, who discouraged frivolity on the part of his daughter in favour of 'making very serious work of prayer & Bible study, and rejecting all reading that is inconsistent with such habits' (WCJ to Mary Cowper Johnson, 17 January, 1869). In many points of character, then, Theodore resembles his distant kinsman, the poet William Cowper (1731–1800). For example, both suffered from lifelong fits of depression, and both sought relief in 'a retired and quiet life of simple domestic and rural pleasures' (Drabble, 1985, 236). It is also hard to read Cowper's letters without recognizing sentiments that Theodore would have endorsed and might even have articulated. In the end-pages of his disbound copy of Cowper's *Private Correspondence* (1824), Theodore has jotted down '155 style' in evident approval of Cowper's observation that 'there is a certain *style* of dispensations maintained by Providence in the dealings of God with every man, which, however the incidents of his life may vary ... is never exchanged for another.' It was *his* fate, Cowper believed, to be subjected to 'sudden, violent, unlooked-for change'. Theodore Powys, it would appear, saw himself as similarly afflicted. In her journal for September 26 1932, Alyse Gregory noted that 'He sleeps and wakes always with his mistress — death ...' (cited in Humfrey, 146) and that he revealed that 'FEAR had been the whole centre and driving force of his life' (Humfrey, 147).

## 2. DEATH IN THE FAMILY: THE DEATH OF THE SON

A death in the family provokes many emotions: grief, of course — but also anger, bewilderment, despair. Sometimes these emotions are exorcised by action of one sort or another, and, in the case of an artistic temperament, creatively exorcised. The death of Katherine Mansfield's brother, Leslie, in World War One in 1915 'completely changed the balance between her cynical side and the other, and so released her main creative stream' (Alpers, 1982, 183). D. H. Lawrence, perceptive as ever, wrote to her consolingly: 'Do not be sad. It is one life which is passing away from us, one 'I' is dying; but there is another coming into being, which is the happy creative you. I knew you would have to die with your brother; you also, go down into death and be extinguished. But for us there is a rising from the grave, there is a resurrection' (December 20 1915). Here, of course, Lawrence goes beyond consolation in trying to get Mansfield to embrace his own phoenix mythology. When Rudyard Kipling lost his son, John, in the same war in the same year, he plunged himself into work for the War Graves Commission and into writing that was far more spiritual, recognizing both the redemptive value of suffering, as in 'The Gardener' (collected in *Debits and Credits*, 1926) and also — in a few stories — the healing power of the English countryside. But the persistence and intensity of his personal loss is heard most poignantly in the refrain to his poem, 'The Children,' which asks the world the always unanswerable question:

'But who shall return us our children?'

The war affected the Powys family less than many — largely because John, Theodore, and Llewelyn were all at one time or another declared unfit to serve — though Bertie was taken prisoner on the Western Front and Willie served in East Africa. None of the three, however, went un-scarred by its effects. Llewelyn, for example, who took Willie's place on the farm while his brother was in the army, found conditions grim and his situation not without danger. In a letter to John on September 23 1917, he refers to a nearby settler murdered in the night by natives and confesses that 'sometimes when I sit alone at night ... I think this may be my end'. Theodore, who could claim little success after years of writing, was humiliated by his poverty, experiencing marital troubles, and almost suicidally depressed, sometimes yearning for 'the peace that passeth understanding' (TFP to JCP, March 16 1918) and sometimes expressing fear of death: 'True is it, as Dr. Johnson said "We shall receive no letters in the grave" ... But I'm terrified of it.' (TFP to JCP, Sept 29 1916). He was twice summoned to Dorchester Barracks for possible induction into the army — the last time on May 26 1917, and one suspects that, had he passed his physical, he might have gone to war with something of a sense of relief. Ironically, his escape from the army came at the price of unwanted intimations of mortality; for the examining doctor detected a disqualifying heart condition which led Theodore — cautious as ever — to abandon swimming. Small wonder then that even the end of the war failed to shake his gloom, and he could imagine himself dead all too easily:

> What a queer thing too it is to think of, that in a very short time we shall be dead, quite dead. Fancy a person standing by the bed and saying quite loudly so that anyone really ought to hear — 'Theodore'. And there would be no reply, only silence.
> (TFP to JCP, Dec 5 1919)

Both John and Theodore were destined to lose sons. John's would die as the indirect result of a motorcycle accident; but, in October 1931, Theodore's son, Theodore Cowper or 'Dicky', as he was generally known, met a death that surpassed in violence and grotesquerie the worst excesses of his father's imagination. At first glance, it seems surprising that the obsessively cautious Theodore should ever have allowed a son of his to venture so far from home. When Dicky was ten, he was scheduled to go off to Sherborne Prep, just as his father had. So painful were Theodore's memories of the experience that he could not even contemplate delivering Dicky to the school himself. Instead, he wrote to his sister, Gertrude: 'If Dicky does go to Sherborne next Autumn, if I bring him to Montacute, would you take him? ... I think I might cry and cry if I took him up that road.' The key to understanding Theodore's willingness to send the same son to Africa that he had been unwilling to take to school in England lies in Dicky's desire to be a farmer, particularly a sheep farmer. The frustrated hopes of Theodore, the father, of becoming 'good shepherd' to his own flock might yet be realized through Theodore, the son. So Dicky, still a youthful seventeen, sailed for East Africa aboard *The Gloucester Castle* on December 6 1923 bound for life as a sheep farmer under his uncle, Willie. But Theodore's acquiescence — it was probably never much more — in Dicky's emigration did not mean that he stopped worrying about him. For example, on the date of his first birthday abroad, Theodore wrote to John: 'I do pray that he will be careful when he rides the motorbicycle. He had a number of adventures when he looks, like Saul, for the lost asses of the King' (October 26 [1924]). Only one of Dicky's early letters to his father survives; there he describes himself, almost triumphantly, as 'busy with 20,000 sheep' (November 10 1926). He must also have tried to allay his father's well-known anxiety, for Sylvia Townsend Warner records in her diary for August 5 1928 that 'At tea Theo spoke of Dicky knowing no fear in Africa. Theo said in a harmless country full of lions and tigers there would be little opportunity to learn that useless lesson' (STW Diary, Dorset County Museum). It would be six years before Dicky returned home for a visit. His father wrote to Sylvia Townsend Warner (October 8 1929) recording the event:

> Dicky does not seem to have altered in the least. He arrived rather suddenly with the same overcoat that he went away in six years ago. His hat was different that was all. He does not take all the cream for breakfast, which is what I expected him to do, and so I am very pleased with him.

He quickly won the affection of his father's circle of literary friends, especially Valentine Ackland and Sylvia Townsend Warner. He went to Dorchester with Sylvia in late October 1929, and visited her in her Bayswater flat a couple of times during January 1930. She was struck from time to time by his resemblance to Theodore, 'Theo's upper-lip, and Theo's nose set on at Violet's angle' (STW Diary, October 25 1929) and 'a tone strangely like Theo in Dicky' (STW Diary, January 4 1930). On January 7, Dicky and Sylvia went to the London Zoo and then to dinner with Charles Prentice who wrote to his father: 'Sylvia, Dick and I had a very happy dinner last night. Afterwards we went a walk along the south side of the river between Hungerford Bridge and London Bridge, through desert streets, past still blank towering buildings, and the strange secret noises of hidden machines ...' (CP to TFP, January 8 1930). The following evening Valentine — with whom he had flirted in Chaldon — escorted him around town. She describes him as 'shy and amorous' in her account of their near-affair in *For Sylvia* (1985,117–18).

The first news of Dicky's death came in a cable from Willie on October 21 1931, saying that Dicky had been killed while out riding. This was soon corrected by another to the effect that he had been killed by a lion. Bad as that must have seemed, the truth was far worse: Dicky had actually been murdered — speared, beheaded, and his head and testicles carried off as trophies by Samburu warriors fulfilling a manhood initiation rite. He had ridden out on his white pony as usual on the morning of October 19 to inspect the flocks and his pony had returned riderless a few hours later. He was only twenty-five. The fate that Llewelyn — who, curiously enough, also rode a white pony in Kenya — had imagined for himself had befallen another member of the family, his nephew. The fullest account of this gruesome episode is to be found in Elspeth Huxley's *Out in the The Midday Sun* (1985). Another version is to be found in Jack Smith-Hughes, 'Songs of the Vultures or Samburu Witchcraft, The Powys Mystery, 1931.'( *Nine Verdicts On Violence, London, 1956, 109–38).

The day after he received the news, Theodore sat down and dutifully wrote letters to family and friends, informing them of Dicky's death. His letter to his brother, Bertie, outlines no more than the painful 'facts'; his letter to Sylvia Townsend Warner adds that 'Violet, though of course terribly upset, goes on just as usual' and asks her to inform Charles Prentice. She must surely have regretted her explicit mockery of his 'unappeasable imagination' and 'insatiable carefulness' at the time of Dicky's departure in 1923 (*Chatto & Windus Miscellany*, 1928, 55). The letter to Francis has a quintessentially Theodorian edge to it: 'Well, I remember Dicky falling down a bank once and saying "That's done for him." This time it has' (October 23 1931). In replying to a letter of sympathy from Charles Lahr, the bookdealer, Theodore's anguish is barely suppressed: 'Perhaps God is treating us less kindly by letting us live than Dicky who he has killed' (October 24 1931). Some days later, he is particularly revealing in a letter to Bertie: 'I certainly never knew before that one could feel quite so strangely as Violet and I feel. — Violet is a little better — But I don't expect that the world will ever be the same world to her again now that Dicky has ceased to live — She looks strangely about her, missing something' (October 29 1931). Meanwhile, in East Africa, British Colonial rule proved itself totally inadequate to dealing with a ritual killing such as that of which Dicky was the victim. Half-a-dozen Samburu warriors who had been heard boasting of their feat were brought to trial but never convicted (See Scutt, 94–5. In this matter Theodora Scutt's source is mistaken. Compare Huxley, 143). On behalf of the family, Willie commissioned 'a proud casting in bronze' to mark Dicky's lonely grave, with a verse from Isaiah 29.10 selected by his father (WP to A. R. 'Bertie' Powys, August 15 1932). The plaque read:

HERE LIES

THEODORE COWPER POWYS

OCT 26 1906

OCT 19 1931

FOR THE LORD HATH POURED OUT

UPON YOU THE SPIRIT OF DEEP SLEEP

As the anniversary of Dicky's death approached, Theodore wrote to John in terms that — importantly, from a biographical point of view — seem to connect Dicky's death with Theodore's abandonment of writing: 'It is now almost a year since Dicky was killed ... It is now too nearly a year since I wrote any fiction. And I begin to wonder how I ever came to do such a thing. I am sure I could never do so again ...' (October 14 1932). The implicit linking of these two events looks very like *prima facie* evidence. On the other hand, one of the few surviving letters from Dicky to his father — dated only December 5, but probably 1930 — seems to constitute possible counter-evidence. Dicky wrote: 'The Kukes [Kikuyu] pinch a lot which always makes everybody furious ... I am awfully sorry you are going to stop writing books as I love reading them.' Now the reference to 'books' may simply mean that Theodore had given up writing novels or it may mean that he was declaring his intention to give up *all* writing at least ten months before Dicky's murder. Even if we accept the latter reading, we may wish to explain it — and a number of other such statements made after the completion of *Unclay* — as the kind of thing that an author often says at the end of his latest creative struggle. In the face of this ambiguity, we need evidence of a different sort. Llewelyn's letter to John (February 12 1933) would appear to confirm Theodore's abandonment of writing, at least soon after he and his wife had adopted Susan in January 1933: 'Theodore is very fond of his Susie. He is in fair spirits but drawing himself back to his old way of living and has given up writing' (February 12 1933). Yet, only seven months later, we find Theodore writing to Charles Prentice, his editor at Chatto & Windus, to promise that 'In about two months time, I hope to have enough of these new short stories that I have been doing, almost enough for a book' (September 17 1933). At best, then, we can say that Theodore vacillated and that his inclination to give up writing extended over a considerable period of time. But what are 'these new short stories'? The three long stories in *The Two Thieves* (1932) were all written by September 1931, as were 'The Better Gift' (originally intended for *The Two Thieves*, but not published until 1937 as *Goat Green*), and 'The Sixpenny Strumpet'; so the book in question could only have been *Captain Patch* (1935). Now one of Theodore's surviving notebooks in the Francis Feather Collection (No 73 in Riley's list) contains the manuscript of an essay on 'Summer' — one of his rare non-fiction publications — which appeared in the *Daily Herald*,

June 2 1933. In all likelihood, this occasional piece was written that year; thus the ten stories in the same notebook (five of which were included in *Captain Patch*) can also be assigned to the same period. Such indirect dating by association is necessary, since Theodore eschewed, for the most part, any effort to date stories. If we remember the reason he offered in 'Why I have given up writing' (*John O'London's Weekly*, October 23 1936) for having begun — 'At one time I hoped to find happiness in writing, like Burton of *The Anatomy of Melancholy*, who professed to discover in writing a cure for depression' — we may even venture to suggest that perhaps, after all, he meant what he said about giving up writing in his letter to Dicky, and that, in fact, it was Dicky's death that led him to *resume*. In any case, this last burst of creative energy faded within a year or so, and there is not much disputing Theodore's 1936 statement that 'I have written nothing for two years ... A writer should know when to stop, when he has said enough.' Louis Wilkinson's comment in a letter to Theodore that he was 'pleased to see in the papers that you were writing again' (December 18 1937) was probably prompted by the recent publication of *Goat Green* by the Golden Cockerel Press. Wilkinson no doubt assumed that the work was newly written, when, in fact, as we have seen, it was written six years earlier.

For Theodore, the memories of his first-born were buried with him: Dicky at Sherborne, Dicky on his motorbike, Dicky 'at the same table with me learning Swahili' (December 24 1922) — and in later life he rarely mentioned the son he lost to Africa and his own dream. But Violet kept his photograph by her bed and kissed it each night before retiring (Scutt, 93; for other details, see Scutt, 163–4). Little wonder that when Willie Powys volunteered to let Susie / Theodora live with his family in Kenya, Violet 'nearly went into hysterics, saying that Africa had taken too much from her already' (Scutt, 223). Did she ever know the facts about her son's death? I cannot say. But Theodore chose to present — to casual acquaintances at least — the more palatable account of Dicky's death given in Willie's second cable. Thus, in his letter to the composer Christopher le Fleming (February 15 1932), he apologizes for being unable to offer hospitality as his wife was still recovering from the death of their eldest son who was killed by a lion in Africa. And four years later, the evidence of her diary for 23 January 1935 suggests that his sister, Gertrude Powys, may have been shielded from the truth. She notes there: 'Dicky's friend Carpenter was killed by a rhinosaurus. I wonder if his horse that shied was the one Dicky rode & that shied with him?' (HRHRC ms.) His memory haunted her. When she went to tea with her brother, Littleton, and his wife, Mabel, in Weymouth just before World War Two, they strolled by the former family residence in Greenhill Terrace and Gertrude wrote in her diary, 'I thought of Dicky's head at his bedroom window so often' (Thursday, March 23 1939).

## 3. THEODORE'S FINAL DAYS: THE DEATH OF THE FATHER

The churchyard of St Nicholas in East Chaldon is now full of individuals from the Powys circle — among them Katie Powys, Bob and Flo Legg of the *Sailor's Return*, Farmer James Cobb of West Chaldon Farm, Betty Muntz, sculptor of the head of Theodore now in the Dorset County Museum. The words on her tombstone — 'I will lift up mine eyes unto the hills' — uncannily echo one of Theodore's oft-quoted lines from the Bible, and suggest his influence upon her. Others include Valentine ('Molly') Ackland (1906–69) and Sylvia Townsend Warner (1893–1978), both of whom were good friends who left valuable impressions of him in their writings. Strangely absent from this company is Theodore Powys himself whose final journey to his resting place in Mappowder churchyard must now be recounted.

The heart problem detected by the army doctor in 1916 when Theodore was forty-one led him to claim hyper-sensitively that 'I have felt that organ rather prominent of late' (TFP to LlP, 22 June 1916). In fact, the problem was probably no more than an innocuous irregularity, a murmur, and it never again features in reports on his health. But for a while he could, with some satisfaction, set his 'heart problem' against John's ulcer and Llewelyn's consumption in the family list of complaints. His fear of death, of course, never needed any sanction from reality and was omnipresent. Writing to David

Garnett in 1927 about Theodore's attitude to death, Sylvia Townsend Warner observes:

> It is the judgement of a child to compare him with Donne and Webster ... for they could not keep away from the thought of death, it was like pressing the sore tooth to them, but with Theo it is the only tooth that will not fail him. (STW to DG, 25 September 1927).

Two years later, after an afternoon walk with him during which they discussed *Unclay*, Sylvia came to appreciate for the first time just how real his fear was: Theodore confessed that 'I never go to bed without thinking of my death' (Harman, 33; STW Diary, April 3 1929, Dorset County Museum). Llewelyn was, in his own way, every bit as obsessed with death as his older brother, though his very real illness undoubtedly gave him more justification. Inevitably, when the two brothers got together — one the creator of John Death, and the other given to exclaiming 'Timor mortis me conturbat' (an epigraph taken from William Dunbar in *Love and Death*, 1941) — the conversation often turned morbid. Llewelyn wrote to John describing Theodore's reaction to a conversation with one of the locals, 'old Dickon.' Llewelyn had asked bluntly 'Are you afraid of death?' and the old man had replied sagely, 'No ... *Because it is natural.*' It was the word 'natural', says Llewelyn, 'that provoked the humorous malice of Theodore, who after all has always distrusted nature and is to his very marrow bone a puritanical visionary'. (LlP to JCP, January 1933; C.U.L.)

By 1938, Theodore was sixty-three and well into his 'retirement' from writing. He suffered from headaches and high blood-pressure, and his hand trembled somewhat; and, after Bertie, who was six year younger than Theodore, died in 1936, death must have seemed far from a distant prospect. During this period, Gertrude usually went to tea at Beth Car on a Tuesday, and reported Theodore 'not at all well' on January 11 1938. But it was not until Monday, March 28 1938 that she reported 'Theodore felt giddy when he got up and fainted. He has to be kept quiet in bed. It was like a stroke.' In fact, his good friend, Dr Charlie Smith confirmed that he had indeed suffered 'a slight stroke' (Llewelyn Powys to H. Rivers Pollock, April 20 1938).

Llewelyn in Clavadel heard of Theodore's 'alarming attack' from Littleton, and quoted back Littleton's remarks about 'that white head that has harrowed so many hells of which you & I know nothing, lying so white upon a white bed' (*Collected Letters*, No 276, April 1938). Theodore's recovery was very slow so that he was still complaining about his head in October, and in 1939 Violet wrote to David Garnett's wife, Ray that 'Theodore is far from well. Last March he had a stroke & it's taking such a time for him to get better. His head is still bad & he can't talk but for a few minutes.' By October of that year, however, he was well enough to walk with Gertrude on High Chaldon when she came for her usual Tuesday tea (GP Diary, October 17 1939). Unfortunately, neither the world news nor the news from Switzerland about Llewelyn's health was good: in mid-November he had a stomach haemorrhage and December 2 brought Alyse's telegram to say 'Darling Lulu died this morning'. A few days later Theodore, who had grown very close to Llewelyn while he lived nearby at Chydyok, spoke fondly of his brother visiting White House Farm, Sweffling so many years ago. Gertrude recorded in her diary:

> Theodore said today he never saw anyone so happy as when as a boy Lulu arrived at Saxmundham [Suffolk] to stay with him & ran out of the station in his Eton coat to him. (GP Diary, December 5 1939)

Theodore's sense of personal loss lingered and, even years later, was still strong. Thus, on August 5 1948, he wrote sadly to Penn Kine: 'Llewelyn has now been dead nearly nine years. I have no words to say how much I miss him.' For Llewelyn, confronted with the same fears as his elder brother, had done what Theodore could never have done: he had chosen to rush out and embrace life, to celebrate 'the glory of life', to seize not love *or* death (the two vintages of wine available to Mr Weston's clients) but love *and* death (as in his autobiographical novel of that name). When Llewelyn died, so died the risk-taker, the womaniser, the *bon vivant* that a secret Theodore would dearly have liked to have been. Theodore's recognition of the contrast between his timidity (something like Joyce's 'paralysis') and Llewelyn's boldness came early in life, as we see from the words he puts in Llewelyn's mouth in one of his dialogues (28 August 1911): 'You dare not taste the apple because you fear the worm in the core.' Precisely. Sylvia Townsend Warner saw the same phenomenon from a different perspective — his problem was 'ennui — the ennui of a violent character constrained to a doctrine of non-offensiveness' (STW Diary, September 4 1953, Dorset County Museum).

A few months after Llewelyn's death, Theodore was shocked to learn of the death of artist Ray Garnett, who had done woodcuts for a number of his books, including *Black Bryony, Mark Only*, and *Mr. Tasker's Gods*. The Garnett family had also visited Chaldon in the twenties; and Ray, then a young mother of two boys, got on famously with all the inhabitants of Beth Car. Theodore wrote a remarkable letter of consolation to his friend David:

> I am quite unworthy of Ray's love and of yours too David, and now that Ray is dead I feel so sad. You were very good to write and tell me — somehow one can bear sorrow better from the fountain head of that sorrow, than if the word comes from elsewhere. Ray was here, and it seems only like yesterday, when she was at Lulworth with Richard and William. And I remember earlier playing with her and Richard near Jar's Stone [on High Chaldon] — she never seemed to me to want much to make her happy, she could be happy so easily. It is easier to follow than to lead David. I am sitting by the fire and the sunlight is slowly moving across my bed, for I sleep downstairs now. When your letter came I had taken up a book of poems[in fact Arthur Quiller-Couch's *Oxford Book of English Verse*] —
>
> > 'Tis true — with shame and grief I yield
> > Thou, like the vain frost took'st the field
> > And gotten hast the victory
> > In thus adventuring to die
> > Before me, who more years might crave
> > A just precedence in the grave.
> > But hark! my pulse like a soft drum
> > Beats my approach, tells thee I come

And show howso'er my marches be
I shall at last sit down by thee.'

For Theodore, poetry — here the work of Bishop Henry King—
offered a special kind of consolation. That is why John Death very
much approves Mr. Hayhoe's choice of poet: 'I believe that you have
Keats' *Odes* in your pocket. He's a fine poet and knows whom to
praise when he listens in a darkening evening to the song of a
nightingale' (*Unclay* 146). In *Still The Joy Of It*, Littleton Powys, the
athletic schoolmaster of the family, recalls with bewildered amusement the letter of sympathy *he* received from Theodore on the death
of his wife: 'My brother Theodore ... introduced this quotation from
the Arabic: "In the Garden of Life a bird sang on the highest branch,
and then soared away (cited also in Graves, 313)."'
Violet was a devoted wife to Theodore and, especially after his
stroke, a good nurse who danced attendance on his every need.
However, from time to time, she had health problems of her own. At
the beginning of July 1949, Theodore related how 'Poor Violet had a
dreadful bleeding of the nose the other day, though it may have saved
her from a stroke. We were very frightened. She is better now but still
feels her head rather bad and is sometimes giddy' (TFP to JCP, July 4
1949). The account Theodora gives of the same incident is both funny
and indicative of Theodore's desperate dependency: 'at the sight of
the ghastly blood-stained apparition that was his wife ... Daddy
completely lost his head; he dived down between the sheets and called
out 'Oh, don't die, Violet! Don't die!' (Scutt, 280).
Since Theodore, Violet, and Susan had moved to Mappowder in
1941, they had lived in The Lodge, a damp and cramped cottage right
next to the churchyard. As Peter Riley put it so well: 'he ate and slept
on the horizon of the dead' (*PR3* 29). Here he found peace and
became friends with the rector, Dr Samuel Francis Jackson — 'old
Frank' to Theodore — who shared some of his bookish interests.
Theodore seems to have been instrumental in the revival of Compline
and would recite the responses from the back of the church. The
effects of his stroke lingered on. Violet reported to Alyse Gregory,
Llewelyn's widow, that he complained a great deal about his head and

that 'he has numbness in his arm & can't use it very well. I have to help him on with his clothes' (VP to AG, 17 November 1942, HRHRC). In fact, it seems to have been his ill-health that caused him to worry about visitors and to 'hide away from them' whenever he could (VP to AG, n.d., HRHRC). His favourite retreat was atop one of the oldest flat-top gravestones under the yew tree where he might read a little William Barnes or Shakespeare or just sit in silent contemplation. It was at this time that 'he began to refer too frequently to the time when he would be "underneath the grasses" in that same churchyard' (Scutt, 226–7). One of those visitors he could *not* escape was the American Elizabeth Wade White, Valentine's friend, who insisted upon a photograph to mark the occasion. In the photo of them arm-in-arm, Theodore looks as grim as Elizabeth looks gleeful at cornering her prey. She later sent him a copy of Christina Rossetti's *Poems* inscribed 'For Dear Theodore, with Elizabeth Wade White's love, & remembering Sunday 10th April 1949'. In the summer of 1951, a new visitor to Mappowder, Gerard Casey, would prove far more welcome to Theodore, given his readiness to indulge discussion of the Theodorean canon of writers: Richard Baxter, Jacob Boehme, Meister Eckhart, William Law and, of course, Jeremy Taylor.

The year 1952 was not a good one for the Powys family. Gertrude died quite suddenly in April and Theodore was not well enough to attend the funeral in Montacute. The brother and sister had always been close, a closeness forged in their youthful days together at White House Farm in Sweffling, Suffolk. John's son, Littleton Alfred, was terminally ill, and Theodore's younger sister, Lucy was in a sanatorium at North Allington, Dorset. Theodore's sight was now failing, probably on account of cataracts. Responding to John's usual birthday gift of money, he said: 'I don't see very well. But I rather like not seeing very well. You don't want to see everything' (TFP to JCP, December 20 1952). The last line is vintage Theodore — 'You don't want to see everything'. In fact, one of his troubles in life had been seeing too much, the skull beneath the skin. The combination of grief and dimmed vision seemed to precipitate a slow withdrawal into himself, the hermit without the soliloquy. Now he would sit cradling some familiar volume like an old friend without turning as much as a

page or he would take up the knitting he had begun as therapy. He
certainly would not have wanted to see very clearly what lay before
him.

When Sylvia and Valentine visited Theodore in mid-July of 1953,
they found him alone, looking 'marked for death' and 'terrified of
falling into the hands of a hospital' (Harman, 198; July 17 1953) —
just as brother Bertie had been in 1936. Five days later they heard from
Violet that Dr Smith had told her the nature of Theodore's malady [it
was cancer of the bowel]. Upon their next visit at the end of July,
'Theo wore his guise of 17th cent[ury] stoicism' (STW Diary, 199;
July 31 1953). The following day they called to drive him to Sherborne
Hospital. Theodora couldn't remember who took him, but her
description of the sick man is evocative: 'He went, beautifully dressed
in his best suit and looking like the dying Merlin' (Scutt, 288). At the
hospital, he was admitted to a private room with a pleasant view. After
Valentine returned with string she had bought for his dressing gown,
she was overcome by emotion. When Violet later entered the empty
house, she burst into tears and Sylvia wrote in her diary 'it is a time for
autumn sowing, whether T. F. lives or dies' (consciously or uncon-
sciously echoing her own epigraph for *Summer Will Show*). On
August 8, he was discharged and Valentine drove him home to
Mappowder. He had been given drugs to take at night and was
scheduled to return on September 9 for an operation. When Sylvia
next saw him on August 11, they chatted about her latest novel (*The
Flint Anchor*) and 'somehow we got round to God being a shy being,
in agonies at public appearances ... but behind all this peaceable
chatter, I saw his eyes roving to next month' (STW Diary, Dorset
County Museum). In fact, ten days before the date set for his
operation, Theodore mustered enough will-power to refuse to
undergo it, choosing what he was told would be 'a year of life rather
than two years perhaps with tubes in his belly' (Harman, 200;
September 4 1953). Harold Raymond, who had replaced Charles
Prentice as Theodore's contact at Chatto & Windus, sent Violet a
reassuring letter when he heard the news: 'Yes, I am sure you are right.
The choice lies with Theo. It is his life & his mind is clear, and capable
of making a decision. Whatever some doctors may think of the

decision, he has come to, I am positive that many of them, if they themselves at his age were faced with the same dreadful choice, would decide as he has done' (HR to VP, October 22, 1953). But the choice was no easy one for Theodore. At times he would be calm and resigned, at others he would be overcome by intense fear and melancholy, even threatening to hang himself (STW Diary, 7 September, 1953; Dorset County Museum). Dr Charlie Smith had meanwhile retired and the new doctor, Eccleston, prescribed no pain-killing drugs, saying that 'when the pain began, Theo would be willing enough to go back to hospital' (STW Diary, Dorset County Museum; October 18 1953). On her visit of October 18, Sylvia kissed his forehead while he lay asleep. He awoke and she said: 'We have loved each other for such a long time' and he replied 'Yes, my dear, we have loved for a very long time'. This may have been the last coherent exchange between the two old friends. When the stress of coping with a dying man became too much for Violet, even with Susan's help, Francis's wife, Sally, took over some of the duties. Of course, at this point, Theodore was well aware that his life was ebbing away.

By this stage, word had spread about Theodore's condition, and a procession of relatives and old friends began to appear at Mappowder or to write. Littleton visited in October and discreetly gave Violet £100. The two brothers 'had a delightful talk for an hour, both knew it was the last', according to Littleton (LP to Vera Wainwright, 27 December 1953; British Library). One childhood friend, Marjorie Philips, of Montacute House, wrote in a shaky hand from Hampshire: 'Those old days at Montacute are still very happy recollections & I can remember a lot of amusing incidents … I shall think of you' (Bissell Collection, Dorset County Museum). Louis Wilkinson who lived close by in Hazelbury Bryan visited more than once and wrote to John with details of his visits. Later he wrote: 'When I last saw him, very soon before his death, of which he had thought and written so much, he was serene, he was at peace and content' (Brocard Sewell 1964, 13). This statement, repeated for a booklet in the Mappowder Church in 1967, smacks more of reassurance than reality. Angus Davidson had heard the news from Sylvia Warner and visited early in September; he told David Garnett over dinner in London who then wrote to

Theodore on November 6, asking to visit on Thursday, November 12. By then, Theodore was too weak to reply and Francis did so instead, reporting that:

> Theodore, I am afraid, is now very weak and getting frailer every day. His mind is as alert as ever. He talks a great deal & with happiness of the old times. He is at present without much pain, and our only hope is that he will not have to suffer. Your visit will give him great pleasure & comfort (FP to DG, November 8 1953).

Alas, by the time of David's visit, the situation had deteriorated and Theodore was confused and slipping in and out of consciousness. It must have been just before this period that he allegedly cried out 'Belle!' Belle!' But whether this was a reference to Bernie O'Neill's long-dead wife or to a church bell (a favourite motif, as in *The Market Bell*; see also Peter Riley in *PR* 3, 1978) we simply cannot say. He lapsed into a coma so that when Katie visited from Chaldon on November 26, it was too late for farewells ('Katie' Powys to Louis Wilkinson, December 1953). Later she wrote to Lucy who had accompanied her: 'I feel glad I went. But oh what a sad sight it was ... I was grateful that we both could stand together at his feet, knowing what he has been to us and what we lose by losing him' ('Katie' Powys to Littleton Powys, November 27 1953). Sylvia Warner was reading David Garnett's autobiography when Valentine took the phone call that Theodore was 'sinking', so she had trouble sleeping:

> That night — there was a wind — I woke many times thinking of Theo; and once, hearing him say [in] that familiar voice of quiet violence, "A leaf has been blown away." I knew it was part of a sentence about an autumn morning in Madder or Dodder, and one morning seeming like another. But A Leaf has been Blown Away. After that I slept, as I hope he does. But I wish he had read my book (STW Diary, November 26, 1953, Dorset County Museum).

Sylvia may have been remembering the fable of 'The Withered Leaf and the Green' where the chestnut represents the false optimism of youth and the oak represents the pessimistic fatalism of age. In any case, Sylvia gave a rather different version of the story to Katie Powys in a letter, saying that she dreamed she was reading a manuscript by him of how 'one morning looks like another, but is not the same' and then 'I heard Theo's own voice continuing the sentence and saying "A leaf has been blown away"' (STW to CP, 27 February 1954?).

Theodore died the next day, Friday, November 27 1953 at 6.45 in the evening, just before it was time for his favourite service, Compline. Only Violet and two local nurses were present at the moment of death. These two women, Lottie Garrett and Bess Trevett, then took on the task of laying him out.

When his death was announced on the BBC, he was misidentified as a novelist and poet, which suggests some confusion with John Cowper Powys. Oddly enough, in far-off Corwen in Wales, John first got the news from this announcement. Writing to Lucy, he says: 'We were not a little startled by the news of his death last night, <u>Friday night</u> on the wireless. But your heavenly letter to Phyllis came safely this morning and you can believe how we studied every word of it … especially those words of his "I will … come … back."' And, just as Theodore's thoughts were drawn back to his brother's childhood when Llewelyn died in 1939, John's took him back to schooldays at Sherborne when Theodore died, albeit articulated in his familiar style of tortured particularity:

> Aye Aye how clearly can I see his figure when as a little boy he came down through the field up towards the Yeovil Rd. at Sherborne when L[ittleton] and I came out of Wildman's House and went up that long field to the Yeovil Rd. to meet him on his way to the Trent Lanes from wh[ich] you could see Montacute Hill. (JCP to Lucy P, November 28 1953. Courtesy of Louise de Bruin)

Sylvia Townsend Warner once tried, in 1927, to write Theodore's 'Life' but had to abandon the project, in part because her would-be subject had serious reservations about it. But he surely would have approved her evocative coverage of his death, especially the funeral on December 1 1953. A portion of her description was included in *The*

*Diaries of Sylvia Townsend Warner* (Chatto & Windus, 1994, 203) edited by Claire Harman. Here I will cite a later unpublished section of the diary itself:

> The starlings brattling against the solitary church crow ... Susie coming out, just after the coffin, in a pre-raphaelite beauty of entranced sorrow. Violet, as though she would fall into the grave as the coffin was lowered, and Francis with a stern set gravity, holding her back, his gaze averted. Old Mr Jackson [the minister], after the last blessing, standing still beside the grave, his foot on the wooden cross-bar ... with a most moving air of having broken off a conversation that would later be resumed, of having, only temporarily, the last word; and old Mrs Lucas, delivering Katie's bunch of bayleaves into the grave.

At last, Theodore Powys, the creator of John Death, had found rest in 'God's Acre', as he liked to call the churchyard. Like Matthew Hurd in *Black Bryony* (1923), 'the perfect stillness had called him, and he had accepted it ... as the kindest of God's gifts to man' (*BB*,183). He had never wanted a tombstone, telling Violet during the war: 'No Violet, I know you cannot afford a tombstone for me, indeed I hate tombstones. I won't have one' (TFP to JCP December 25 1941). But he got one anyway: such memorials are for the living. It is in the shape of an open book, upon the left-hand page of which is inscribed 'IN LOVING MEMORY OF / THEODORE FRANCIS / POWYS / AT REST / 27TH NOVEMBER 1953 / AGED 77 YEARS'. Upon his grave in spring celandines sometimes grow; these were among his favourite flowers because of their link with Wordsworth's poem.

In *The Rules and Exercises of Holy Dying* (1651) one of Jeremy Taylor's precepts is that 'He that would die well must always look for death, every day knocking at the gates of the grave' (*HD*, 37). In this matter, Theodore followed the advice of the seventeenth-century divine, as a way of conquering his fear of death. But he remembered, too, Nietzsche's advice in *Thus Spake Zarathustra* on how to survive life: 'Creating — that is the great salvation from suffering, and life's alleviation' (*TSZ*, 99). Reflecting upon his career, he once said with characteristic humility : 'When I look back I wonder that I ever wrote at all. I suppose it was fright. Fright that when God says to me "Show me your work" I should have had nothing to show.' We can only be grateful for the 'bondage of fear' that drove him to such a productive response.

## ACKNOWLEDGMENTS

I would like to express my appreciation to the following for help in granting access to manuscript materials under their control: Louise de Bruin, Mappowder; Richard Garnett, Hilton Hall; Claire Harman, biographer of Sylvia Townsend Warner; Cathy Henderson, The Harry Ransom Humanities Research Center, University of Texas at Austin; the late Mary Cowper Johnson; Morine Krisdóttir, The Bissell Collection, Dorset County Museum; the Library staff, Cambridge University Library; Stephen Powys Marks.

## REFERENCES

Ackland, Valentine, *For Sylvia: An Honest Account* (London: Chatto & Windus, 1985).
Alpers, Antony, *The Life of Katherine Mansfield* (New York: The Viking Press, 1980).
Ault, Norman, *Seventeenth Century Lyrics* (London: Longmans, Green, 1928 [copy in Bissell Collection, Dorset County Museum]).
Clemo, Jack, 'Pilgrimage to Mappowder', in Humfrey, 1980, 164–7.
Cowper, William, *Private Correspondence of William Cowper Esq.*, 3rd edition, Volume II (London: Henry Colburn and Simpkin and Marshall, 1824).
Drabble, Margaret, *The Oxford Companion to English Literature*, 5th edition (Oxford: Oxford University Press, 1985, 236).
Garnett, Richard, 'Theodore Powys and The Garnetts: Records of Friendship', *The Powys Journal*, Volume XI (2001), 9–44).
Graves, Richard Perceval, *The Brothers Powys* (New York: Charles Scribner's, 1983).
Harman, Claire, ed., *The Diaries of Sylvia Townsend Warner* (London: Chatto & Windus, 1994).
Humfrey, Belinda, ed., *Recollections of The Powys Brothers* (London: Peter Owen, 1980).
Huxley, Elspeth, *Out in the The Midday Sun* (New York: Viking, 1987 (first published in London, 1985)).
Kipling, Rudyard, *Debits and Credits* (London: Macmillan, 1926).
Marlow, Louis, *Welsh Ambassadors: Powys Lives and Letters* (London: Chapman and Hall, 1936).

Nietzsche, Friedrich, *Thus Spake Zarathustra*, translated by Thomas Common (New York: Boni and Liveright, 1926).

Powys, Theodore Francis, 'Summer', *The Daily Herald*, June 2, 1933.

——, 'Why I Have Given Up Writing', *John O'London's Weekly and Outlook*, October 23, 1936, Vol. XXXVI, No 915, 145–6, 152.

Quiller Couch, Arthur, ed., *The Oxford Book of English Verse 1250–1900* (Oxford: The Clarendon Press, 1922).

Riley, Peter, 'T. F. Powys at Mappowder: A consideration of his fiction in the light of the twenty years of non-writing', *The Powys Review* 3, Summer 1978.

Scott, J. W. Robertson, ed., *The Countryman Book* (London: Odhams Press, 1948), (Includes reprint of 'The Grave Digger's Diary' from the 1929 *Countryman*).

Scutt, Theodora Gay, *Cuckoo in the Powys Nest: A Memoir* (Harleston, Norfolk: Brynmill Press, 2000).

Sewell, Brocard, *Theodore: Essays on T. F. Powys* (Aylesford, Kent: Saint Albert's Press 1964).

Smith-Hughes, Jack, 'Songs of the Vultures or Samburu Witchcraft, The Powys Mystery, 1931', in *Nine Verdicts On Violence* (London: Cassell, 1956), 109–38.

Taylor, Jeremy, *The Rules and Exercises of Holy Dying* (London: William Pickering, 1845).

Wilkinson, Louis, ed., *The Letters of Llewelyn Powys* (London: John Lane, The Bodley Head, 1943).

Zytaruk, George J., and James T. Boulton, eds., *The Letters of D. H. Lawrence*, Volume II, 1913–16 (Cambridge: Cambridge UP, 1981).

ROBIN WOOD

# Resident Foreigners and Bards!
# John Cowper Powys & James Hanley in Wales

On 22nd August 1936, two writers from England, then resident in
North Wales, John Cowper Powys and James Hanley, were admitted
to the order of the Gorsedd of Bards.[1] Hanley came to Corwen in
1931, from nearby Liverpool, when he had just begun to establish
himself as a writer (Gostick 10). Powys, on the other hand, through
Hanley's encouragement, came to Wales, in 1935, from Dorchester.
This is where he had made a temporary home, after his return from
America in 1934. By this time, the much older Powys was a well-
established writer and had published numerous works, including six
novels. Powys remained in Wales until his death in 1963, whereas
Hanley moved to London, sometime in 1963.

Different reasons led these two important twentieth-century novelists, from England, to settle in Wales in the 1930s. The interaction
between these two 'resident foreigners',[2] and Wales and the Welsh,
also produced distinctly different works of fiction, set in Wales, from
Powys and Hanley. Yet interesting similarities, and shared influences,
do exist, at times, between their novels.

The backgrounds of these two novelists were very different. Born
in Dublin in 1901, Hanley grew up in working-class Kirkdale, Liverpool, in an Irish-Catholic, immigrant family, the son of an engine-
room greaser on a Cunard transatlantic liner.[3] Born in Derbyshire,
almost thirty years earlier, in 1872, Powys, however, had grown-up
largely in the rural West of England where his father had been a
Church of England clergyman, with a private income. Powys had,
over the years maintained his West Country roots, with annual
holidays, even when he was a peripatetic lecturer, based in New York
City. Prior to returning to Dorset, he had lived since April 1930, in

retirement from the lecture circuit, in rural seclusion in Upper New York State. While Powys had experienced the rigours of Sherborne Public School in his youth, Hanley had gone to sea when he was thirteen, in 1915. He served on troopships, until April 1917, when, lying about his age, he joined the Canadian Army in New Brunswick (*Broken Water* 207–13). Hanley reached France in May 1918, and eventually moved to the front line where he took part in the major offensive in late August 1918. He was then hospitalized, on August 27th, a few days before his seventeenth birthday (Canadian Army files). The middle-aged Powys made two attempts to join up in New York, probably in 1917, and then again in Sussex, early in 1918, but was rejected on health grounds, on both occasions (*Autobiography* 584–7).

The friendship between these two men had its origin in a letter Hanley wrote to Powys on 3rd October 1929, asking for a copy of the recently published *Wolf Solent* (Gerard 38). Later, in 1931, Powys was godfather to Hanley's son Liam Powys (Gostick 11), and in that same year Hanley's *Men in Darkness: Five Stories* was published, with a preface by Powys. The friendship was maintained over the years by visits, gifts, and letters. Particularly in the early 1930s Powys wrote lengthy letters that offered not only praise but valuable criticism and suggestions on Hanley's latest novel.[4] Powys also generously suggested that these letters could be used for publicity. According to Powys's diary, they first met in Dorset on 6th March 1935, and it appears that not only the two men, but Phyllis Playter and Timmy Hanley, got on very well.[5] The much younger Hanley reciprocated Powys's help and encouragement, coming up, for example, with a suggestion for reprinting Powys's collection of poems, *Samphire* (1922), in 1932.[6] In 1936, Hanley reviewed Louis Wilkinson's *The Welsh Ambassadors: Powys Lives and Letters*, and later, in 1951, *Porius*. His essay about Powys, 'A Man in the Corner', was broadcast on BBC Radio Wales, November 1953, published in September 1954, and reprinted on several occasions (Gibbs C17, B87).

While the two men wrote very different kinds of novels, they both had reclusive tendencies and chose to live in North Wales because they were attracted to solitude,[7] although, especially in the case of

Powys, other factors influenced the choice of this particular part of Wales.

For one thing Powys's very name linked him with an ancient Welsh kingdom. In his *Autobiography* Powys describes, that when he was a child

> father's eyes used to burn with a fire … like the fire in the eyes of long discrowned king, when he told us how we were descended from the ancient Welsh Princes of Powysland. (26)

There is also evidence of Powys's own early enthusiasm, as when still at school, in 1888 or 1889, he wrote 'Mordaunt ap Griffith. A tale', based on Welsh history (Humfrey 24–8). Then when his son Littleton was born in 1902, he 'suddenly acquired a passion for everything Welsh' and bought whatever books he could lay his hands on 'to do with Wales and with the Welsh people' (*Autobiography* 334). This interest was revived in 1929 when he was researching the Grail mythology for *A Glastonbury Romance* (1932).[8] Powys's reading of Sir John Rhys, Jessie L. Weston, and others led him to emphasize the idea that Glastonbury and the Holy Grail should be associated with the heathen, pre-Christian Welsh. While in Powys's next novel, *Weymouth Sands* (1934), little use is made of Welsh mythology, in *Maiden Castle* (1936), which was begun in Dorchester, in 1934, and completed in Wales, Welsh mythology is an essential element.

A major factor in Powys's decision to settle in Corwen, beyond the encouragement and assistance of the Hanleys, was that it is 'about five miles from Glyndryffwy, the home of Owen Glendower … in the very heart of Powysland' (*Letters to Llewelyn* II 186). He also saw settling in Wales as a homecoming, despite four hundred years of exile, and his claim to only a 'few drops of Welsh blood' (*Obstinate Cymric* 41). His brother Bertie, however, was dismissive of 'all this nonsense of Jack's about our being Celtic or Welsh' (Marlow 46).

Hanley's roots, on the other hand, were Irish. He had been born in Dublin in 1901, and both his parents had also been born in Ireland (*Broken Water* 1, 43).[9] The fact that Hanley chose to settle in Wales, rather than returning to Ireland, may have been because he wished to

be close to his family in Liverpool.[10] But undoubtedly he would also
have been influenced by the infamous problems of writers in Catholic
Ireland. In his 'autobiographical excursion' *Broken Water* (1937),
Hanley describes seeking a copy of Joyce's *Chamber Music* in a
Dublin book store, during the 1920s:

> and the man kindly offered me some sermons by the Reverend
> Father Joyce, and, when I again asked for James Joyce, looked
> very disgusted. (267–8)[11]

Because of what was, for Hanley, in effect, exile from his true
homeland, John Fordham goes so as far as to suggests, that

> Hanley's move to rural Wales acted out the 'fantasm' of a
> spiritual homecoming to a pre-industrial familial past, before
> his family's fatal exile to 'mainland' Britain. (143)[12]

Once Powys had settled in Corwen, he enthusiastically continued
his research into Welsh history and mythology, as well as beginning to
study the Welsh language.[13] Although he never acquired any facility
in speaking or writing Welsh, Powys persevered with literary, critical
and mythological works in Welsh and regularly read Welsh newspa-
pers and listened to radio broadcasts in Welsh, so that by 5th December 1937 he could record in his diary, that he read St Luke in Welsh
'*sans* the translation!' Amongst other things, Powys's diaries suggest
that, from late 1939, he regularly read the popular column of political
comment 'Cwrs y Byd' (World Affairs), by the famous Welsh writer
and nationalist, Saunder Lewis, published in the Welsh-language
weekly newspaper *Baner ac Amserau Cymru* (*Y Faner*).[14]

As soon as he had finished *Maiden Castle*, Powys began his first
Welsh novel, *Morwyn, or the Vengeance of God*, which was published
in September 1937. Powys used a purely heathen Welsh mythology, in
both *Maiden Castle* and *Morwyn*, leaving behind the Christian dimension of the Holy Grail, found in *A Glastonbury Romance*. Another
step had yet to be made, that of adding the further mythological
dimension of the Welsh landscape. This is only incidental in *Morwyn*,
where the main setting is Hell. Indeed, it is perhaps stretching things
a little to call it a Welsh novel. Although *Morwyn* is a minor work that
lacks the depth and complexity of Powys's other novels that use

147

Welsh mythology, it does provide a concise map of his mythological ideas.

In April 1937 Powys began writing the first of his major Welsh novels, *Owen Glendower* (1942).[15] Then, in 1947, *Obstinate Cymric: Essays 1935–1947* was published. Many of these essays have Wales and its people as their subject. This collection was followed by *Porius* (1951), written between 1942 and 1949.[16] The medieval Welsh classic *The Mabinogion*, which Powys had read before 1895, was a major influence on the shaping of both *Owen Glendower* and *Porius*.[17] As Jeremy Hooker comments:

> *The Mabinogion* is a significant presence in [*Owen Glendower*] through characters' knowledge of its stories and identification of themselves or others with figures or incidents in the stories. (106)

Thus when the young man Rhisiart first sees Glendower he is reminded of the Welsh god Pryderi from the *Mabinogion* (146). Glendower is also associated with other Welsh mythological deities, such as Bran and Manywydan, but the dominant identification is with Pryderi, and with the Southern gods who were defeated by 'the cruel "magicians" of the Age of Bronze' (*Owen Glendower* 563). Commenting on *Porius*, Morine Krissdóttir goes even further, describing it as 'a twentieth century *Mabinogion*', and indicating that, in her opinion it, 'comes closest to fulfilling [Powys's] own conception of mythological art' (127).[18] Whereas Glendower just resembles a god from Welsh mythology, in *Porius* actual figures from Welsh mythology appear, including Myrrdin Wyllt (Merlin), Nineue the enchantress, the poet Taliessin, as well as King Arthur and the author of the *Mabinogion*.

In addition to his use of mythology from the *Mabinogion*, Powys creates his own idiosyncratic Welsh mythology, central to which is the idea, that because of the remote mountainous terrain, there has survived in Wales a race, 'who are the direct descendants *in situ* of races that existed at least twenty thousand years ago' (*Obstinate Cymric* 49). Furthermore, according to Powys, an important characteristic of the 'Welsh Aboriginal', as well as their modern descendants, is that 'we lack all belligerency' (7). Powys also stressed his belief, that all the inhabitants of Britain were, in part, descended from the same aboriginals. Writing to Huw Menai, on 27th June 1940, Powys comments:

[Saunders Lewis] forgets that the Welsh used to own <u>all</u> Britain and their kings were always crowned in London and that their attitude was British i.e. <u>belonging</u> to the <u>whole country</u> and a piece of Scotland too! ... And the Welsh element in the blood of not only West Country people but all over the island is the Aboriginal Blood.

This Aboriginal Welsh mythology was a major influence on the way that Powys reshaped Welsh history and myth concerning Owen Glendower. Powys's divergence from the traditional view of Owen Glendower has been criticized, and Roland Mathias has suggested, that while Powys's 'two novels of Wales, *Owen Glendower* (1940) and *Porius* (1951), are in some respect brilliantly evocative ... they were formed philosophically in his native Wessex' (118). Myrrdin, the prophet of some future New Golden Age of peace in *Porius,* was of course created under the influence of the same Powysian mythology.

Discussing *Obstinate Cymric,* Ned Thomas was also critical of these ideas about Wales and the Welsh, of this 'visitor from the dominant culture' (76). In *The Powys Review* 4 (1979), Thomas asked, in 'exasperation', if 'any nation deserves to have inflicted on it the zanier projections of the romantic imagination?' (75). While Thomas also uses the word 'lunacy' to describe Powys's Welsh mythology, he does also note, that 'Here is a harmless kind of old aboriginal, quite capable of stepping out of his romantic clothes and even laughing at himself' (75).

On the other hand, Welsh novelist Emyr Humphreys, in 'The Crucible of Myth' treats Powys, along with *full-blooded* Welshmen, like Saunders Lewis and Robert William Parry, as examples of writers who had kept alive the Welsh literary tradition:

We inherit a landscape which preserves trace elements of the wonders that walked through the imagination of our remote ancestors ... Saunders Lewis takes a melodic line from the ... *Mabinogi* and creates a symphonic variation so that the woman conjured up from the landscape of Ardudwy can be understood as a comment on our twentieth-century experience of science intervening like magic in the process of sexual love. ... [Powys] became so well-versed and so absorbed in the mythological origins of the landscape and history of Wales that he was able to use them as keys to a cosmogony of his own. The strength of his understanding allowed him a control over dynamic forces reminiscent of those possesed by the family of Don in the Mabinogi (14–15).

Unlike Powys, Hanley did not arrive in Wales in 1931 with much, if any, knowledge of Welsh mythology, and in his fiction there is no evidence of the kind of intensive research into Welsh mythology and history undertaken by Powys.[19] According to John Fordham, Hanley did take Welsh lessons (141), but in 1936, Hanley confessed in a letter that he knew only 'thank you' in Welsh, and couldn't really understand why he had been been made a bard at the Corwen Eisteddfod![20] There is, however, evidence of his interest in Welsh writers and literature, including a friendship with the poet, and Welsh nationalist, R. S. Thomas (Fordham 208).[21]

What seems especially to have mattered to Hanley was the belief that Wales had maintained a character and culture distinct from that of England, and that its landscape likewise — if South Wales was left out — was less ravaged by industry and urbanization. Hanley also believed the Romantic myth that life in rural Wales was lived at a different, more heightened, level than in urban, industrial England, stating in 1943, that:

> even a very ordinary journey in a very ordinary little Welsh bus, can by an act of the imagination be turned into the narrative of adventure as thrilling as that of Homer. ('A Welsh Bus Ride' 358)

The main influences on Hanley's use of myth, in those few novels of his set in Wales, is the pastoral tradition, especially as reshaped by Wordsworthian Romanticism, along with the Celtic Twilight myth, with its suggestion that Wales, like Ireland, was a fertile place for the imagination, and myth.

Whereas Powys began writing about Wales soon after he moved there, it was not until the 1950s that Hanley begun to explore seriously his experience of living in a village in North Wales, though he had in fact settled in Wales several years before Powys. The novels that James Hanley published in the 1930s were not about Wales, but about working-class Liverpool, such as the semi-autobiographical *The Furys* (1934). He also wrote about life at sea, including the novel *The Hollow Sea* (1937), which was based on Hanley's experience on a troopship in the Mediterranean in 1916, when he was only fourteen (*Broken Water* 142–206). In 1937, Hanley did, however, publish under commission, his first book-length, Welsh work, a non-fiction study of the unemployed in the Mining Valleys of South Wales, *Grey Children: A Study in Humbug and Misery*. Moreover Hanley had begun experimenting with pastoral pieces, starting with the essay 'The Sower' (1935), his first work with a Welsh setting. 'The Sower' contrast the rural North Wales, where Hanley then lived, with the city of Liverpool, that he had left: 'Away across the mountains I knew there existed the desperate mass of life that symbolises the cities and towns of today', whereas 'Wales is a country most untouched by the modern spirit' (662). Hanley wrote further Welsh stories in the pastoral genre: 'The Lamb' in 1936 and 'Wild Horses and Fair Maidens of Llanganoch'.[22] The latter was published under the Welsh pseudonym Ifan Pughe, in *Welsh Short Stories* (1937).[23] But he also published, between 1936 and 1938, four pastoral stories, set in Ireland,[24] as well as submitting, in July 1938, a play, *We are the Living*, to the BBC, under an Irish pseudonym Seamus O'Hanlon (Fordham 162).

Then somewhat inexplicably, in July 1939, the Hanleys left Corwen. Gostick suggests that they moved because 'by 1939 Tim Hanley was finding the isolation of North Wales too much to bear indefinitely' (18).[25] After a nomadic existence, involving short stays in numerous places, including London, late in 1940 they returned to Wales, specifically to Llanfechain, the other side of the Berwyn Mountains from Corwen.

Hanley's exploration of the pastoral mode, that began in the 1930s, did not, however, develop further until February 1953, when a

ROBIN WOOD

collection of essays and sketches, *Don Quixote Drowned*, was published. In these Hanley uses a fictionally named village, Llangyllwch,
to explore his experience of living in Llanfechain. As Fordham notes,
Hanley is 'highly selective' in what he describes, and 'reduces a highly
complex local hierarchy ... to a simple, traditional society of peasants
and eccentrics' (205). This work also contains a few essays about his
earlier life at sea. In his review of this collection, Emyr Humphreys
criticizes the fact, that '[i]t has become common for English writers
in Wales ... [to] cast an Anglo-Celtic twilight about the only too
matter-of-fact behavior of those around them' (5). Despite containing some interesting writing, *Don Quixote Drowned*, is a minor work.
    Hanley published his first novel set in Wales, *The Welsh Sonata*
(1954), more than twenty years after he had first settled in Wales.
Then, over a period of almost a quarter of a century, appeared his two
subsequent works set in Wales: *Another World* (1972) and *A Kingdom*
(1978). Other than a few plays, broadcast or published in the 1960s
and 1970s, these were the only further works by Hanley set in Wales.²⁶
There were to be several later novels that were not set in Wales.
    Powys described *The Welsh Sonata*, in a letter to Hanley, on 5th July
1954, as a poem to rival the poetry of Dylan Thomas. This opinion was
prompted by the fact that Hanley wrote the novel in a biblically-
influenced, poetic style to to give it a Welsh aura. Kingsley Amis was
less kind about the style, describing *The Welsh Sonata* as, 'a remarkable feat of ventriloquism ... a hodgepodge of Gwyn Thomas ...
Dylan Thomas, and Rhys Davies'. Hanley had already attempted
some passages, in a similar, though less biblical, poetic style, in his first
novel *Drift* (1930), which was written under the influence of James
Joyce's *Portrait of an Artist as a Young Man*. In his efforts to create a
Welsh novel, Hanley had deliberately adopted a 'Welsh style'. Jeremy
Hooker describes, in contrast, the 'great care' that Raymond Williams
took in his novels, 'not to write in what had come to be seen in
England as a "Welsh style" ':

    This was a style of extreme verbal inventiveness, using highly
    coloured figurative language, which derived in part from an
    aspect of James Joyce and was identified most famously with
    Dylan Thomas. In Raymond Williams's view the style served

a version of what he sought in all his writing and thinking to avoid: escapism. (22)

*The Welsh Sonata* is an imperfect novel, largely because of the artificiality of the poetic style. Powys, on the other hand, in *Owen Glendower* and *Porius*, wrote in his usual style, and creates a Welsh aura from the setting and with his use of Welsh history and mythology. The countryside of Corwen, along with the rest of North Wales provided ample Welsh historical and mythological material for Powysian reverie.[27] Setting these novels back in the fourteenth and sixth centuries, respectively, also enabled Powys to avoid the dangers inherent for a newcomer attempting a realistic portrait of contemporary Wales. Powys's diary for the 10th August, 1941 records that he had "chucked" his attempt to write a novel about contemporary Corwen.

In *The Welsh Sonata*, Hanley plays ironically with pastoral myth and with Arthurian mythology. The main character, the tramp Rhys, like Wordsworth's leech gatherer, lives so close to Nature, free from the restrains of society, that he seems to be an ideal embodiment of Romantic values. The Welsh villagers also create mythology about Rhys, through the nick-names and stories that they tell about him. He is called, for example, Rhys the Wound, because 'of a blow that he took when he was young and fiery, when his woman ran off with a sailor named Parry' (15).[28] This suggests The 'Dolorous Blow' and the Maimed King of Arthurian Romance. In Powys's *Morwyn*, the Captain also receives such a 'Dolorous Blow', during the fight over Morwyn with the young vivisector, but in Powys's novel the mythology plays a much more important and complex role, in relation both to plot structure and themes, than is the case in Hanley's (238).[29] Rhys had also been given another nickname, Rhys the Cloud, because of his mop of white hair. This name suggests a halo, and the villagers see him as 'like a prophet ... walked out of a living page of the Book' (10).[30] These names, rather than being part of a complex structure of mythology, are in fact mainly used by Hanley to suggest the ways in which, through the imagination and myth making of its inhabitants, life is lived at a heightened level in the Welsh countryside.

But perhaps the most important myth used by Hanley relates to ideas about childhood. Following the 'Dolorous Blow', Rhys has found a childlike joy and innocence in his life as a tramp, whereas his actual childhood had been a nightmare of abuse, at the hands of his drunken father. Interestingly, this myth of childhood innocence is central to Powys's writing, though this does not necessarily imply any direct influence on Hanley. In fact, it is probably Romanticism, possibly along with Dostoievsky, that is the main influence on Hanley here.

Throughout his life, Powys emphasized his belief that the adult can still experience the ecstatic spontaneity of childhood, and that it is important to cultivate such experiences imaginatively. This quality is something that he inherited from his father, whom he described in his *Autobiography*, as 'more childlike than any of his eleven children' (14–15). This belief was reinforced by his reading of the New Testament, Wordsworth and Blake, amongst others. Thus, in *Porius*, the bard Taliessin is described by Myrddin, as '*an undying child*', and that:

> it may well have been that it was this childishness, showing itself in a stripped and naked objectivity, that explained the magical appeal of the boy-bard and his victory over his rivals. So primeval, so artless, so unadorned, so content with the immediate impression of the object or situation or event was Taliessin's verse, that it left upon the mind a curious feeling of paradisic obscurity, the ecstatic sufficiency in fact of pure sensation about which it was impossible to say anything except what is implied in these childish proclamations so often repeated: "I was," or "I was there," or "I was with," or "I saw." (423)[31]

*The Welsh Sonata*, however, is not an innocent pastoral, nor a work of escapism, for, if Rhys strides the landscape like a prophet and possesses childlike innocence, it is not the total story. Industry in the form of quarrying and mining is not far away, and the novel's ending, with the discovery of Rhys's frozen body, emphasizes the un-Arcadian nature of Welsh winters.

It was almost twenty years after *The Welsh Sonata*, in 1972, that Hanley's next Welsh novel, *Another World* appeared, though it had started life as a radio play in 1959.[32] Set in the holiday resort of Garthmeilo, presumably on the North Wales coast, *Another World* is an ironic exploration of both the pastoral mode and Other World mythology.

This seaside town is at the margin between the urban world and Nature. It is an *other world* into which the inhabitants of Liverpool and Manchester can briefly escape while on holiday. However, it is winter, and the holiday visitors are absent. One of the novel's main characters, Miss Vaughan, lives in a different kind of other world, from that of the urban holiday makers. There are, in fact, two personalities to Miss Vaughan. On one level she is lonely, middle-aged, a spinster typist, without any family, living in a boarding house. But there is another Miss Vaughan, who happily lives a rich inner life. This *other world* involves two fictitious narratives, one about a Captain, and another about a lover, the Colonel. Her imaginative fictionalizing is fed by her reading, and interestingly the only title mentioned is that of the *Mabinogion* (139). Miss Vaughan has in fact achieved an ideal balance between the real world and the other world of her waking dream. That is until the Reverend Mervyn Thomas cruelly intrudes into her life, with his illusion of saving her from her supposed unhappiness. At the end of the novel, Miss Vaughan walks into the sea, which has been traditionally associated with the Other World of Welsh and Celtic mythology. This act does not, however, appear to be suicide, but rather the loss of the balance she had achieved between the real and the imaginary, caused by Thomas's harass-ment.[33] Insane, in an entirely different way, is the clergyman, Thomas, who has an obsessive desire to save Miss Vaughan from the empty life that he mistakenly believes she is living. His imagined picture of her life is as delusional as hers — but less benign — the product of a confused muddle of Christianity, lust, and romantic love and the projection of his own loneliness and unhappiness onto Miss Vaughan.

Powys would have fully understood both characters, as he writes with sympathy and understanding about madness. Amongst his mad men is Sylvanus Cobbold in *Weymouth Sands*, who because he at-tempts to break through to another level of reality — or another world — is placed in an insane asylum. Enoch Quirm, in *Maiden*

155

*Castle,* believes that he is a reincarnation of the Welsh god Uryen and is also trying to reach the Other World. In the chapter 'In Spite of Madness', in his book of popular philosophy, *In Spite Of* (1953), Powys makes his position on mental illness very clear:

> Our Philosophy is entirely, and without reservation, on the side of the insane person, and, as far as the insane person is concerned, against the rest of the world; that is to say as long as his insanity is not homicidal (127).

An entirely different, other world journey, to that of Miss Vaughan, is taken, in *Another World,* by the unromantic couple, Mrs. Gandell and her servant Jones. This is comedy. Their afternoon sexual romps, aided by four gins, takes them 'beyond the frontier of the world' (45), and 'After the crossing of frontiers, after the explosion, Mrs Gandell had conveniently kicked [Jones] off the bed' (66).

Hanley's third Welsh novel, *A Kingdom* (1978), is also his last novel,[34] published just before his 77th birthday, long after he had left Wales. As he had been living in North London since 1963, this work is very much written at a distance. *A Kingdom* is an elegy in the pastoral mode to a dying way of life, that of hill farming in Wales, and here Hanley does not make use of any Welsh mythology. It is also a novel that reveals the influence of Hanley's friend, the Welsh poet R. S. Thomas, both in its subject matter as well as in its plain, but poetic prose style.

In the narrative structure of *A Kingdom,* a contrast is drawn between the depopulated hill-farms of Wales and nearby England, where, as Cadi Evans comments: "'they all go in the end'" (118). The setting is a remote Welsh small-holding: 'Three miserable looking fields and a broken-down house' (66). Cadi's father, Madog Evans, with his daughter Lucy, has moved sixty miles to this remote place amongst strangers, following the death of his wife. At the end of the novel it is revealed that this was as an act of atonement for his adultery (200). Cadi had already made her escape to teach in Manchester, but when her older sister elopes to England, Cadi obeys the patriarchal values of the rural society that she was raised in, and returns to take care of their father.

Hanley contrasts Cadi's stoic spirituality with the shallow, urban world of her sister Lucy and brother-in-law. Even though Cadi has been forced by the patriarchal values of her father and her Welsh culture to give up her freedom and independence, Hanley suggests that Cadi has a more deeply rooted and spiritual life, than her married sister. While there is no doubt that Lucy has found happiness, town life in England across the border is shallow and superficial, as these comments by Lucy reveal:

Averton came alive, with its comforts, a warmth, a contentment, and all those marvellous magazines that David gets for me because he knows that's what I like best, and even saw herself in the snug sitting room, sat on the floor, surrounded by a shoal of women's magazines, of every size and colour, and this was Lucy's real world. (30)

Cadi, on the other hand, is at peace, rooted in the rhythm of farm life and supported by caring neighbours. She asserts:

'I've changed. I'm anchored here, and yet I don't mind. Our lives are reduced to the utmost simplicity. And strange, too, but the harder I worked, the more absorbed I became in everything I did, the further away I seemed to get from myself. It was a curious feeling, and I couldn't explain it' (50).

Cadi, a strong woman, has a distinct individuality, and will stay on and run the farm following the father's death. On the other hand, Lucy is very dependent on David: 'How good David was, a tower of strength, what on earth would she have done without him?' (61).

There is in Cadi Evan's stoicism, kindness, and simple pleasure in the elemental landscape of upland Wales, affinity with the philosophy of John Cowper Powys, in works like *A Philosophy of Solitude,* and *In Defense of Sensuality.* Hanley especially admired the latter work,[35] in which Powys declares that:

There is only one purpose of all conscious life, and that is to grow calmly, steadily, quietly more conscious! It is in loneliness alone that the human soul can achieve this inner growth (127–8).

There is, however, no naïve idealization in *A Kingdom*, for Hanley recognizes that the same Welsh culture which shaped Cadi's strong character, also produced the religious fanaticism of her guilt-ridden father and of the African missionary, who deserted Cadi for God. Hers is a tragic story, and while superficially seeming to support conservative patriarchal values, it in fact criticizes such archaic values and shows Cadi transcending her suffering.[36]

Hanley's interest lies in such seemingly unexciting lives and the failures of ordinary people like Cadi Evans. As he wrote: 'The more insignificant a person is in this whirlpool of industrial and civilized society, the more important he is to me' (quoted in Stokes 12). Hanley focuses on an unromantic world in which love usually fails, though there is friendship and concern for others, and where achievements, even on the small scale and the ordinary, are celebrated. Yet there is none of the heroic celebration of the transcendent power of the human imagination and ecstatic communion with the elements, associated with Powys's heroes and magicians, Wolf Solent, Geard, Owen Glendower, Myrddin. In *Glendower* and *Porius*, amongst Powys's most important characters are Prophets and Princes, engaged in epic events from history, whereas Hanley's protagonists lead unexciting lives in twentieth-century Wales, and include a tramp and a policeman-bard (*The Welsh Sonata*); spinster and clergyman (*Another World*), and another spinster (*A Kingdom*). Jeremy Hooker suggests, that 'Powys is fundamentally a writer with a comic vision, which includes himself and his pretensions to Welshness' (95). Hanley's vision, in fact, is tragic, although irony and humour have an important role in his works; he is especially interested in exploring the psychology of the suffering of characters in extreme situations.

It is surprising that these two friends, thirty years apart in age, and from such dissimilar religious, class and ethnic backgrounds, and whose approach to the novel, and to Wales is so different, should have so much in common. Though they differed greatly in the way that they wrote novels, both in subject matter and technique, as well as how they responded to Wales, they were, as has been seen, alike in their basic human values. There are also similarities in their politics, and though both had leftish tendencies, sharing a suspicion of the power of the State, they were also sympathetic to anarchism. They had more empathy with those who failed or were defeated in life than with the successful, and though they were both agnostics, championed redemptive Christian values.

Hanley and Powys had both been raised in Christian families: Hanley's mother, in particular, was a devout Catholic, while Powys's father was a clergyman on the evangelical wing of the Church of England, and although both men rejected their religious upbringing, their philosophies of life were shaped by Christian values. In this context it is significant that Powys's *Dostoievsky* (1946) was 'admiringly and affectionately dedicated to James Hanley' (6). According to Chris Gostick, Hanley helped Powys find a publisher for it, and Gostick also suggests that: 'It is probably impossible to over-estimate the influence of Dostoievesky on Hanley' (23). Likewise, Powys described Dostoievsky as 'my Master' (*Autobiography* 445, also see 524). Powys's affinity with Dostoievsky can also be seen, for example, in the following comment: 'The deepest emotion that I have is my malice against the well-constituted. ... every type of individual upon whom the world looked down, I loved respected, admired, reverenced, *and imitated*' (*Autobiography* 515–6). Hanley was interested in those on the margins of society. These were often working class men and women struggling to survive in the modern city, with fear of unemployment, old age, and the Work House, but, as is clear from Hanley's Welsh novels, he includes other kinds of people and places. Powys commented, at the beginning of Hanley's career, in his 'Preface' to *Men in Darkness* (1931), that:

> Mr James Hanley's pity is as far removed from sentimentality as it is removed from sadism. It is that rare and uncommon pity, such as certain nuns and priests and doctors have, whose lot has thrown them among the hosts of the damned, and *who understand the damned.* (ix–x)

Despite this affinity between Powys and Hanley, they treat the Welsh landscape, and the relationship between it and characters, very differently. Central to Powys's fiction is his psycho-sensuous philosophy of reverie, which makes use, imaginatively, not only of the landscape and the elements, but history, mythology and memories. This is variously called, mythologizing (*Wolf Solent*, 1929), elementalism (*A Philosophy of Solitude*, 1933), and cavoseniargizing (*Porius*, 1951). There is in Hanley's works, however, none of this intimate, ecstatic involvement, with the natural world that is so important in Powys. Hanley gives only the briefest description of the landscape, even in his Welsh novels. In *A Kingdom*, for example, description of the landscape is used to set up the contrast between the Cheshire town of Averton, with its cinema and plentiful supply of magazines, and the remote hill farm of Pen y Parc, which is three miles from the nearest neighbour. The following passage gives urban Lucy's view of the Welsh landscape:

> [Lucy] stared across three small fields, at the sour wintry grass. And she supposed that something had come out of them. Hay perhaps. She ambled slowly down the path, leaned heavily against the little white gate. The light was coming in fast. She looked up at the sky. What an awful feeling that was, she told herself, suddenly gripped the gate, looked beyond it, longed for her sister's return, listened for the steps in the lane. (42)

Wales also meant something different for each of them. As has been seen, when Powys moved to Corwen in 1935 he totally immersed himself in everything Welsh. The people, language, landscape, history, literature and mythology fired his imagination, and led to the creation, between 1937 and 1949, of his two great historical romances, *Owen Glendower* and *Porius*. Central to Powys's Welsh novels is an imaginative involvement with the landscape and nature, along with the history and mythology associated with that particular landscape.

Hanley, on the other hand, never immersed himself in Welsh mythology. His major concern was more with the psychology of lives lived in extreme situations: the solipsist, Miss Vaughan, whose rich imaginary life protects her from trauma caused by the death of her father; Rhys the tramp who lives on the edge of society because of childhood and adult trauma, and who then dies of hypothermia; or Cadi who courageously faces the isolation and loneliness of a remote hill farm and a dying rural culture. While Welsh mythology is a central element in Powys's Welsh works, for Hanley, Welsh mythology is not present in either *The Welsh Sonata,* or *A Kingdom.* The allusion to the 'Dolorous Blow' in *The Welsh Sonata* is just an incidental, ironic detail and an allusion to Arthurian or Celtic myth, rather than anything specifically Welsh, whereas in *A Glastonbury Romance* and *Morwyn* the 'Dolorous Blow' is part of a fully developed mythological structure that is integral to the plot. Neither is the single allusion to the *Mabinogion,* nor the Other World element, intrinsic to the themes, or to the plot structure of *Another World.*

Whereas *Owen Glendower* and *Porius* are amongst Powys's finest achievements, Hanley's Welsh novels, at their best, stand shoulder to shoulder with the numerous other novels, set in a variety of places, that he wrote while living in Wales. However, *A Kingdom,* along with, *The Welsh Sonata,* were described, in 1978, by the American critic Harvey Curtis Webster, as showing 'again why Hanley has been called a major novelist by critics as disparate as Edwin Muir, E. M. Forster, … C. P. Snow, Herbert Read, and J. C. Powys' (19–20). Unfortunately, there has been little evaluation by Welshmen, or Anglo-Welshmen, of those works of Hanley set in Wales.[37]

In 1955, Powys moved deeper into Wales, to Blaenau Ffestiniog, where he remained until his death on 17th June, 1963. Despite his deep attachment to the land of his forefathers, Powys's ashes were scattered on Chesil Beach, near Weymouth, Dorset. But, of course, Powys had believed that the original inhabitants, not only of the West of England, but of <u>all</u> of England had been the Welsh Aboriginals. Sometime after June 1963, the Hanleys moved to London,[38] probably at Timothy's insistence, though for two more years, they stayed frequently in a cottage on their friend Richard Rhys, Lord Dynevor's, estate at Llandillo, and, but for Rhys's financial problems, might have settled there, in South West Wales.[39] Hanley deeply regretted this move to London, and his friend, the Welsh writer and theatre director, James Roose-Evans, has affirmed, that: 'Though Liverpool-Irish in origin, Hanley regarded himself as wholly Welsh by adoption' (320). When he died on 15th November, 1985, Hanley was buried in the village of Llanfechain (Harrington 34).

WORKS CITED

Amis, Kingsley, 'New Novels', *Spectator*, 13th August 1954.
Birch, J. Roy, 'Writer for a Lit-up People?', *New Welsh Review* X/III (40) Spring 1998, 58–63.
BBC Written Archives, Caversham.
Brown, Tony, 'The Heart is a Terrible Prison', *New Welsh Review* X/III (40) Spring 1998, 63–5.
Canadian Army, James Hanley's army service file (National Archives of Canada, Ottawa).
Fordham, John, *James Hanley: Modernism and the Working Class* (Cardiff: The University of Wales Press, 2002).
Gerard, David, '"Ever your Faithful Friend": Letters from John Cowper Powys to James Hanley', *The Powys Review* 25 (1990), 39–50.
Gibbs, Linnea, *James Hanley: A Bibliography* (Vancouver: William Hoffer, 1980).
Gostick, Chris, *Lord Jim, and Lady Tim and the Powys Circle* (London: Cecil Woolf, 2000).
Hanley, James, *Another World* (London: André Deutsch, 1972).
——, *Broken Water: An autobiographical excursion* (London: Chatto & Windus, 1937).
——, *Don Quixote Drowned* (London: Macdonald,1953).
——, *Drift* (London: Eric Partridge, 1930).
——, 'Far Horizons', *The New Statesman and Nation*, 1st May 1937, 721–2.
——, *Grey Children: A Study in Humbug and Misery* (London: Methuen, 1937).
——, *A Kingdom* (London: Deutsch, 1978).
——, Letters to Liam Hanley (National Library of Wales, Aberystwyth).
——, Letters to John Cowper Powys (National Library of Wales, Aberystwyth).
——, Letters to John Cowper Powys (Liverpool Public Library).
——, 'A Man in the Corner', *John O'London's Weekly*, September 3rd, 1954, 877–8.
——, *Men in Darkness: Five Stories* (London: John Lane, 1931).
——, *People Are Curious* (London: John Lane, 1938).
——, 'Powys and Company', Review of *Welsh Ambassadors* by Louis Marlow, *The Left Review* vol. 2, No 6, March 1936, 279.
——, 'The Sower', *Spectator*, 25th October 1935, 662.
——, 'The Spirit of Wales', *Britain Today* 72, April 1942: 21–3.
——, *A Stone Flower* in *Plays One* (London: Kaye & Ward, 1968).
——, 'A Welsh Bus Ride', *Time and Tide*, 1st May 1943: 358.
——, 'Wild Horses and Fair Maidens of Llanganoch' (under the pseudonym of Ifan Pughe), *Welsh Short Stories*, ed. — (London: Faber, 1937).
——, 'A Wonderful Picture of Ancient of Days' (review of *Porius* by John Cowper Powys), *The Recorder*, 18th August 1951:4.
——, *The Welsh Sonata: Variations on a Theme* (London: Derek Verschoyle, 1954; New York: Horizon Press, 1978).
Hanley, Timothy Letters to Liam Hanley (National Library of Wales, Aberystwyth).
——, Letters to John Cowper Powys (National Library of Wales, Aberystwyth).
Harrington, Frank G., *James Hanley: A Bold and Unique Solitary* (Francestown, NH: Typographeum, 1989).
Hooker, Jeremy, *Imagining Wales: A view of modern Welsh writing in English* (Cardiff: University of Wales Press, 2001).
Humfrey, Belinda, 'John [Cowper] Powys "Mordaunt Ap Gryfith. A Tale"' (1888?), *The Powys Review* 18:24–28.
Humphreys, Emyr, *Emyr Humphreys: Conversations and Reflections* (Cardiff: University of Wales Press, 2002).
——, 'Home from the Sea', *Times*, 15th March 1953: 5.
Krissdóttir, Morine, *John Cowper Powys and the Magical Quest* (London: Macdonald, 1980).
London University, Manuscript of *Drift* (Sterling Collection).
Manx National Heritage, Crew agreement for 6 months to December, 1903 for *Mona*, Isle of Man

Steam Packet Company (Lloyd's registration 96575).
Maritime History Archives, Memorial University of Newfoundland, St. John's, Newfoundland, Canada. Crew Agreements for *Scythia* 1922,1926, 1930 and 1931.
Marlow, Louis (Louis Wilkinson), *Welsh Ambassadors: Powys Lives and Letters* (1936) (London: Bertram Rota, 1971).
Mathias, Roland, *Anglo-Welsh Literature: An Illustrated History* (Brigend: Poetry Wales Press, 1987).
Owen, D. E., Review of *The Welsh Sonata* by James Hanley, in *The Anglo-Welsh Review* 65, 1979.
Peate, Iorwerth, *John Cowper Powys: Letters 1937–1954* (Cardiff: University of Wales Press, 1974).
Phelps, Gilbert, *The Russian Novel in English Fiction* (London: Hutchinson, 1956).
Powys, John Cowper, 'Preface' to *Men in Darkness* by James Hanley .
——, *Autobiography* (1934) (London: Macdonald, 1967).
——, *Diaries* (unpublished) (National Library of Wales, Aberystwyth).
——, *Dostoievesky* (London: John Lane, 1946).
——, *A Glastonbury Romance* (1932). (London: Macdonald, 1955).
——, *In Defense of Sensuality* (New York: Simon & Schuster, 1930).
——, *In Spite Of* (1953) (London: The Village Press, 1974).
——, *Letters of John Cowper Powys to his Brother Llewelyn*, vol. II, ed. Malcolm Elwin (London: The Village Press, 1975).
——, *Letters to James Hanley* (Liverpool Public Library).
——, *Letters to James Hanley* (Temple University Library, Philadelphia).
——, *Letters to Huw Menai* (The Powys Collection, Dorchester Museum).
——, *Maiden Castle* (1936) (Cardiff: University of Wales Press, 1990).
——, *Morwyn, or the Vengeance of God* (1937) (London: The Village Press, 1974).
——, *Obstinate Cymric: Essays 1935–1947* (Carmarthen: The Druid Press, 1947).
——, *Owen Glendower: An Historical Novel* (New York: Simon & Schuster, 1940).
——, *A Philosophy of Solitude* (London: Jonathan Cape, 1933).
——, *Porius: A Romance of the Dark Ages* (1951) (Hamilton, NY: Colgate University Press, 1994).
——, *Weymouth Sands* (New York: Simon & Schuster, 1934).
——, *Wolf Solent* (1929) (London: Macdonald, 1961).
Reading University, Publishers Archives: Chatto & Windus.
Roose-Evans, James, *Contemporary British Dramatists*, ed. K. A. Berney (London: St James Press, 1994).
Stokes, Edward, *The Novels of James Hanley* (Melbourne: F. W. Cheshire, 1964).
Thomas, Ned, 'Obstinate Cymric', *The Powys Review* 4 Winter/Spring 1978/9, 75–78.
Webster, Harvey Curtis, 'A Protean Imagination', *New Leader*, vol. lxi, No 20, 9th October 1978, 19–20.

NOTES

1 See John Cowper Powys's 1936 diary and a letter from James Hanley to Harold Raymond of Chatto & Windus, dated 26th October 1936. There was also an earlier ceremony on 16th May, according to Powys's diary.
2 The term 'resident foreigner' is used by Roland Mathias to distinguish between incomers like James Hanley and John Cowper Powys, and (a) The Welsh speaking writers of Wales; (b) English speaking writers of Welsh ancestry, the Anglo-Welsh. The term Anglo-Welsh is, however, sometimes used confusingly to include such resident foreigners (116).
3 Edward Hanley worked regularly on the *Scythia* in the 1920s until he retired in 1931. I have Chris Gostick to thank for the discovery of this fact, in the Maritime History Archives at Memorial University of Newfoundland.
4 See Gerard 39–50.
5 See Gostick 11 and Powys's 1935 diary. A fuller discussion of the friendship between James and

Timothy Hanley and Powys, and Phyllis Playter, as well as their respective families, can be found in Chris Gostick's monograph.

6 See letter from Powys to Hanley dated 30th November 1932 (Liverpool Public Library).

7 See, for example Powys's *Obstinate Cymric* 55 (also *A Philosophy of Solitude*) and Hanley's *Broken Water* 247, 259.

8 The first Welsh allusions in fact come in *Wolf Solent*, where Christie's mother was Welsh and claimed descent from Merlin (233, 238). The major influence on Powys's use of Welsh mythology was Sir John Rhys's *Studies in the Arthurian Legend* (1891), which he first read in 1898, in preparation for a lecture on the Arthurian legend (*Autobiography* 284). He also read R. S. Loomis's *Celtic Myth and Arthurian Romance* (1927) (*A Glastonbury Romance* 807), as well as Jessie L. Weston's *From Ritual to Romance* (1920) (*Autobiography* 285, 270, 337). In addition, Powys had also read Lady Charlotte Guest's translation of the *Mabinogion* (284), and was aware of Matthew Arnold's *On the Study of Celtic Literature* (1867) (25-6). He also admired W. B. Yeats's, and was influenced by the Celtic revival movement, and therefore probably read Yeats's 'The Celtic Element in Literature' (1897) (224).

9 While Hanley was born in Dublin in 1901, the Hanley family may have moved to Liverpool by 1903, if not earlier, where Hanley's father worked as a greaser in the engine-room of various ships, including a number of Cunard transatlantic liners, according to crew agreements held by Manx National Heritage.

10 It is worth noting that the manuscript of Hanley's first novel, *Drift* (1930) indicates that it was completed in Cork, in 1926 (London University).

11 In Hanley's first novel, *Drift* (1930), the protagonist Joe's mother destroyed a copy of *Ulysses*, that he has borrowed from a middle-class friend (113, 145).

12 Fordham suggests, that 'An actual return was ruled out by Timmy's and James's family responsibilities' (143). Hanley also had strong negative feelings about the Irish Civil War, which had followed the partition of Ireland in 1921, and the granting of independence to the South (*Broken Water* 263).

13 Powys's unpublished Diaries for 1935-1939 provide a wealth of detail.

14 See, for example, Powys's diary for 17th November, 3rd and 30th December 1939, and 20th September 1941.

15 Powys diary, for 15th May 1935, records the fact, that Phyllis wanted him to write a romance about 'Owain Glydwr'. Powys's 1937 diary records that began writing *Owen Glendower* on 24th April 1937.

16 See Powys's diary entry for 18th January 1942; and letter to Iorwerth Peate dated 9th March 1949 (79-80).

17 See Belinda Humphrey *The Powys Review* 18:24-8. Also diary for 19th November, 1939.

18 See Jeremy Hooker for a full discussion.

19 But see Fordham 144, re letter to Harold Raymond of Chatto & Windus, as well as his note 42; Powys's diary also records that Hanley attended a lecture, on the *Mabinogion*, given in Corwen by Powys, on 20th November 1936.

20 The letter, mentioned at the beginning (note 1), dated 26th October 1936, to Harold Raymond of Chatto & Windus.

21 In a letter to Powys, dated 1st October 1955, Hanley claims to know R. S. Thomas very well (National Library of Wales). See also letter 23rd April 1947 to Powys, where Hanley recommends the poetry of Vernon Watkins (Temple University). In another letter to Powys, dated 15th October 1957, Hanley refers to his Welsh friend Mr Ellis planning to translate *The Welsh Sonata* into Welsh (Temple University). The 1978 American edition of *The Welsh Sonata* is inscribed, 'For Islwyn Ffowc Ellis', the Welsh-language novelist. Fordham also refers to his friendship with Idris Parry, the German scholar and translator of Kafka (229).

22 See Fordham 153. On 23rd July 1937 Hanley advised Raymond that he planned to submit a kind of pastoral work (Reading University).

23 July 27th 1937, shortly after the Corwen Eisteddfod, Hanley sent Harold Raymond a short story

that he planned to publish under a Welsh pseudonym. Raymond's reply on the 30th July indicates the pseudonym to be Ifan Pughe (Reading).

24 See Fordham 153. The stories are 'The Butterfly' (*Spectator* 10th April 1936), 'Afternoon at Miss Fetch's', 'Beyond the Horizon', and 'The Tale' (*Half an Eye: Sea stories*, 1937). The last three appear to be set in Cork, where Hanley's mother was born. These four stories were included in the short story collection *People are Curious* (1938).

25 A letter to Powys, dated 1st November 1940, refers to the Hanleys moving to Llanfechain (Liverpool Library).

26 *Miss Williams*: Radio play: Canadian Broadcasting Commission 1959, BBC 1960; *The Inner World of Miss Vaughn*: play: BBC Television: 1964 (Gibbs); *A Stone Flower :Plays One* (London: Kaye & Ward, 1968) (Their were earlier versions of this play for radio and television).

27 See *Obstinate Cymric* 56–8,71–2.

28 See also Fordham 211.

29 It is, however, possible to suggest a mythological pattern, thought this is not reinforced or underlined, nor is it essential to the overall plot structure, as with Powys's use of myth. Thus Rhys following the blow leaves society for the wilderness, or Waste Land of Arthurian Romance. He also loses his adulthood, like the Fisher King, though Rhys receives his blow to the head, not to the groin, when he becomes an asexual being, a child. It might also be suggested that his happiness is analogous to that of someone who has seen the Holy Grail. There is, however, nothing mythological about the novel's ending with Rhys freezing to death!

30 In 'The Sower' the Welsh peasant 'is almost biblical ... [and] looked like one of the old prophets' (662).

31 I was reminded of this by Jeremy Hooker's discussion (109). Powys also states in his *Autobiography* that he 'always had a very strong, an almost hurtingly strong sympathy with tramps. I would identify myself, in a sort of imaginative projection of my spirit, with these strange wayfarers' (276). It is possible that this shared interest in tramps, has its origin in the writings of Dostioevsky. Gilbert Phelps refers to his influence in the early twentieth century: 'There were too the numerous inspired simpletons such as Hugh Walpole's Harmer John ... the saint-like tramps whom we encounter in so many of the short stories of the period' (179).

32 *Miss Williams* first broadcast by the Canadian Broadcasting Corporation in 1959; then by the BBC in 1960. It was then re-shaped for BBC Television in 1964 as *The Inner World of Miss Vaughn* (Gibbs C 48,C51, C62).

33 There is a possible parallel with the drowning of Geard in *A Glastonbury Romance*.

34 *Against the Stream* (1981) was originally published as *The House in the Valley* (1951) under the pseudonym Patric Shone; *What Farrar Saw and Other Stories* (1984) contained stories first published in 1946/47.

35 See 'A Man in the Corner'.

36 Hanley explored the darker side of Welsh non-conformist religion, more thoroughly, in his play *The Stone Flower*, published in 1968.

37 Hanley's early works in the 1950s were received somewhat critically by Emyr Humphrys and Idris Parry. In 1979 D. E. Owen reviewed *The Welsh Sonata* in *The Anglo-Welsh Review*. More recently, Welsh institutions have acknowledged Hanley: *The New Welsh Review*, in the Spring of 1998, with articles by Roy Birch and Tony Brown; and in 2002, The University of Wales Press, with John Fordham's book on Hanley. Roy Birch was born in Wales, and returned on retirement, while Tony Brown lectures at the University of Wales, in Bangor.

38 Timothy Hanley wrote to Phyllis Playter, on 21st June 1963, from The Cottage, Llanfechain, following the death of John Cowper Powys (National Library of Wales).

39 The correspondence between both James and his wife Timothy and their son Liam documents this, and as well indicates James Hanley's regrets about the move.

ANDREW NASH

# Frank Swinnerton on John Cowper Powys

In an earlier number of *The Powys Journal*, James Knowlson and I published an essay on the relationship between T. F. Powys and Charles Prentice, senior partner of the publishing firm of Chatto & Windus.[1] Additional research into the Chatto & Windus archive has thrown up further evidence about the publishing history of the Powys brothers, this time in relation to John Cowper.[2] A valuable feature of the archive is the sequence of readers' reports on incoming manuscripts that begins from around 1915. Most of the early reports in this sequence were written by the young novelist Frank Swinnerton (1884–1982), who had been appointed as the firm's first salaried reader in 1909. Over the period 1915–25, Swinnerton commented on no fewer than six titles by John Cowper. At a time when Powys's reputation in the United Kingdom was still largely that of an unknown writer, these reports offer a valuable insight into the way his work was viewed, critically and commercially, by a significant literary figure of the day who was not only a publisher but also an accomplished novelist and literary critic.

My interest in this material lies principally with Swinnerton and in the role of publisher's readers in the history of publishing and the formation of literary taste. I am not a John Cowper Powys scholar and in what follows I have not attempted to analyse in any detail Swinnerton's critical assessment of the various works. Instead, I have presented the full text of each of the reports together with a brief commentary that draws attention to the operations of the firm at the time and comments on Swinnerton's own values and tastes. My hope is that this material will prove a useful resource for more specialist Powys scholars.

✻ ✻ ✻

For much of the twentieth century, Frank Swinnerton was one of the most significant figures on the London literary scene. Author, publisher, broadcaster, and reviewer, he wrote over forty novels — the earliest of which, including the best-selling *Nocturne* (1917), won considerable critical approval. He spent much of his early adult life in publishing, working first for J. M. Dent and then for Chatto & Windus, where, between the years 1909 and 1926, he played a major role in helping to transform that firm into one of the most important literary publishers of the 1920s.[3] When Swinnerton took up his official role as reader in 1909 (he had first joined Chatto & Windus some two years earlier) the firm was going through something of a crisis. Andrew Chatto had been an innovative Victorian publisher but in his later life had rather lost touch with new developments in the trade. As a consequence, Chatto & Windus lost the capacity to attract and retain the sorts of authors that gave credibility to a publisher's list. Chatto missed out on the chance to publish the young Kipling, lost patience with Arnold Bennett — who took *The Old Wives Tale* to Chapman & Hall from under his nose — and steered Hall Caine's best-selling novels into the hands of Heinemann when he refused to give the author royalties. As Swinnerton himself correctly judged of Chatto, 'in losing touch with popular taste and with rising standards of execution he had lost also much of the prestige which his genius had formerly created'.[4]

Chatto retired in 1911, but that event did not signal any clear break with the past for control of the firm passed to Percy Spalding, who had assisted Chatto with the firm's finances from as far back as 1876. Spalding, by all accounts, was much loved by those who worked for him, but had what Swinnerton called 'a great, even sublime, ignorance of literature, which he never attempted to conceal'.[5] For this reason, Swinnerton was able to acquire a much stronger editorial role than might have been possible had his senior partner been more in touch with literary developments. Indeed, until the mid 1920s, when two younger partners, Harold Raymond and Charles Prentice, became established in the firm, Swinnerton and Geoffrey Whitworth (the firm's art editor) enjoyed 'exceptional liberty' in editorial affairs. As Swinnerton later recalled in his *Autobiography*, so long as Spalding was consulted and satisfied, he 'let us do as we wished'.[6]

What Swinnerton wished to do was to raise the quality of the firm's fiction list, which had always been the backbone of the business. The loss of Bennett meant that the writers who featured most prominently under the Chatto & Windus imprint in the Edwardian period were names that have been completely, and no doubt deservedly, lost to posterity. One by one, Swinnerton managed to drop the firm's close association with the likes of Constance Smedley, John Ayscough, J. E. Preston Muddock and F. E. Penny, whose sundry titles cluttered the list. When he left the firm in 1926, writers of the calibre of Aldous Huxley, Lytton Strachey, Constance Garnett (whose translations of Chekov and other Russian authors were secured as a direct result of Swinnerton's initiative) and, briefly, D. H. Lawrence had appeared under the Chatto & Windus imprint.

Given this commitment to quality, one might have expected Swinnerton to have been more interested in the work of a writer as talented and unusual as John Cowper Powys. He seems, however, to have been one of those critics who saw nothing in the eccentric style but the empty posturing of a charlatan. Indeed, as a literary historian Swinnerton appears to have discounted Powys's achievement altogether for he is nowhere mentioned in *The Georgian Literary Scene* (1935), an otherwise comprehensive and still very useful survey of the literature of that era.[7] Paul Roberts has suggested that this exclusion might be explained in part by Powys's residence in America and subsequent absence from the national literary culture:

he was out of England for almost the whole period 1905–34, during which many of his contemporaries established their reputations, and could not, therefore, participate in what Frank Swinnerton has called 'The Georgian Literary Scene', even if he had been temperamentally capable of doing so.[8]

The point of temperament is well made and strikes at the heart of the difference between Swinnerton and Powys as novelists and critics, a difference that undoubtedly fuelled the negative response Swinnerton gave to the various books by Powys on which he reported. Yet for all his distrust of experimental techniques in fiction, it is easy to be misled by the title of Swinnerton's study. The avoidance of the word 'modernism' is clearly deliberate, but he covers the full range of literature in the period and includes discussions of Eliot, Joyce and Woolf among others. The absence of any coverage of the Powys brothers (both Theodore and Llewelyn are excluded from the discussion as well) thus cannot be put down to a narrowness of focus. Roberts is right, however, to lay emphasis on John Cowper's American residence when assessing his critical reputation in the UK, and it is an important factor in understanding the publishing history of his works as well. Powys's distance from the British literary scene meant that his work was always on the margins of a publishing culture that was traditionally hesitant about works published in the American market.

We can see this hesitancy at work in the case of Powys's first novel, *Wood and Stone*, which was also the first of his books to be reported upon by Swinnerton. The novel had been published in New York by G. Arnold Shaw on 5 November 1915.[9] Thanks to the work of Paul Roberts, a good deal is now known about Shaw who was a crucial early sponsor of Powys's career as both lecturer and author.[10] As Roberts notes, the overnight decision Shaw took in 1914 to set up as a publisher 'galvanised' Powys into activity, 'and released at last the flood of books on which he had made so many false starts during the past twenty-five years'.[11] *The War and Culture* (1914) and *Visions and Revisions* (1915) appeared first, with *Wood and Stone* following shortly after. Shaw mounted a large publicity campaign for the novel, which included a full page advertisement in *The Publishers' Weekly*.[12] It was this very advertisement that prompted Chatto & Windus to make an approach to Shaw on 13 December 1915 enquiring whether *Wood and Stone* was available for the British market. This unusual course of action gives some indication of the success of Shaw's publicity strategy, for Chatto & Windus was not in the habit of approaching American publishers (especially new and unestablished publishers such as Shaw) on the strength of announcements in trade journals. The firm asked Shaw to send a copy of the book together with a quotation for an edition of 500 or 1000 copies, bound or in sheets. Shaw complied on 28 December 1915, at the same time informing Chatto & Windus of the book's early success in America: the first edition of 3000 copies had been sold within three weeks and a second edition of 5000 had been printed. In view of these figures, Shaw felt confident in telling the British firm 'we feel sure that you will agree that the book has real merit despite its length'.

The customary procedure for incoming manuscripts was that Swinnerton would write a report, which would then be read by Percy Spalding, the senior partner, who would act on the recommendations made. Swinnerton began his report on *Wood and Stone* by offering some explanation as to why a novel set in England might be coming to Chatto & Windus via an American publisher. It was important for him to establish Powys's cultural origins and the location and setting of his work because the firm was sceptical at this time about the market for American fiction in Britain. The overall report, however, was short and not at all positive:

> Mr Powys, I think, is an Englishman turned American; but he may not be. At any rate, the scene of his very long novel is Southern England, upon the boarders [*sic*] of Somerset and Dorset. He is a great admirer of Thomas Hardy, and I suppose that this book is intended as an imitation of Hardy. It is lacking, however, in one of Hardy's essential attributes — clearness; and in another — convincingness. His book is a sprawling uncharacterized mass of talk and description and incident, from which nothing clear emerges.

The criticism of the 'sprawling' nature of Powys's writing is not, of course, unusual, and Swinnerton was not alone among contemporary readers and reviewers in failing to see beyond the diffuse form of the novel.[13] His emphasis on 'clearness', however, gives some indication of his own particular values and tastes in fiction. By 1915 Swinnerton had himself published five novels; his greatest critical success, *Nocturne*, would appear two years later in 1917. His early novels are mainly tales of suburban life and in terms of form and style show the influence of Arnold Bennett, whom Swinnerton much admired and about whom he wrote several books. Whilst he was by no means blind to the values of alternative modes of writing, the clarity and conviction which he thought lacking in Powys's work were clearly important criteria in his assessment of the quality of fiction. It seems doubtful that Powys was ever very close to receiving a recommendation of publication.

Some mystery surrounds the reading of *Wood and Stone*, however. It was not until November 1916, nearly twelve months after Chatto & Windus had first requested the book, that the firm finally reported its decision not to publish. On 22 November the firm wrote to Shaw apologising that the decision 'has been so long delayed and that it is an adverse one. We have given very careful consideration to the volume, but we regret to say that we are unable to handle it for this market.' Why the firm should have taken so long to reach its verdict, particularly given Swinnerton's succinct dismissal of the book in his report, is not at all clear. It seems incredible that it took them almost a year to inform Shaw of their verdict, so we have to conclude that debate within the firm about the volume was ongoing during that time. There is, however, no recorded evidence of such a debate and certainly no evidence in the firm's archives of any communication between Chatto & Windus and Shaw between January and November 1916.

Swinnerton's association with *Wood and Stone* did not end with this rejection. Shaw eventually sold sheets of the novel to Heinemann and shortly after the book was issued in the UK in early 1917 Swinnerton reviewed it for *The Manchester Guardian*.[14] We can only speculate whether he read the book again (or, indeed, if he had read it again during the eleven months that it took Chatto & Windus to return their copy to Shaw). It is noticeable that in the review Swinnerton focuses much more on the style of Powys's writing than the content of the novel, which perhaps suggests he was relying on his earlier impressions of the book. *The Guardian* then, as now, appealed to an educated audience but it was not a literary periodical, and Swinnerton's dense, almost opulent, critique, seems almost too specialist for the casual reader of a national newspaper. The review is very clear and detailed on what Swinnerton took to be the artistic failings of the book, and I have quoted it in full partly because of its density and partly to give an illustration of Swinnerton's own critical style:

Mr Powys essays in "Wood and Stone" the presentation of a philosophical romance in which actions are derived not from impulses but from the general principles which seem to the author to govern human character. The aim is an interesting one, and the book contains work which one must respect, but it can hardly be said to succeed artistically. The persons of the romance are many, the author's philosophic demonstrations are similarly numerous, and the whole vast and loquacious novel impresses one as a rough scaffolding or first draft of a work of art rather than as a finished performance. Long pages of natural description — many of them excellent in vision despite their turgidity — are confused with philosophic inter-pretations and a crude yet sometimes penetrating analysis of character. One is introduced in chapter after chapter to per-sons who illustrate in themselves innumerable attitudes to life, lusts, temperamental conflicts with environment etc.; but these people do not breathe, and the result, in spite of all grandiose endeavours after exactitude, is at best an air of galvanised matter. The author too constantly takes up the too numerous persons and nonchalantly lets them fall again, so that they do not compose. He furthermore explains every-thing, every character and motive and scene, with an obscur-ing amplitude. In his wish to make every individual illustrate the conflict between what he styles "the will to power" and "the will to sacrifice" Mr Powys allows nothing for growth or reaction. He does not imagine. He grapples with conceptions of life-forces. He arbitrarily and clumsily moulds his ascetics, his schemers, his sensualists, his priests, and his draggled young women into representations of type. The reader, ab-sorbedly aware that behind the novel there is a personality that interests him, forgives much, seeks out the symbolic values of all the quaintly-named and personality-laden creatures who are subjected to the author's exegesis and made thereupon to behave very grotesquely; but no principles and no exposition can ever vivify work that has not been imagined or characters whose conduct is fantastically squalid.

It is interesting to compare the criticisms here with those Swinnerton shared with his colleagues a year earlier and which he never intended for public view. The basic opinion on the novel remains unchanged but in the review Swinnerton gives fuller expression to what he refers to in the report as 'a sprawling uncharacterized mass of talk and description and incident'. The analysis of character is 'crude yet sometimes penetrating'; the people in the book 'do not breathe' and 'do not compose' and Powys 'does not imagine'. All of these observations on the creation of character and incident contribute to Swinnerton's general criticism of the book: that it 'impresses' as a 'first draft' rather than 'a finished performance'. To Swinnerton, the book is more an exercise in philosophical meditation than imaginative creation, hence his criticism that 'Mr Powys allows nothing for growth or reaction'. Growth is a word that Swinnerton would use again in connection with Powys (in his report on *Ducdame*) and it indicates a significant point of difference between his ideas on fiction and aesthetics and Powys's own style of writing.

It was another eight years before Chatto & Windus received any further works by Powys. Although, thanks to Shaw, a good number of John Cowper's books were published in America in the intervening period, these were mainly concentrated in the year 1916, and the only novel to appear, *Rodmoor*, remained unpublished in the UK until 1973. Powys's critical and commercial reputation was still very small, especially outside America.[15] Any reputation that he did have in the UK would not have much influenced Swinnerton's opinion on the various titles on which he reported in the mid 1920s; they were evidently judged entirely on Swinnerton's assessment of their intrinsic merits.

In the intervening years since the war, Chatto & Windus had experienced something of a renaissance. Partly as a result of Swinnerton's influence, the firm had begun to attract more distinguished names to what had become a rather undistinguished list. The writers of the Bloomsbury group (including Clive Bell, Roger Fry and Lytton Strachey) now graced the shelves alongside fiction by such authors as Aldous Huxley, David Garnett, R. H. Mottram and, of course, T. F. Powys. It might, therefore, have been expected that John

Cowper's various books would receive serious attention, but the
flurry of titles that passed through Swinnerton's hands over 1924–5
met with almost total disapproval. The first of these, *Suspended
Judgments*, was received by the firm on 14 July 1924, almost eight
years after it had first been published in New York by Shaw in
December 1916. The book had been reissued in 1923, however, with
new material by the American Library Service and it was a copy of this
edition that was sent to Chatto & Windus by the literary agents Curtis
Brown. Swinnerton's opinion was categorical:

> Mr Powys thinks of a thing to say about a man, doubles it, and
> keeps on doubling until he is tired. That is the method of these
> essays, which are decidedly not sound. The hit or miss nature
> of the estimates, the habit the author has of following out one
> momentary judgement until it yields no more words, gives the
> book liveliness, but no value.

Again, the opinion is not unusual. In his helpful study, W. J. Keith
has shown how Powys's criticism stands apart from the various styles
of academic and professional criticism that were becoming more
dominant in the early years of the twentieth century.[16] In this context
it is important to note that at this stage in his own career Swinnerton
was himself an accomplished critic. He wrote a regular column for the
*Bookman*, was a frequent reviewer for the *Observer*, the *Evening News*
and, as we have seen, the *Manchester Guardian*. He also published
critical books on Gissing and Stevenson in 1912 and 1914 respectively.[17] If his critical style inclined more towards that of the journal-
ist than the academic, he was nevertheless very much a learned
professional and practised in his art; he clearly had little patience with
the protracted, undisciplined, subjective style he detected in Powys's
criticism. *Suspended Judgments* was returned to Curtis Brown on 22
August 1924.

Shortly after making this rejection, Swinnerton was asked to
comment on Powys's novel *Ducdame*. Slips of the American edition,
which was poised to appear in the following February from
Doubleday, Page & Co., were sent to Chatto & Windus, again by
Curtis Brown, on 11 December 1924. Swinnerton's report suggests

that he read the novel carefully — over Christmas? — but there was no disguising his distaste for the content and style:

> A very long novel — much longer, in a way, than its length. It is the story of a decadent family, obsessed by the need for continuance of its breed. The hero has a mistress living in the same house as the rest of his family; he has love affairs also with two other ladies. Idiot boys, monstrosities and grotesques populate the book. There are chunks of description, tombstones, woods, and other accumulated horrors. At times the book is almost impressive; but on the whole it is exhausting, and it has no momentum. Each paragraph is splodged down, carries its meaning, and drops into oblivion. It does not lend meaning or growth to the story. Consequently, as the book is long, improbable, humourless and horrible, but in a ghoulish rather than in a popular style, I think we should pass it. The Mr Powys who has written it is brother to T. F. Powys.

That final observation was probably incidental and not designed to influence any of the partners in the firm. Chatto & Windus had begun to publish T. F. Powys's work by this time but Charles Prentice, Theo's great admirer, was evidently less enamoured of John Cowper or Llewelyn. He later told an American publisher that as a writer Theodore 'knocks his two brothers into a cocked hat'.[18]

Swinnerton's criticisms of *Ducdame* are hardly surprising in view of the response he had given to *Wood and Stone* some nine years before. They are also, of course, characteristic of the usual criticisms drawn against John Cowper's work — the length, the formlessness, the lack of momentum. Swinnerton's emphasis on 'meaning' and 'growth' (the echo from the *Wood and Stone* review) in terms of 'story' nevertheless captures the distrust of modernist techniques that characterised so much of his critical writing. *Ducdame* was returned on 1 January 1925, one month before it appeared in America. It was published in London by Grant Richards in August of the same year.

On 19 January, just over two weeks after the firm had returned

*Ducdame*, Chatto & Windus received two further books by John Cowper, again sent by Curtis Brown. The first of these was the American Library Service edition of *One Hundred Best Books*. It was quickly dismissed by Swinnerton:

> A futile little work which ranges from the Psalms to Cannan's "Round the corner". Mr Powys's comments are naïve and useless.

Perhaps the frequency with which he was now being confronted with John Cowper's work was beginning to test Swinnerton's patience. His report on the other book, the Manas Press edition of *Confessions of Two Brothers* (co-written, of course, with Llewelyn), was equally terse:

> There is a failure in proportion here. The sort of stuff Mr JC Powys writes about himself — very fluent, very amazed, very sesquipedalian — could only interest a reader already interested in Mr Powys. That is, only in a great and famous man could such statements have interest. From Mr Powys they are windy and strained. Mr L. Powys seems less windy, but prattling.

The dismissal here has a double edge. John Cowper's 'confessions' are not only uninteresting to Swinnerton, he finds them unworthy of record because they are the observations of a man who is neither great nor famous. Swinnerton's opinion of Powys was now clearly fixed, and when he received a copy of the Dodd, Mead edition of *The Religion of a Sceptic* just three months later, on 22 April 1925, he adopted the same dismissive tone:

> In America just now there is a theological row going on. I heard all about it when I was there, but could learn nothing of the beliefs separating the modernists from the Fundamentalists. Mr Powys, being on the spot, has added a small stone to the fight in this pamphlet. He dislikes both the contending parties, and instead of their dogma offers his own faith, which seems to be the usual love of beauty, love of literature, love of

nature, and marvel at the universe and 'all created things' to which we are accustomed. Not a very distinguished piece of work, and not at all one that English people would buy in large numbers. Intellectually it is negligible.

As with the two immediately previous titles on which Swinnerton reported, *The Religion of a Sceptic* was returned to Curtis Brown just two days after it had been sent.

* * *

What are we finally to make of this glimpse into one man's opinions of the work of John Cowper Powys? We should not be too surprised that Swinnerton advised Chatto & Windus not to publish books like *The Religion of a Sceptic*, *One Hundred Best Books* and *Confessions of Two Brothers*. Although the firm published editions of Shakespeare and Medieval literature, and by the 1920s had begun to issue the essays and biographical works of Lytton Strachey, it did not publish many non-fictional works, and those that were published generally formed part of a series or appeared in the same format as fiction (generally at a retail price of six shillings or seven-shillings and sixpence). Even if Swinnerton had not been so dismissive of their intellectual qualities, the difficulties of marketing Powys's non-fiction titles would likely have been too great an impediment to recommendation. It is the rejection of the two novels that is more significant because fiction had always been the backbone of the Chatto & Windus list and Swinnerton was particularly keen to capture works of fiction that were of conspicuously high quality. The publication of Theodore's work, among other novelists of the time, proves that the firm was not unprepared to take commercial risks with the work of original writers. But Swinnerton simply saw nothing of value in John Cowper's books, and the decisions he took in the name of Chatto & Windus appear to have been prompted primarily by literary and aesthetic judgements rather than commercial demands.

NOTES

1 'Charles Prentice and T. F. Powys: a publisher's influence', *The Powys Journal* XII (2002), 35–66.

² The archive is held on deposit in Reading University Library. All quotations from manuscripts and unpublished sources are taken from this archive. As ever, I am grateful to Mike Bott for his assistance. For permission to quote from Swinnerton's unpublished writings I gratefully acknowledge the kind permission of Miss Olivia Swinnerton.

³ For a full account of Swinnerton's role as reader to the firm, see my essay 'A Publisher's Reader on the Verge of Modernity: The Case of Frank Swinnerton', *Book History* 6 (2003), 175–95.

⁴ Frank Swinnerton, *Swinnerton: An Autobiography* (London: Hutchinson, 1937), 121.

⁵ *Ibid.*, 164.

⁶ *Ibid.*, 161.

⁷ Frank Swinnerton, *The Georgian Literary Scene 1910–1935* (London: Hutchinson, 1935, revised 1954, 1969).

⁸ Paul Roberts, 'John Cowper Powys and his Popular Contemporaries', *The Powys Journal* IX (1999), 39–61, 40.

⁹ This and subsequent bibliographical information is drawn from Dante Thomas: *A bibliography of the writings of John Cowper Powys: 1872–1963*, (Mamaroneck: Paul P. Appel, 1975).

¹⁰ See Paul Roberts, *The Ideal Ringmaster: a biographical sketch of Geoffrey Arnold Shaw (1884–1937)*, (Kilmersdon, Somerset: The Powys Society, 1996).

¹¹ *Ibid.*, 20.

¹² *Ibid.*, 21.

¹³ Most reviews of *Wood and Stone* criticised the excessive length and loose construction of the novel. See Roberts, 'John Cowper Powys and his Popular Contemporaries', 41–2.

¹⁴ 9 March 1917, p. 3. I am very grateful to Professor Claude Gibson of Texas A&M University for drawing my attention to this review. It is signed 'F.S.' and appears under the section headed 'New Novels'. The review is cited by Paul Roberts in his essay on 'John Cowper Powys and his Popular Contemporaries', but not identified as by Swinnerton.

¹⁵ Paul Roberts (*Ibid.*, 40) notes that many reviewers took *Ducdame* (1925) to be Powys's first novel.

¹⁶ W. J. Keith, 'John Cowper Powys: the Literary Criticism of a Book-Worm', *The Powys Journal* IX (1999), 62–80.

¹⁷ *George Gissing: a critical study* (London: Martin Secker, 1912); *R. L. Stevenson: a critical study* (London: Martin Secker, 1914).

¹⁸ See Nash and Knowlson, 'Charles Prentice and T. F. Powys', 49.

PAUL ROBERTS

# John Cowper Powys
# and The Cambridge Summer Meetings

## I  INTRODUCTION

As far as I am aware, none of the published accounts of John Cowper
Powys's work as a University Extension lecturer make any reference
to his participation in the Summer Meetings held by the Cambridge
Delegacy. Stuart Marriott and Janet Coles, in their magisterial study
of Powys as an Extension lecturer,[1] tell us that Powys delivered a 'trial
lecture' at the Oxford University Summer Meeting in 1899 and Derek
Langridge informs us[2] that Powys also took part in the Oxford
Summer Meetings for 1901, 1903 and 1905: but of the Cambridge
Summer Meetings there is no mention.

The Oxford and Cambridge Summer Meetings were held throughout August on alternate years, an arrangement introduced in 1900 to
enable delegates to attend at both universities. They were hugely
popular affairs that had been established as biennial events as a result
of the demand from local groups. Between 700 and 900 delegates
regularly attended, about a third of whom were teachers from elemen-
tary and secondary schools around the country. Many of those
attending would have attended local University Extension courses,
but there were also usually between 150 and 200 students from
overseas. In 1902, for example, students were recorded in the annual
report as having travelled from Austria, Belgium, Denmark, Finland,
France, Germany, Holland, Hungary, Norway, Sweden, Switzerland,
the United States and 'the Colonies' to attend the Meeting. It was also
not unusual for students from China and Japan to attend, as they did
in 1906.

Records held by the University of Cambridge Board of Continuing Education show that, having been approved by the Lectures Committee on 1 March 1899, Powys participated in the Summer Meetings for 1900, 1902, 1904 and 1906.

In August 1900, when the theme for the Meeting was 'Life and Thought in England in the Nineteenth Century' Powys delivered a lecture on 'Three Poets of To-day', choosing as his subjects W. B. Yeats (1865–1939) (from whom he had received a treasured, but no longer extant, letter of congratulation on the publication of his first collection of verse, *Odes and Other Poems* in 1896), William Watson (1858–1935) and Francis Thompson (1859–1907).

In 1902, when the Meeting ran from 1 to 26 August, the theme was 'Some Aspects of Life and Thought in Europe and America in the Nineteenth Century' and Powys delivered two lectures under the title 'Some Modern Poets'. The first of these dealt with Rudyard Kipling (1865–1936) and Stephen Phillips (1864–1915); the second was concerned with the poetry of George Meredith (1828–1909) and Thomas Hardy (1840–1928), although Powys did manage to introduce a reference to his elderly friend Alfred de Kantzow.

The Summer Meeting of 1904, which ran from 29 July to 23 August, was held not at Cambridge, where there was a large meeting of the British Association, but at the Royal Albert Memorial College in Exeter. The theme this time was 'The Age of Elizabeth, in History, Literature, and Art' and Powys delivered a series of three lectures on 'Certain of Shakespeare's Plays', taking as his examples *Richard III*, *Macbeth* and *The Taming of the Shrew*.

In 1906, the year in which Llewelyn Powys failed his Tripos at Cambridge, Powys returned to the Summer Meeting to take part in a conference devoted to 'The Eighteenth Century' where there was a particular focus on the years 1714–89. Powys gave two lectures on 'The Sentimental Comedy'. The first of these was concerned with Goldsmith (whose play *The Good-Natur'd Man* was performed twice during the conference under the direction of William Poel) and the second with Sheridan. Powys's syllabuses for these lectures, published by the Cambridge University Press, were as follows:

# THE SENTIMENTAL COMEDY
## BY J. C. POWYS, M.A.

### I. GOLDSMITH.
*English Comedy before Goldsmith. Elizabethan Humour. Romantic farces. Shakespeare and Ben Jonson. The New Style. Beaumont and Fletcher. The Comedy of Manners. Dryden and the Drama of the Restoration — Congreve, Wycherley, Farquhar, etc. The Sentimental style in England and France. The Writings of Richardson and Rousseau. Steele's Plays. Influence of the* Spectator *in refining morals. Influence of the French "genteel" Comedy. Fielding's struggle against the sentimental spirit.*

*The life and genius of Goldsmith. His plays partly "sentimental" and partly a return to the earlier model.*

*"I confess I was strongly prepossessed in favour of the poets of the last age and strove to imitate them. The term "genteel" comedy was then unknown among us and little more was desired by an audience than nature and humour in whatever walks of life they were most conspicuous."*

*The beginnings of the dramatic instinct in Goldsmith. The Man in Black. Mr Tibbs. Goethe's criticism of the* Vicar of Wakefield. *"The Goodnatured Man"[sic] produced at Covent Garden Theatre, Jan. 29*[th]*, 1768.*

*Johnson's Prologue. The Plot and the Characters. The character of Croaker borrowed from Suspirius in Johnson's Rambler (No.59). Mr Lofty an enlargement of Mr Tibbs. Reception of the Play. The bailiff scene regarded as an offence to the "genteel" spirit.*

She Stoops to Conquer *acted for the first time at Covent Garden Theatre, March 15, 1773. The Plot and the Characters. Horace Walpole's opinion. "Dr. Goldsmith has written a comedy – no, it is the lowest of all farces: it is not the subject I condemn, though very vulgar, but the execution. The drift tends to no moral, no edification of any kind...."*

### II. SHERIDAN.
*Sheridan's character and adventures.*

The Rivals, *produced Jan 17*[th]*, 1775. Its plot and characters. Sheridan's literary borrowings. His mother's comedy. A trip to Bath. Mrs Tryfort the original of Mrs Malaprop. The claims of Mrs Slipslop and Mrs Tabitha Bramble.*

*Miss Lydia Languish. This type of sentimental heroine compared, on*

*one hand, with the heroines of Congreve and, on the other, with those of
Shakespeare.*
Bob Acres. Sir Lucius O'Trigger. Sir Anthony Absolute.
*Sheridan has more of the true non-moral spirit of the classic comedy of
manners than Goldsmith and so his Faulkland and Julia are deliberately
introduced as a sop to the sentimentalists and their taste – a taste not quite
converted yet, even by* She Stoops to Conquer.
The School for Scandal *first performed at Drury Lane Theatre, May
8th, 1777.*
The Plot and the Characters. *A play better* acted *than* read. *The most
popular of all English Comedies. Its cunning theatrical craft, its almost
complete moral detachment — its wise dramatic artificiality. A pure work
of art. Its main appeal being not to Sentiment, but to that "middle"
emotion, described by Charles Lamb. The actors in the* School for
Scandal. *An actor's Play. Sheridan's anxiety to fit them all with appropriate parts. In fact it may be said that the play was* written up to *the actors.
Charles Lamb's description of the true artificial comedy and its relation to
the audience.*

"*This secret correspondence with the company before the curtain which
is the bane and death of tragedy has an extremely happy effect in some kinds
of comedy, in the more highly artificial comedy of Congreve or of Sheridan
especially, where the absolute sense of reality (indispensable to scenes of
interest) is not required or would rather interfere to diminish your
pleasure.*

"*The fact is you do not believe in such characters as Surface — the
villain of artificial comedy — even while you read or see them." Garrick's
opinion runs on the same line. The "fall of the screen" must be acted lightly:
not as though it were serious tragedy.*
The <u>Critic</u> *brought out Oct. 30th, 1779. The Play within the Play.
Former examples of this device. Fletcher's* Knight of the Burning
Pestle. *Duke of Buckingham's* Rehearsal. *Fielding's* Pasquin.
*Sir Fretful Plagiary, Dangle, and Puff. Influence of Sheridan upon
modern English Comedy. We can discern the same mixture of Sentimental
and Artificial motives in* Lady Windermere's Fan. The Importance of
Being Earnest, *is pure Artificial Comedy, while a play like* Candida *has a
serious or psychological value. Thus the present situation reproduces the
dramatic issues of the eighteenth century, in a new form.*

By a happy chance, an account of this Summer Meeting, written by

Eleanor E. Helme, was published by the journal *School: A Monthly Record of Educational Thought and Progress* in December 1906. Although it makes no mention of Powys or his lectures, it gives a lively account of the Meeting and makes it clear that the event made a considerable impact on its participants.

## On Summer Meetings
### By Eleanor E. Helme

*UNIVERSITY Extension is a name which conveys to many people nothing beyond the idea of courses of lectures delivered from time to time in various provincial towns, and they probably are quite ignorant of the workings of that organisation. "Delegacy for the extension of teaching beyond the limits of the University" is the title to which it lays claim, and at a summer meeting it more than justifies that claim. For it is then that the University herself is thrown open to the extension students and they are able for a time* qua *alumni to live within her walls and to breathe the unique atmosphere which belongs to either of our great University towns. What an aroma of learning, past history and new ideas hangs over them, not merely suggestive of "lost causes and forsaken beliefs and impossible loyalties," as Matthew Arnold tenderly infers, but an air instinct with the lessons to be learnt from enterprises and ideals which have left some impress on the place of their birth.*

*Oxford may be more pregnant with associations of the past because her part in English history has been so large, but Cambridge during a summer meeting can speak more vividly of the present. Unlike to Oxford's routine, Cambridge has a term during the Long Vacation and so, up to the middle of August, university life still continues: the college chapels are open daily for service — and those who have once heard the choir at King's College will not speedily forget what that means, — whilst the town is not wholly deserted by the under graduates. Hitherto the summer meetings have begun in the first week of August and lasted till the end of the month, but there is a movement afoot to put the date of Cambridge meetings a fortnight earlier. If this could be carried out, then the university term would be in swing during the whole time, whereas at present those able only to attend the second half of the meeting have no opportunity of seeing university life. [This change did, in fact, take place in 1908. PR.]*

*There is a mysterious "something" in the air of Oxford or Cambridge which acts as an incentive to study. Perhaps it is the sight of so much* antiquity around one, perhaps the industry of the extension students, but whatever the cause, idleness would be an impossibility, even if it could for a moment be contemplated by those for whom so much is done to make this month one of real help and stimulation. The method adopted of taking one period and studying it from every side, in history, literature, art, architecture, and music, is one which needs no defence, since it is at once the most logical and complete as well as the most attractive way of studying the past. Its efficacy was well proved this year when the period dealt with was that perplexing epoch the eighteenth century. At first sight it seems an age of such conflicting results, and it is only by a clearer knowledge of its history that one can account for the artificiality and "correctness" of its literature as typified by the poetry of Pope; that one can trace the rise of the modern novel and see the first efforts towards a reaction to romanticism: it is only through acquaintance with all these things that it is possible to account for the pedanticism of the architecture as exemplified in such buildings as Blenheim Palace. These art and architecture lectures are well illustrated by lantern slides, and in the case of those dealing with music, ample examples are sung or played.

Following out this illustrative method, organ recital were given this year in the chapels of King's, Trinity, and St. John's Colleges, where eighteenth-century compositions formed the chief part of the programme. This is an extremely vivid way of learning about an epoch, and in addition to this a performance of The Messiah was given — a performance full of historical interest, as the oratorio was given under the conditions intended by Handel, i.e., twenty-four picked voices and thirty-five instruments. This summer meeting was particularly rich in musical pleasures, as yet another concert was arranged, when the combined choirs of the three colleges of best musical repute gave an unaccompanied sacred concert in King's College Chapel.

For those to whom the present offers more attraction than the past, there was a welcome variety in lectures, debates and conferences on social and economic problems, astronomy, Jewish art and customs, and theology.

The system of tangible illustration of the lectures is insisted on throughout, and excursions are arranged under the guidance of lecturers to view the colleges and their points of historical or architectural interest, and to see famous places in the neighbourhood. Every possible provision is made that this month may be one of enjoyment in a social as well as an educational way. Tennis courts are placed at the disposal of the students, and even a cricket match organised, so that there need be no lack of variety in the life *there. With this end in view evening receptions and boating parties are planned by the indefatigable committee, whilst garden parties are given at various colleges.*

*In this way intercourse is made possible with people from all parts of England, and, it may be said with perfect truth, from all parts of the world, and this free circulation of ideas on every subject is undoubtedly one of the greatest benefits of a summer meeting. Year by year a larger number of foreign students flock there, and every European country is represented, with additions from China and Japan. They are delighted to make friends, to talk of their countries and discuss our own, with the result that one's horizon is broadened, and one is led to take a more intelligent interest in the affairs of our country. For foreigners demand such encyclopedic information on everything connected with England that it is startling to find how little the average English men or women know of their national life, and one welcomes with avidity lectures primarily intended for foreign students such as those delivered this year by the Rev. J. H. B. Masterman, on "British Institutions," including the King, the Cabinet, Local Government, and so on.*

*For those who have had no opportunities for travel, here are means of intercourse with people of other lands, and even possibilities of talking with them in their own language, thus refurbishing knowledge perhaps grow rather rusty, or of acquiring such as can never be gained through written instruction, or conversation with English teachers. Social evenings are even arranged, when the singing of national music by the foreigners forms one of the attractions.*

*Doubtless the best way of insuring this intercourse is to stay in one of the colleges which remain open for residence by extension students. Here the foreigners do chiefly congregate, knowing that they will be well and cheaply provided for without further arrangement on their part. In one of the men's colleges this year no fewer than sixteen nations were represented, and even the women's college could boast of just over half that number!*

*In addition to the foreign element, there is the advantage of tasting for a short time the pleasures of college life, as the authorities, who take the greatest trouble for the extensionists' comfort, arrange that life shall go on as far as possible in the same way as in term time. The same order of proceedings is observed, for instance, at meals, which are taken all together in one of the dining-halls; and this makes the time spent there interesting, and yet no tiresome restrictions are imposed on the students' liberty.*

*In the matter of expense there is little to choose between staying at a college or in lodgings, whilst the greater pleasure and comfort of the former is undoubted. The colleges charge £6 inclusive of* everything *for the whole meeting of four weeks, or for a shorter time on the same scale of 4s a day. Board and lodging are advertised in the town at from 25s a week, but it is open to question whether those extra five shillings are not better invested in obtaining the friendly life of a college with the use of its good garden, and the gain of a more airy situation and excellent feeding. These sound small matters, but they are worth considering if this is to be a month of real enjoyment and profit.*

*Many people are frightened away from attending summer meetings by the mistaken idea that a large expenditure is entailed. But this is a fallacy. Ten pounds is a liberal computation for the entire cost, and it might be done for a somewhat smaller sum. There is the initial outlay of £6 for board and lodging, and about £1 10s. for the ticket for all the lectures, receptions and organ recitals, but the amount of this varies according to the extension examinations the student has passed and a scholarship can be obtained by a system of prize essays. An extension student's or a teacher's ticket is £1 10s. at Cambridge ; £1 at Oxford. Railway companies issue return tickets to the meeting for a single fare and a quarter, and the most expensive of the excursions arranged for do not exceed 10s., the college visits being free. Specially cheap tickets are also obtainable for concerts, and for the play, illustrative of the period studied, which usually forms a part of the programme, but of course these and the excursions are entirely optional.*

*An extra expenditure which is well repaid is to take or hire a bicycle for the meeting. In the first place, it economises time and energy in going to the lecture rooms. After all, the lectures are not so much an end as a means, and if they send away students, satiated, with knowledge, but too tired out in mind and. body for the work for which they should fit them, their end has failed. It is a common but a most regrettable mistake that many, especially teachers, who come to the meeting for a well-earned, but withal profitable, holiday, should wear themselves out by attending perhaps six lectures a day, or nearly 140 during the month. Far better that they should omit a few, and go back with minds refreshed and broadened in other ways! There is no denying that our Universities in August are hot and tiring, and one cannot recommend too strongly the benefit of seizing any spare time to get outside them into the surrounding country, and so relax for a little the tension of work or architectural sightseeing. If the student has a hobby, such as sketching, photographing or flower-collecting, let that hobby have free rein—the results will not only form a pleasant memento of the time spent in Oxford or Cambridge, but will give a variety and zest to the all-too enthralling pursuit of lectures there. Of the excellence of these lectures in themselves there is no need to speak. Such names as Professor Churton Collins, Mr. Herbert Paul, Professor W. Raleigh, Sir Alfred Lyall, Mr. George Wyndham, Mr. Sidney Lee carry their own recommendation with them, and these are only a few of those whom summer meeting authorities manage to secure to lecture on their special subjects.*

*The result of all these good things to teachers and others should be to send the students away not only with greater knowledge but with greater wisdom — the power to reason for themselves more logically and more rightly and to draw just inferences; with material for future reading and study; with an horizon of outlook broadened and enlivened by cosmopolitan interests.*

*Surely these are aims which make it worth while to attend a summer meeting, and those who think of doing so at Oxford next August will have as attractive a programme as ever. The history of the part played by Oxford in English history forms the main course, with special reference to the events of the seventeenth century since the sixteenth was the period treated in the last Oxford meeting. Oxford herself and the neighbourhood is rich in connections with the seventeenth century, and one feels sure that the meeting will be no less successful than its predecessors.*

*" It is a despair to see such a place and ever to leave it, for it would take a lifetime, and more than one to comprehend and enjoy it satisfactorily. "*

*So wrote Nathaniel Hawthorne; but nevertheless, there will be many extension students next August capable of enjoying Oxford very thoroughly in one brief month, and of leaving it with an insight into its history and environments, both ancient and modern.*

Miss Helme was not the only one to commemorate the Summer Meeting of 1906, however. It seems to have been during this conference that Powys wrote an unpublished comic short story of thirteen manuscript pages, which is currently held at the Harry Ransom Humanities Research Center, the University of Texas at Austin.[3] The story which, in common with most of Powys's manuscripts, is heavily revised, was originally called 'From Addison in the Shades to Steele', but this has been crossed out and replaced with 'From Nance Fresport to Mistress Margery Loveit', the title which has been retained for this edited text.

Paul Roberts

187

NOTES ON THE INTRODUCTION

[1] Stuart Marriott and Janet Coles: 'John Cowper Powys as University Extension Lecturer 1898-1909', *The Powys Journal* IV (1994).
[2] Derek Langridge: *John Cowper Powys : A Record of Achievement* (The Library Association, London, 1966).
[3] The manuscript can be found at HRHRC, Austin, Texas indexed as follows: Powys, John Cowper: Works: HANLEY II B: (Untitled short story) Ams/inc. A Revisions, 13pp. on 711, n.d.

ACKNOWLEDGEMENTS

I owe a debt of gratitude to Barbara Pemberton, Librarian of the University of Cambridge Board of Continuing Education for her help and advice in preparing this text and also for providing copies of the relevant documents.

I am also grateful to Robin Patterson who sent me a photocopy of Eleanor E. Helme's essay 'On Summer Meetings'.

Like so many Powysians before me, I am also grateful to the staff of The Harry Ransom Humanities Research Center for their assistance in providing a photocopy of the original manuscript of John Cowper Powys's previously unpublished short story which appears below.

## 2   JOHN COWPER POWYS

### From Nance Fresport[1] to Mistress Margery Loveit
Rose Bower, In the Happy Fields, Elysium

### "Let it be remembered that we sport in fabled stories"

To gratify your amiable wish, my dear friend, I now take up my pen to convey to you some imperfect relation of the prodigious adventure into which chance — if I may use that word to one so well acquainted with the lucubrations of the admirable Mr Boyle[2] — has plunged me since we last walked together among the rose-gardens of Elysium. You recollect as we were arranging amaranth leaves in those adorable blue vases and you were wishing, you naughty minx, that the shade of Will Honeycomb had not been escorted elsewhere, how that extraordinary person arrived — that person so vexatiously plump and opaque

— who presented me, for you retired in a fit of the vapours, with an invitation to the Summer Meeting at Cambridge.

Under the delusion, which you I am sure would have shared, that what was referred to was a meeting rather for pastime than for learning, I lost no time in accepting it. I was conveyed by my mortal acquaintance in a mysterious chariot, of a shape so elegantly contrived that I was not offended by the least sight of the ruffian who drove it, to a door by the side of a small chapel upon which was written in fair large characters the words "Reception Room".³

Here it first became obvious to me that something other than sport was the object of this elegant assembly. My guide, however, informed me that I need be under no anxiety — I could go everywhere, see and hear everything, without anyone perceiving me. Nor indeed was I long ignorant that there were many other persons in the same condition as myself moving surreptitiously and in absolute secrecy among the living members of this gathering.

Among these unrecognised visitors were some that came not from the happy Elysian bowers where I left you, my dear Margery, but — I am afraid — from Tartarus itself. A sort of sulphurous fume accompanied these visitors; though to say the truth this may have been produced by the infernal machines in which they had been fetched.

You will ask what my first feelings were on returning to the Earth after so many years. Well, I must admit to you that I felt a little uneasy. The scene in the "Reception Room" reminded me rather of the sedater parties at Vauxhall than of the meetings we used to have at our club of She-Romps. Here there were no broken fans, torn petticoats, no spoilt flounces and ruined furbelows. Nor could it be said that these devotees of culture are wanting in those graces and elegancies which we used to be taught, my dear Margery, to value higher than anything else. I saw two or three most handsome beaux and one charming wench who looked as though she had stept out of a picture. I could not help smiling at seeing so many pretty girls and charming ladies going to and fro with books in their hands. I thought of the days when we, my dear, used to poke such fun at Mrs Hypatia and her grave airs — such jests would have been totally out of place on this occasion.

Before leaving the "Reception Room" I observed a little group of shades watching with amusement and interest all that went on. Among them I recognised at once that dear Dr Johnson by his wig and twitching face and dramatic manner. He saw me and pointed me out to a little ugly shadow who was by his side, who at once came over to me and with a low bow introduced himself as the author of *The Good Natur'd Man* ,[4] a play that is going to be acted here. You will laugh at my folly, but I want to confess to you that since that first introduction I have got quite to like my little friend. He took me to hear a lecture on himself and even held my fan and counted the cupids in the prettiest shy manner. You would have loved him. He is adorably ugly.

The lecture we went to was given by a certain Mr Powys, the most stiff and pompous speaker I have ever heard. He reminded me a little of our dear Bishop Rubric whose sermons you used to say were like September mists.

My little beau kept fidgeting uneasily with the handle of his sword all the time and I believe if he had not been _____ — you know what I would say; etiquette forbids mention of the word — there would have been bloodshed at the close of the performance.

O, but I must tell you, my dear Madge, about the lecture I went to on our sweet Prince Charlie. Such a dear sentimental professor — a priest, I think he must have been, of the old faith. He told us the prettiest anecdotes. I thought of you and of that rose-leaf you have kept so carefully. What a nice, kind place this Cambridge must be to produce men of such elegance and refined taste. I wish Mr Hogarth could have been there. I am sure he would have brought him into his "Marriage à la Mode". By the way, I hear Mr Hogarth *is* at this meeting. I hope to meet him at some nice little respectable café before long. They say he is painting a wonderful picture called "The Lecturer's Progress", which is to begin with a scene in a girls' school and end — but I will not bore you with description.[5]

By the way, the use of the word "bore" seems to be the distinguishing mark of the present English aristocracy. They say "how boring" when we would have said — but my pen runs away with me.

On Sunday I went to hear what they call the University Sermon and was never so scandalized. It was all about the duties of the Educated and the duties of the Rich. I began to be quite alarmed. I thought reference might even be made to the duties of the ___. Fortunately, I had with me that sweet good-looking Dr Snape's [6] sermon on charity — you remember Dr Snape? Well, I read the passage where he said The Wise Providence has amply compensated the disadvantages of the poor and indigent in wanting many of the conveniences of this life by a more abundant provision for their happiness in the next. Had they been higher born or more richly endowed they would have wanted this manner of education, and after perusal of these eloquent and consoling words my nervousness vanished as quickly as it had come.

Last night, my dear, I had such a shock! I was walking down what they call Regent's Street when who should I see coming towards me swinging a golden-handled cane and smiling wickedly at everyone he passed, but that dreadful old heron Monsieur de Voltaire. I had not seen him since our visit to France, not since that most fortunate event occurred which relegated him to the shades. But I knew him at once by his silver buckles. I am afraid there can be no doubt as to where he comes from. It is scandalous that he should be allowed here at all.

However, of course, I had to speak to him. After all, one cannot be rude to an old acquaintance. Besides, he is a gentleman, certainly better dressed than anyone else at this meeting, either living or ___. He at once gave me his arm and took me to hear a lecture by the Bishop of Durham[7] on a poet called William Cowper. (Do you remember the elaborate preparations made in Elysium to receive him? It was not long after *we* arrived. He was given a little arbour and lawn to himself. I recollect it all as though it was yesterday. We were told to be careful about mentioning theatres or music-halls in his presence.)

Monsieur de Voltaire was delighted with the Prince-Bishop's manner of delivery and choice of language. He said it reminded him of Monseignour Buille de Bois Chatellaine. He especially admired the freedom from anything like sentiment of the address and the mordant irony with which the great Durham illuminated his massive grasp of facts. In connection with this, Monsieur de Voltaire showed me a little commonplace book, handsomely bound in Russian leather, in which he entered all the especially pungent or piquant remarks he had overheard. He permitted me to glance at a few of them. I recollect only the following:

Cowper was an exponent of unaffected simplicity.
Hogarth had much humour.
Dr Johnson was famous for common sense, morality and wit.

I saw several of the younger ladies smoking cigarettes when they thought they were alone. As far as I could ascertain, none of them indulge in *our* vice. In fine, my dear girl, remembering our romps at No. 30 Tavistock Street, how your Nancy pined — among all these learned assemblies — for a pinch, yes, I must say, — for a pinch of snuff. This only offers one more proof of the truth of what the elegant Dr Tillotson [8] says in his sermon entitled "The Value of Contrast upon Earth". "Even in Heaven," says he, "unregenerate people desire Heavenly pleasure and the inhabitants of Felicity find the greatest pastimes disrelishing and dull."

I was surprised yesterday by an unusual noise in the street opposite the theatre. A tolerably large crowd had collected, but pushing my way through as well as I could (it is so hard, my dear Margery, to remember that one is a shadow) I found that a certain poor dear professor — it was the one that had the temerity to say that Blue Stockings were more beautiful than stars — had fallen into a fit and lay prostrate in the road. No one present, so I gathered from my observations of the crowd, understood how this calamity had occurred. One profane voice went so far as to put it down to love at first sight. But I quickly discerned that the real cause was the conduct of one of ourselves. A strange and formidable shade. They tell me that in life he was a Dean of Dublin [9] and that by means of his terrific rage at this unusual speech he had actually succeeded in visualizing himself before this poor man and then had contorted his visage into such a horrible scowl that the result was the unfortunate collapse I witnessed.

However, to eliminate the memory of this dreadful event (for they say the poor learned gentleman has not yet recovered), I must tell you of an amusing episode that occurred at the end of the meeting.

We shades were invited to a garden party in Christ College gardens, with the topic arising as to suggested improvements on the occasion of the next meeting.

Mr. Secretary Addison, ensconcing himself in the recesses of Milton's Mulberry Tree — for, as you know, it is against our etiquette to permit our negative qualities to appear in public — uttered the following words: "Among the monuments, galleries and museums of this learned town, I have not noticed a Temple of Fashions", and recommended the erecting in Cambridge of a museum in a style something between the Fitzwilliam Museum and King's Chapel, devoted to the perpetuation of changing fashions.

"Let there be a repository built for fashions," said he, "as there are chambers for medals and other rarities. The building may be shap'd as that which stands among the pyramids, in the form of a woman's head. This may be raised upon pillars whose ornaments shall bear a just relation to the design. Thus, there may be an imitation of fringe carv'd in the base, a sort of appearance of lace in the frieze and a representation of curling locks with bows of ribband sloping over them may fill up the work of the cornice. There is to be a picture on the door with a looking glass and a dressing chair in the middle of it. There, on one side, are to be seen above one another, patch boxes, pin-cushions and little bottles: on the other, powder bags, puffs, combs and brushes; beyond them, swords, with fine knots, whose points are hidden and fans almost closed with the handles downward are to stand out interchangeably from the sides till they meet at the top and form a semicircle over the rest of the figures: beneath all, the writing is to run in this pretty-sounding manner:

"Adeste, o quotquot sunt Veneres, Gratiae, Cupidines
    In vobis adsunt in promptu
      Faces, Vincula, Spicula,
Hince eligite sumite, regite."[10]

"We desire," so Mr. Secretary Addison was pleased to murmur on in his persuasive way, "we desire also to have it taken notice of that because we would show a particular respect to foreigners, which may induce them to perfect their breeding here in a knowledge which is very proper for pretty gentlemen, we have conceived the motto for the house in the learned language."

This motto, my dear Margery, which I will not insult you by translating into English ought, when I consider all I have seen in the course of this brief visit, to be promptly forwarded to all the fair sex in the United Kingdom.

We have learnt now, as you know, to regard bull baiting and cock fights and public hangings as unsuitable amusements for a Lady of Quality, but I must confess that the difference of fashion in these latter respects and the ones we remember as ours made me feel, when I first returned among mortals, somewhat forlorn and desperate. A walk through the streets, even of Cambridge, is not what it was. However, I begin to see that these differences are largely superficial. Though they don't bait bulls they still eat beef and though they don't hang the beggars they still starve them.

I am, dear Margery, your affectionate friend and humble servant, Nance Fresport.

NOTES TO THE STORY

1 The spelling of the name is hard to distinguish. At its first appearance it seems rather to be 'Freeport' or 'Freepost', but the second and final appearance seems to support the spelling as given here and this spelling has been adopted as more appropriate to the context.
2 Robert Boyle (1627–91), chemist and natural philosopher.
3 During the Summer Meeting of 1906 the Reception Room was managed by Miss Hargood and her committee.
4 The author of *A Good Natur'd Man* was, of course, Oliver Goldsmith (1728–74), the Irish born playwright, novelist and poet.
5 Clearly, Powys's own career, which had begun in a girls' school, would have been the source material for this imaginary work by Hogarth.
6 Dr Andrew Snape (1675–1742) was Provost of King's College, Cambridge and a famed controversialist.
7 Bishop Handley Moule was the first Principal of Ridley Hall Theological College, Cambridge and then Bishop of Durham from 1901 to 1920. A popular evangelical Christian, he was closely associated with the setting up of the Keswick Convention and the author of many books, as well as being a regular contributor to the Cambridge Summer Meetings. His brother Horace Moule was a friend of Thomas Hardy.
8 Dr John Robert Tillotson (1630–94) was brought up as a Presbyterian, but

accepted the Act of Uniformity and became Dean of St Paul's in 1689 and Archbishop of Canterbury in 1691. Tillotson published *The Rule of Faith* and *Lectures on Socianism* and his sermons were long regarded as among the best of their time.

9 Jonathan Swift (1667–1745) became Dean of St Patrick's in Dublin in 1714.

10 The sense of this is: 'Come, your every desire can be satisfied here: put away all your troubles and irritations.'

## 3   APPENDIX

**Syllabuses for the lectures of John Cowper Powys delivered at the Summer Meetings of the Cambridge Delegacy in 1900, 1902 and 1904.**

1900

### THREE POETS OF TO-DAY.
### W. B. YEATS, WILLIAM WATSON, AND FRANCIS THOMPSON.
### BY J. COWPER POWYS, B.A.

*W.B. Yeats.* Celtic poetry. Its polytheism. The making of Myths.

The Poet of Ireland. His poetry based on Irish folk-lore is an organic growth, not merely an individual appreciation of life.

Irish mirth and melancholy. Natural magic. Interest in quaint animals, wild birds and fishes. The naturalness and simplicity of Yeats' style. The Poet of Fairy Land. Revolt of the child in us against the man, of the dreamer against the realist —

" For I would mould a world of fire and dew
  With no one bitter, grave, or over wise,
  And nothing marred or old to do you wrong."

The desire to escape from drudgery and routine, from domestic and social restraint back to an earlier freedom.

" Come, fairies, take me out of this dull house,
  Let me have all the freedom I have lost,
  Work when I will and idle when I will,
  Come, fairies, take me out of this dull world,
  For I would ride with yon upon the wind,
  Run on the top of the dishevelled tide
  And dance upon the mountains like a flame."

The wanderings of Usheen. The Land of Heart's Desire.

*William Watson.* The poetry of culture and criticism.

The influence upon him of Wordsworth, Landor, Tennyson and Matthew Arnold. His interest in social, philosophical and political questions compared with W. B. Yeats's attitude towards these things. His correct, reticent and epigrammatic style. His manly self-assertion and poetic egoism. " Vita Nuova." " Apologia." His blank verse, its excellencies and defects. His want of overpowering inspiration. Compensations for this. The province in Poetry of Rhetoric and Wit.

His complimentary verses " To Richard Holt Hutton."

His Sonnets, " I think the immortal servants of mankind."

His imaginative poems, " Hymn to the Sea."

His "Autumn," in its scholarly treatment of Nature compared with Thompson's "Corymbus."

His lyrics, their polished perfection.
    "Sweetest sweets that Time hath rifled
    Live anew on lyric tongue."

His critical poems. Wordsworth's grave.

*Francis Thompson.* The poetry of mystical religion.

Influence over him of Donne, Crashaw and Vaughan.

" The Hound of Heaven." Its imaginative audacity.

His sense of richness in colour. The poetry of colour compared with the poetry of form.

"Corymbus for Autumn." Thompson's use of metaphors drawn from Catholic ritual. His hieratic use of gold and silver, jewelry and gorgeous stuffs, as in early Italian pictures.

The fantastic elaborateness of his verse.
Its subjectivity.

" Love in Dian's lap." His quaint Idealism.

His poems on children. Their pathos.
    "Nothing begins and nothing ends
    That is not paid with moan,
    For we are born in other's pain
    And perish in our own."

His power in single passages
"Who dare, who dare
Adulate the Seraphim for their burning hair?"

"How shall I gauge what Beauty is her dole
Who cannot see her countenance for her soul
As birds see not the casement for the sky?"

"Our looks and longings which affront the stars
Most richly bruised against their golden bars."

*Summary.* Various tendencies of our latest poetry.

REFERENCES FOR READING.
*Poems,* by W. B. Yeats. Fisher Unwin. *7s 6d*
*Poems,* by William Watson. John Lane. *3s 6d* net
*Odes and other Poems,* by William Watson. John Lane. *4s 6d.* net.
*The Father of the Forest and other Poems,* by William Watson John Lane. *3s. 6d.* net.
*Poems* by Francis Thompson. Elkin Mathews and John Lane. *5s.* net.


1902

SOME MODERN POETS.
BY J. C. POWYS, M.A.
*Two Lectures.*


1. THE POETRY OF MR RUDYARD KIPLING AND MR STEPHEN PHILLIPS.

The Muse justified of all her children. Value of contrast in literary criticism. Opposite types of feeling. The authors of Barrackroom Ballads and Paolo and Francesca. The Pioneer and Æsthetic spirit; value of both. Mr Kipling's poems in Classic English and poems in rank-and-file slang. How far the language of the camp, the ship and the jungle can claim the privileges of a provincial dialect. It is not so deeply rooted in the Past or consecrated by so many homely usages. It is expressive of more transitory modes of life. It is nomadic, cosmopolitan, without household gods. Mr Kipling's rendering of the inarticulate half-bestial jargon of brutalized Man, Stephano and Trinculo out-flouting Caliban. He represents the revolt of "unaccommodated Man" against the amenities and urbanities of civilization. He turns away from the carefully cultivated instincts of centuries of Cloister and Studio — to Tommy Atkins and the Lost Legion. His patriotic poems. A Song of the English. The English Flag. The Recessional. Value to the race of his warnings and encouragement. His devotion, first to the Blood and then to the Country. His religion; obeisance to the God of battles: the virtue of strenuousness: *laborare est orare*. His ultra-Teutonic attitude towards life. The antithesis of the Celtic temper. His fearless assertion of the Romance of To-day and of the Art which cares only for Actuality.

"And only the Master shall praise us and only the Master shall blame,
And no one shall work for money, and no one shall work for fame,
But each for the joy of working and each in his separate star
Shall draw the Thing as he sees It for the God of Things as They Are."
L'Envoi. *The Seven Seas.*

Mr Stephen Phillip's Poems. The peculiar appeal which his poetry has made to modern ears. Causes of its popularity. How it expresses what is most characteristic in the desire of modern sensibility for passion, colour and fragrance. The evasive magic and dream-like charm of it at its best. The touch of morbidity in it at its weakest. Its central and recurring mood, a wistful tenderness for the sorrows of Lovers. The passion of a God with all his splendours (Marpessa), of a Goddess with all her wiles (Ulysses), contrasted with simple human love. His use of mythology. Strange intermingling of Christian and Pagan elements (Christ in Hades), as in a picture by Boticelli. His Dramas. Absence of Humour. Peculiar accompaniment of faraway music in the verse, as though the characters moved and spoke in a dream. His sense of the dramatic value of single lines.

"I did not know the dead could have such hair."

His use in impassioned dialogue of a kind of lyrical chant with a musical refrain of deliberate simplicity.

"*Pao.* So still it is that we might almost hear
The sigh of all the sleepers in the world.
*Franc.* And all the rivers running to the Sea."
*Paolo and Francesca*

## 2. THE POETRY OF MR GEORGE MEREDITH AND MR THOMAS HARDY.

Peculiar interest attaching to the poetry of our greatest living Novelists. The

Philosophy of Mr Meredith and the Philosophy of Mr Hardy. The one a modified Optimism, the other an unmodified Pessimism. Their different forms of expression; the one complex and many-coloured, the other simple and monumental; the one veined with the subtle possibilities of the Intellect, the other graven with the tragic certainties of the Heart.

*Mr Meredith's Poems.* Their tantalizing obliquity of style. How far this springs from obscurity, how far from compression, of thought. His main doctrines: Man, a material animal, evolving, by way of Mind, into a spiritual king of the Earth. He must adhere closely to the Earth, serve her, wrestle with her, love her; she is her beginning and his end, his parent and the mother of his children. The old Dragon, Self. He advocates obedience to social laws, but their revision according to the laws of Nature. His Religion, a faithfulness to the Earth. His Ethics, a following of her intentions. The personal craving for Immortality to be transcended; man to live in his offspring and the fruit of his labours. Only through struggle and contention is the good corn set free.

> "Behold the life at ease — it drifts —
> The sharpened life commands its course
> She winnows, winnows roughly; sifts
> To dip her chosen in her source."
> *Hard Weather, A Reading of Earth.*

Earth cares only for Beyond-Man. The giant race of the Future. Mind not Sentiment understands her.

*Mr Hardy's Poems.* Their trenchant originality and weird demonic power. Their Promethean pity for a world that "groaneth and travaileth in pain." Their volcanic outbursts of long-smouldering wrath at the cruelty of Fate. The terrible directness of the passions they dramatize. Mr Hardy's unshrinking insight into the ironic substratum of Things. He sees Incongruity, an impish Goblin, seated on the Throne. His style, bound as though with bands of steel about its subject; driving as though with the blade of a ploughshare through the flowering weeds that clothe the Skeleton Truth. Mr Hardy apprehends the world rather by way of Form than by way of Colour. Men, trees and houses appear darkly silhouetted against a pale sky. His Titan's grasp upon the rim o' the world trembles sometimes in heartbroken tenderness over the anguish of mortal love. To him there is no beneficent purpose in life. Man is the creature of Chance and a blind Mother who knows not what she bears and wounds where she would cherish. "The

Lacking sense." " The Sleep-worker."
"Unenlightened, curious, meek
She broods in sad surmise...
Some say they have heard her sighs
On Alpine height or Polar peak
When the night tempests rise."

Death is regarded as "a consummation devoutly to be wished "but Mr Hardy
has a weird fancy about the Dead, that they retain a shadowy consciousness
as long as they are remembered by Lover or Friend : to this they cling; but
this they must lose at last. Living Poets who bear a resemblance in mood and
feeling to Mr Hardy. The Poems of Mr de Kantzow.

## 1904

### THREE LECTURES ON CERTAIN OF SHAKESPEARE'S PLAYS.
### BY J. COWPER POWYS, M.A.

### I. RICHARD III.

Shakespeare's first dramatic period.

The influence of Marlowe. The Predominance of Richard over the other
characters, and the predominance of one master passion over Richard, is as
characteristic of Marlowe's conception of the drama as the violence of
certain passages — *i.e* Margaret's curses — is characteristic of the "blood and
fire" of Marlowe's style.

*Richard's character.* His need of violent action His passion for power. His
intellectual irony and mental superiority over all he encounters. His grim
humour. He is not essentially evil in the way Iago is evil. There are elements
of greatness in him. He uses evil as a means
  "I am determined to prove a villain."

Not only his intellectual audacity but his candour wins our admiration. He
does not deceive himself. He knows himself for what he is. A few slight signs
of indecision lessen the abnormal nature of his will and increase our
admiration for it:
  "*Rat.* Your highness told me I should post before.
  *K. Rich.* My mind is changed, sir, my mind is changed"

Or again, even before the ghostly visions on the eve of the battle, he

confesses:
"I have not that alacrity of spirit
Nor cheer of mind that I was wont to have."
His last soliloquy. The Tragedy of Egoism. The sense of loneliness.
'There is no creature loves me
And if I die no soul shall pity me."
His furious courage at the end. His oration to his soldiers – more inspiriting
and poetic — though less moral than Richmond's. Brandes compares it to
the Marseillaise:
"Remember whom you are to cope withal: —
A sort of vagabonds, rascals, runaways.
(*Que veut cette horde d'esclaves ?*)"
Richard the symbol of Titanic Individualism dashes himself to pieces against
Richmond the symbol of Social Law yet, even so, Shakespeare compels us to
feel sympathy with him, at the last, rather than with his rival; as Milton, in
spite of himself, made a hero of Satan.


II. MACBETH.


Shakespeare's Mid-period. The four great tragedies. Their conjectural connection with his life. Date of the composition of Macbeth,1605-1606.
External and internal evidence in favour of this date. Sources and Authori-
ties. Holinshed, Bocce, Bellenden, Fordun. The stories about Macbeth.
"Theatris aptiora quam historiae." Shakespeare's manipulations of, and
deviations from, the Chronicles. Holinshed's *Macbeth.* Donwald and Duff.
The "local colour" of Celtic Scotland in *Macbeth* compared with the "local
colour" of Celtic Britain in *King Lear.* The question of the supposed
"Interpolations." Was the speech of Hecate written by Shakespeare? Is the
Porter's speech genuine? If so, how is it to be justified on dramatic
principles? The Witch of Middleton. Shakespeare's treatment of Evil in his
tragedies. His interpretation of Destiny, of Free-will. The extraordinary "
atmosphere" of Macbeth. Natural and supernatural deviations from the "
Good and the Beautiful." The ever-felt presence of the Sinister and the
Demonic. "Fair is foul and foul is fair." "The Raven himself is hoarse." "I
heard the owl scream and the crickets cry." " Is't night's predominance or the
day's shame, that darkness does the face of earth entomb'?" " Good things of
day begin to droop and drowse." The antique and heroic simplicity of the

action of this play. The plot moves breathlessly forward undeterred by philosophy or description. The grandeur of the two central figures. Their magnanimity in crime. The character of *Macbeth*. The latent dangers: ambition and imaginative superstition. The mixture of physical courage and moral cowardice. The sympathy which we feel with him in his desolation and final turning to bay. The imaginative passion displayed in his speeches and hallucinations :

"Methought I heard a voice cry ' Sleep no more !
Macbeth does murder sleep.'"

*Lady Macbeth.* Her extraordinary power of will. Her practical insight. Her influence over Macbeth. Was it by means of will-force or feminine charm ? Her inability to foresee the moral consequences of the deed. Her unselfish devotion to her husband. The overthrowing of her mental balance. The sleep-walking scene. Her death. Macbeth's stupor and indifference.

*Summary.* The Psychology of Murder — a nature of grand dimensions and noble affections, ruined by ambition and the Evil powers, but discovering at the last how it has been tricked.


## III. THE TAMING OF THE SHREW.

Probable date of the play. It belongs to the comedies of Shakespeare's second period. The old play of 1594. " A Pleasant conceited Historie called The Taming of a Shrew." The relation of the present text to this. The portions of the play which are unmistakably Shakespearian. Theory of an intermediate reviser who introduces the Bianca "intrigues."

The traditional Petruchio. Necessity of protesting equally against a too farcical and a too pedantic interpretation of the Play. The wisdom and real subtilty of Petruchio's method. How far any evidence of personal feelings' can be legitimately drawn from Shakespeare's treatment of this subject.

Shakespeare's attitude towards women. The three general types.
(1) Witty and shrewish — Katharine, Beatrice. (2) Unselfish and womanly — Cordelia, Desdemona. (3) Innocent and girlish — Perdita, Miranda.

The elements of feminine character which both in their positive and negative aspect can be shown as most important in Shakespeare's eyes.

The Induction. Christopher Sly. The serene good-natured animalism of this fellow compared with the romantic grossness of Caliban or the intellectual grossness of Falstaff. The suitable and well-rounded-off close of the older play:

"*Slie.*　　But Ile to my
Wife presently and tame her too
And if she anger me.
*Tapster.* Nay tarry, Slie, for Ile go home with thee
And heare the rest that thou hast dreamt to-night."

The acquired knowledge of Italian "local colour" and the native knowledge of English "local colour" which this play displays. The peculiar Shakespearian attitude towards life discoverable in the best scenes.

PETER J. FOSS

# An Inventory of the Llewelyn Powys Holdings: Manuscripts of Works (Part One)

The following inventory will provide as near as possible a comprehensive list of the manuscript and typescript holdings of Llewelyn Powys's works (exclusive of diaries and letters) that are deposited in public, university or institution archives in Britain and America. (It does not include notebooks containing only working notes, of which there are many.) This is not a *catalogue raisonné*, and the information it provides is still provisional; but it will be the fullest list available of the whereabouts of his manuscripts and of their identification on the basis of current knowledge (even, in some cases, providing a usable catalogue of uncatalogued collections). The inventory is in two parts as follows:

PART ONE (printed here):
    1. Manuscripts of complete books              p.207
    2. Typescripts of complete books            p.209
    3. Manuscripts of essays, stories and reviews in
        Notebook Drafts                          p.210
PART TWO (to follow):
    1. Manuscripts of essays, stories and reviews
        on loose separate sheets
    2. Typescripts of essays, stories and reviews.

My policy here is to list the items according to two schemes; that is alphabetically, in the case of individual books, stories and essays, and where that is not possible, as in the case of Notebook drafts of material, numerically by the numbers provided on the items by Llewelyn Powys or his wife, Alyse Gregory (though there are some overlaps here). Where there is an archive reference number I put that at the beginning of the item, but I also include, in square brackets, a number which corresponds to the numbering in the *Catalogue of the Llewelyn Powys Manuscripts* published by George Sims in 1953, when Sims came to sell the manuscript collection for Powys's widow Alyse Gregory. In that Catalogue there are five sections, of which section I and section II include many of the books and Notebook drafts which found their way into the institutional archives. Thus the reference I give quotes both the section and the number in that section where I have identified the material described. Notwithstanding this, there are problems with Sims's numbering system, in that errors were made and some of the numbers do not exactly match the numbers on the books. This is shown in my own enumeration. However, the advantage of this numbering method is that it imposes at least a provisional order on a vast array of diverse material, much of which is not properly catalogued or identified in the various archives in which it is currently deposited.

In the case of the collection at the Harry Ransom Humanities Research Center, Austin, Texas (which constitutes probably 80% of the extant holdings of Llewelyn Powys's manuscript and typescript works), I realise this is a problematic method, in that the collection there is catalogued (on index cards) alphabetically under the headings of several purchased collections, mainly those of T. E. Hanley. This system, however, makes little sense and has its drawbacks as a means of identifying the material, particularly on untitled items or notebook drafts. I have wished particularly to distinguish the Notebook drafts from the individual manuscript sheets in the collections (since the Notebook drafts were the original versions whereas the loose manuscript sheets were the fair copies). In the case of the HRHRC's holdings I have included the Center's index card identification (eg. 'Hanley II: (Works 4)') after the description of the item; but the order I place it in will correspond with the numbering on the item (in the case of the Notebooks) and that with the numbers in Sims's *Catalogue*. Some items are not identifiable from Sims's Catalogue, and some have no number on them at all. These are distinguished separately (there is also another series of numbers used, as described in the

HRHRC's section below). A few other Llewelyn Powys items, I have since discovered, are lodged in other collections at the Harry Ransom Humanities Research Center but are not cross-referenced under Powys.

Llewelyn Powys's compositional method was fairly straight-forward. His writing period covered, roughly, 1913 to 1939, and he generally made drafts of articles, essays or stories in hardback or softback notebooks, sometimes even in large-format desk diaries (in which case, of course, the date of the diary may not correspond to the date of the material in it). The early drafts were often in pencil, the later ones in ink; in the early period (say, 1913 to 1923) he often made several attempts or versions, whereas when he became more confident as a writer, his first version was his only one, with emendations. The next stage was often a corrected manuscript copy in fountain pen ink made usually on foolscap paper for typing up. These copies would often have many extra corrections and emendations. The third stage was a typescript, in the early days made by one of his sisters, later by a paid typist. The top copy of course was sent to the publisher, and usually has not survived, but one or more carbon copies were made and have sometimes survived. A further complication arises from the fact that Alyse Gregory went through all Powys's notebooks and diaries in her widowhood and typed up much of that material, so that many of the typescripts that exist in the archives were made by her in the 1950s from material that was left over, much of it unpublished. In the case of Llewelyn Powys's books, the manuscripts survived in his possession, or in some cases were given away. These sometimes came back to public archives, others (as in the case of the manuscript of *Glory of Life*) have disappeared from view into private hands. (I have not of course sought to trace private collections.)

As I have already stated, my method here is limited. Under the various headings I give the name of the archive in alphabetical order (with the main name of the collection or university underlined), then list the items alphabetically with an accession number if there is one. In the case of the Notebook drafts, which cannot be catalogued alphabetically, I arrange them in the numerical system I have described, listing the items inside . Some of these have no titles or titles provided later, so some of them are identified from my own knowledge. The titles of the items either on the pages inside or on the cover of the book are given in bold. I also provide a brief description of the appearance of the Notebook itself, so as to confirm identification. I attempt to identify each item and provide its published title, date and place of publication in an abbreviated form (full details will be available in my forthcoming *Bibliography*). In addition to this data I will give any additional information which is of interest or usefulness. There has been no attempt at this stage to examine properly the different versions of items other than a rough identification. I refer readers to my article on 'The Llewelyn Powys Holdings at the HRC, Austin, Texas' in *The Powys Society Newsletter* No 45, pp.37–40 to give an idea of the complications involved in identifying the material in that particular collection.

## 1.1   MANUSCRIPTS OF BOOKS

### (a)   IN THE <u>BISSELL</u> GIFT, POWYS SOCIETY COLLECTION, DORSET COUNTY MUSEUM, DORCHESTER, ENGLAND:

[Sims I:7]
**APPLES BE RIPE**
*MS in three foolscap marbled stiff-backed notebooks, in pencil with ink corrections, Volume 1 (green), Chapters 1-14, Volume 2 (red marbled), Chapters 16-42, Volume 3 (blue marbled), Chapters 43-64*
[Written in the last notebook: 'This manuscript belongs to Llewelyn Powys, White Nose, Warmwell, Dorchester, Dorset, England. If lost please return to the above address. It is very valuable to the owner. Bellay, Ain, France, September 11th 1928'.]
•
[Sims I:6]
**THE CRADLE OF GOD**
*MS in three small thick quarto stiff-backed green marbled notebooks, with a half spine, in ink with many corrections*
[Dated November 25th 1928. It was meant to be presented to William Dibben, but *The Pathetic Fallacy* was given instead, 9 March 1933.]
•

PETER J. FOSS

[Sims I:9]
IMPASSIONED CLAY
*MS in ink in two stiff-backed notebooks, one red quarto, the other green marbled foolscap, with the original title 'Earths Pastures' (replacing 'The Epicurean Vision') written on the spine*
[It was begun on 1 June 1930; the notebooks were a gift from Philippa Powys, Xmas 1929.]
•
THE PATHETIC FALLACY
*One quarto marbled hardback notebook, 215pp., bound in red box-case with gilt-lettered spine, written in ink with pencil corrections, a gift to William Dibben*
[Not included in Sims's catalogue because given away beforehand; it seems it was sold in 1949 to Bissell, perhaps via Sims]

---

(b) AT CAMBRIDGE UNIVERSITY LIBRARY MANUSCRIPTS DEPARTMENT, CAMBRIDGE, ENGLAND:

---

Add. 7664 / 1-3
LOVE AND DEATH
*MS in ink in three large quarto maroon hardback notebooks*
[The original title is given as 'After Death by Llewelyn Powys' followed by an alternative title 'The Death of a Consumptive: An Imaginary Autobiography'; Volume 2 beginning at Chapter VII. LIP: 'I began writing this book on Oct 28th']

---

(c) AT THE HARRY RANSOM HUMANITIES RESEARCH CENTER, AUSTIN, TEXAS, USA:

---

[Sims I:2]
BLACK LAUGHTER
*MS in pencil in six quarto hardback notebooks, boxed*
[In the first notebook (black) is the draft of a letter to Mr Harcourt, agreeing at his suggestion to put titles to the chapters, and sending him a list. In the third notebook (red) is the draft of an essay entitled 'Sanctuaries of Civilization']
•
[Sims I:5]
HENRY HUDSON
*MS in pencil with ink emendations in two thick dark blue foolscap stiff-backed notebooks, given him by CEPP in 1926, marked Volumes 1 and 2; her inscription reads: 'Llewelyn Powys with much love from CEPP. For the love of the Hudson River at whose mouth stands the great city of New York'.*
[There are no titles to the chapters. Sims's *Catalogue* mentions 'Notes on Henry Hudson' in a separate book, which may be the notebook at HRHRC catalogued as HANLEY II (WORKS 1) — see Notebook drafts, unnumbered section.]
•
[Sims I:10]

## NOW THAT THE GODS ARE DEAD
*MS in ink in marbled quarto hardback notebook, boxed, 56pp.*
[Original title, 'The Secret of Life'; at back is a fragment of a story about an Archdeacon Laud and his son, Hubert, whom he wishes to go into the church.]
•
[Sims I:8]
## A PAGAN'S PILGRIMAGE
*MS in ink in one thick red quarto stiff-backed notebook, boxed, 144pp* [Second notebook missing; this is recorded among AG's papers. Sims's Catalogue describes the two books.]
•
[Sims I:3]
## SKIN FOR SKIN
*MS in pencil in five quarto hardback notebooks, boxed*
[In the fifth book (black) is a Preface of 4½ pages by LlP; Sims's catalogue mentions the Introduction by JCP to be sold alongside; this is now catalogued under Works of John Cowper Powys. Both Preface and Introduction were published in *The Powys Society Newsletter* 48 (April 2003), pp.19–24. ]
•
[Sims I:4]
## THE VERDICT OF BRIDLEGOOSE
*MS in pencil in five quarto hardback notebooks, boxed*
[Original title, 'The American Jungle'. The second notebook is missing, AG recorded this elsewhere and said 'it might turn up']


## 1.2 TYPESCRIPTS OF BOOKS

### (a) IN THE BISSELL GIFT, POWYS SOCIETY COLLECTION, DORSET COUNTY MUSEUM, DORCHESTER, ENGLAND:

### EARTH MEMORIES
[TSS of some of the essays, set up for the publisher in a bundle, with some represented by cuttings from their first printing, interleaved with MS preliminaries and proofs of the wood-engravings by Gertrude Mary Powys]
•
### NOW THAT THE GODS ARE DEAD
[21 pp of loose quarto leaves with MS corrections and alterations, and the date 'March 1st 1932, Chydyok']
•
### SWISS ESSAYS
[two versions on loose quarto leaves, one with corrections by LlP and queries by Alyse Gregory and Louis Wilkinson; and a sheet of MS notes by LlP and Rivers Pollock on the choice of illustrations]

## (b) IN THE CASE LIBRARY SPECIAL COLLECTIONS, COLGATE UNIVERSITY, HAMILTON, NEW YORK, USA:

### SWISS ESSAYS
[bound corrected typescript, dated 1947, 213pp., with MS corrections. A late version; information supplied by Colgate]

## (c) AT CAMBRIDGE UNIVERSITY LIBRARY MANUSCRIPT DEPARTMENT, CAMBRIDGE, ENGLAND:

### Add. 7664 / 4-8
### LOVE AND DEATH
[Much annotated typescript bundles, five in number, bound with ribbons, some with red boards, others with brown boards. Three of them are top copies, of 233pp., 287pp., and 289pp., the other two copies of the same. One has Alyse Gregory's typed Introduction. Some of the boards have ankh and sun designs in ink. The original title was 'The Death of a Consumptive', replaced by 'Death and Life'.]

## (d) AT THE HARRY RANSOM HUMANITIES RESEARCH CENTER, AUSTIN, TEXAS, USA:

### A PAGAN'S PILGRIMAGE
[Prepared typescript with MS corrections in pencil on 156 quarto sheets, bound with ribbon. Original dedication, 'with love to T. F. Powys']

## (e) AT THE BEINECKE LIBRARY, YALE UNIVERSITY, NEW HAVEN, CONNECTICUT, USA:

### SWISS ESSAYS
[with MS corrections. No more known]

## 1.3   NOTEBOOK DRAFTS

## (a) AT THE CUSHING LIBRARY, TEXAS A&M UNIVERSITY, COLLEGE STATION, TEXAS, USA:

[Sims II:65]
*Marbled quarto hardback notebook, boxed*

Of the Sun
Of Romance
Of a Gannet
Of Egoism (*New Statesman* 6 November 1926)
Of Goodness
When the Unicorn 'Cons' the Waters (*Weymouth and District Carnival Programme* 1932)
[This MS notebook was given to George Sims by Alyse Gregory as a gift for his handling of the sale of the manuscript collection in 1953. It was acquired by A&M through the sale of Sims's archive]

## (b) IN THE BISSELL GIFT, POWYS SOCIETY COLLECTION, DORSET COUNTY MUSEUM, DORCHESTER, ENGLAND

[These are MS notebooks acquired chiefly through Sims's 1953 Catalogue, although later Alyse Gregory did present Bissell with some extra items as gifts for his collection]
•
1 [Sims II:1]
*Marbled quarto hardback notebook*
**The Poems of W. B. Yeats** [2 versions in ink, one abandoned, 3pp, the other 8pp]
Untitled [in pencil, 9pp; AG's title on front: '**Account of Visiting Home of Dead Child and Reflections on Death**'.]
Untitled [in pencil, 9pp; AG's title on front: '**Attending Meeting of Adult School**'. AG adds: 'Story later with same theme — the man strangled by his tie. These have not been copied' (crossed out). AG typed up later as 'The Adult School']
**The Confession** [at back, in pencil, two beginnings, 13pp]
•
3 [Sims II:3]
*Black quarto hardback notebook with label*
Poem by JCP [in ink in LlP's handwriting, 5pp] ('Psyche', *The Powys Journal* VI (1996), pp.62-5, with Note by P. J. Foss)
**Don Quixote** [in ink, dated 1913]
**Death** [in ink much scored out, 18pp] (*New Age* 10 April 1913)
**Perhaps Yes, Perhaps No**
•
7 [Sims II:9]
*Quarto hardback notebook*
**Memories of Thomas Hardy** [in ink; on front: 'Thomas Hardy'] (in an altered version as 'Recollections of Thomas Hardy', *Virginia Quarterly* July 1939)
**August Bank Holiday** [in ink] ('Let's Make Merry This Moon-day', *Daily Herald* 3 August 1936)
draft of a letter [re. the Secretary of the Christian Evidence Society]
•
9 [Sims II:7]
*Marbled red quarto hardback notebook*
**The Epicurean Vision** ('The Epicurean Vision', *Rationalist Annual* 1931)

**The Poetic Vision** ('The Poetic Vision', *Rationalist Annual* 1932)
**The Unveiling of the Memorial Statue of Thomas Hardy OM, September 2nd 1931** [titled 'Unveiling of Hardy's Statue' in Sims] ('At the Unveiling of the Memorial Statue of Thomas Hardy, 1931' in *A Visit to Thomas Hardy*, 1919 (Toucan Press, 1971))
draft of Note for *The Life and Times of Anthony à Wood*
•
**47 [Sims II:48]**
*Grey quarto hardback notebook*
Untitled [in ink, 18pp; '**MS of Body Snatchers**' written on front; 'Bodysnatchers' in Sims] ('Body Snatchers', *The Powys Journal* VI (1996), with a Note by P. J. Foss)
•
**58 [Sims II:58]**
*Green quarto hardback exercise book*
Untitled [in ink, '**Christmas Charity**' on front] ('Christmas Charity', *Daily Herald* 19 December 1936)
Untitled [in ink, '**Christmas Day**' on front] ('Heigh-ho! The Holly', *Daily Herald* 24 December 1936)
Untitled [in ink, '**The New Year**' on front] ('The New Year', *Western Gazette* 1 January 1937)
Introduction for Millard Hudson, 2pp
•
**63 [Sims II:63]**
*Black mottled quarto hardback notebook*
**Morality Without God** ('Morality Without God', *Rationalist Annual* 1939)
Untitled [in ink, about his crossing of the Furka Pass, called 'Incident at Clavadel' in Sims] ('The Walk Over Furka Pass, 1912', *The Powys Journal* IV (1994), with a Note by P. J. Foss)
Moilliet pedigree [on last page]
•
**80 [Sims II:80]**
*Thick red quarto hardback notebook*
**The Craft of Happiness or The Devil's Handbook** (2 chapters) [AG: 'intended for the beginning of a book but abandoned' and dated 'June 15th 1935, the day Jack is coming to stay one night'; called 'two chapters of an untitled book' in Sims]
••
[The following Notebooks are numbered but not in Sims where section Two of the Catalogue ends at 81]
•
**82**
*Thin pink quarto softback notebook*
**Visit to Thomas Hardy at Max Gate, 1919** [written on front] (*A Visit to Thomas Hardy 1919*, Toucan Press, 1971)
•
**86**
*Blue quarto softback notebook, with label*
Untitled [AG's title on front: 'Fragment about CFP at Weymouth, not copied'] ('In His Great Old Age', *The Powys Journal* V (1995))

Untitled [AG's title 'Review of Jane Austen — not copied'] (in part as 'An Imperfect Lady', *Freeman* 12 January 1921)
Untitled ['Why should you come to hear JCP ...' AG not copied]
Untitled ['Why is John Cowper Powys different from all other lecturers?' AG not copied]
Untitled ['John Cowper Powys, lecturer, poet, philosopher will be in New York during the month of January ...' AG not copied]
list of subjects for *New York Evening Post* articles [on back page]
Untitled [about Tim Smith — 'read by AG in March 1956']
Untitled [first page of review of Jane Austen]
Untitled [review of the *Diary of John Korb*] (in part as review of *Scenes from the Court of Peter the Great* in *Freeman* 2 March 1921)
**Monkeys in Africa** [in pencil, 20pp] ('Adventures with Baboons in British East Africa', *New York Evening Post* 6 May 1922)
Untitled [AG has written: '**Snakes**'; in pencil, 18pp] (in part as 'Snakes in East Africa', *New York Evening Post* 8 July 1922)
**African Birds** [in pencil. 17pp; AG not copied, then 'article of African Birds — published'] (in part as 'Some African Birds', *New York Evening Post* 19 November 1921)
**Warthogs** [in pencil, 7pp]
Untitled [in pencil, 5pp; AG: 'not copied — see last chapter BL'. About locusts, vultures and his red shirt.]
**African Buck** [in pencil, 20pp] ('Death Always Runs with the African Antelope', *New York Evening Post* 3 September 1921)
Untitled [in pencil, 11pp, about shooting warthogs; AG: 'not copied']
⁝
[The following Notebooks are unnumbered]
⁝
*Fawn quarto softback empire exercise book*
**Venice MS 2** [in pencil, 40pp] ('The Venice Manuscript', *The Powys Journal* III (1993), with a Note by P. J. Foss)
⁝
*1912 Desk Diary notebook [marked by AG 'Diary No.15']*
Untitled [AG: '**Black Gods**' and on front] ('Black Gods', *New Statesman* 10 July 1920)
Untitled [AG: '**Black Laughter — Writing in the Dust**' and on front, but not the same]
Untitled [about his return to England after Africa, beginning 'It was my first Sunday in England ...']
Untitled [simulated diary of his return to England in 1919; AG copied up later] ('An Exiles Return', *The Powys Journal* X (2000), with a Note by P. J. Foss)
Untitled [called by AG on front '**The Mad Manager** — see 51'; AG copied up later]

## (c) AT THE BRITISH LIBRARY, LONDON, ENGLAND:

[These three Notebooks were gifts from LlP to Lloyd Emerson Siberell, and contain the latter's bookplates and in some cases slips with Siberell's notes on. On the front of them are labels on which LlP had briefly written the contents, for Siberell's use, together with in some cases the location of the first publication of the articles, but some of these are incorrect.]

**Add. 65157 A**
*Blue quarto hardback notebook*
**Cardinal Newman** (*Congregational Quarterly* January 1934, pp.38-42)
**An African Mule** ('Animal Love', *Weymouth and District Hospital Carnival Programme* 1933)
**African Birds** (material used in 'African Birds', *Modern Reading* Summer 1951)
Aborted piece on fairies
**Shakespeare's Fairies** (*Dublin Magazine*, April 1934)
Untitled item ('Classical and Romantic', letter to *Week-End Review*, 15 July 1933)

**Add. 65157 B**
*Black mottled quarto hardback notebook*
**Fifth of November** ('Please to Remember the Fifth of November', *Dorset Daily Echo* 30 October 1937)
**Children of the Mountains**
**Christmas Day 1937**
**Montacute Christmas** ('Forty Years Ago', *Western Gazette*, 24 December 1937)

**Add. 65157 C**
*Blue mottled quarto hardback notebook*
**Journey** [aborted beginning of essay on gulls]
**Herring Gulls** ('Herring Gulls in Winter', *Manchester Guardian* 18 January 1937)
**Memory of a Day** ('The Memory of One Day', *Dorset Daily Echo* 13 March 1937)
**Pitt Pond** (*Western Gazette* 5 February 1937)
**A Priest Plot**
**Christmas Day** ('Christmas, the Great Day of Merriment and Charity', *Dorset Daily Echo* 24 December 1936)
**Witcombe** [not the same as the essay in *Western Gazette*, 20 May 1938, though LlP seems to have thought so]
**Sports** ('In Switzerland. Life in a Valley', *New English Weekly* 11 March 1937)

[These three notebooks are described and referenced, not wholly correctly, in *British Library Catalogue of Additions to the Manuscripts* n.s. 1986-1990 (BL, 1993), pp.268-9]

---

## (d) AT THE CASE LIBRARY, <u>COLGATE</u> UNIVERSITY, HAMIL-TON, NEW YORK, USA:

---

66 [Sims II:67]
*Blue quarto hardback notebook, boxed* [*with 1920 written on box*]
**African Wisdom** [32pp] ('Africa's Wisdom' in *Damnable Opinions* (1934))
Letter fragment to Darvall?
**Good Hope Lies at the Bottom** [11pp] ('Old Threads for New Weavers', *The Outrider* January 1934)

A Pond [8pp] (*Atlantic Monthly* March 1932)
Another letter fragment to Darvall?
Another letter fragment
[The date on the box is erroneous; the number on the cover was changed by AG
to accord with the numbering in Sims, 6 replaced by a 7]

(e) AT THE KARL KROCH LIBRARY, <u>CORNELL</u> UNIVERSITY,
ITHACA, NEW YORK, USA:

4621 [Sims II:10]
The Wordsworths in Dorset [with TS] (*Dorset Daily Echo* 1 August 1936)
Review of Havelock Ellis's *From Rousseau to Proust*

(f) AT <u>DARTMOUTH</u> COLLEGE LIBRARY, HANOVER, NEW
HAMPSHIRE, USA:

[from information provided by Dartmouth]
•
[Sims II:71]?
*Notebook*:
Snobbishness
The Hedgehog (?'Thrice and Once the Hedgehog Whined', *Dorset Daily Echo* 14
November 1936)
Introduction to *The Book of Days*?
•
*Notebook* [possibly notes only]
Thoreau
The Cradle of God
•
*Notebook*
Thomas Hobbes
December
•
*Notebook*
Riddles (? 'Riddles Are an Old Pastime', *Farmer's Weekly* 6 December 1940)
Proverbs (? 'Proverbs, the Peoples Wisdom', *Reynold's News* 28 May 1939)
Whitsuntide 1939 (?'This Should Be a Happy Whitsuntide', *Dorset Daily Echo*,
27 May 1939)

(g) AT <u>NORTHWESTERN</u> UNIVERSITY LIBRARY, EVANSTON,
ILLINOIS, USA:

84
*Brown quarto softback notebook [marked Manhattan]*
[essay on] Edna St Vincent Millay, 16pp ('The Poetry of Edna St Vincent Millay',

*Double Dealer* June 1921)

## (h) AT THE HARRY RANSOM HUMANITIES RESEARCH CENTER, AUSTIN, TEXAS, USA:

[This major collection is listed numerically in accordance with the numbering on the books where that is visible; the HRHRC's catalogue reference is given after the description of the Notebook]
•
4 [Sims II:4]
*Blue quarto hardback notebook* [HANLEY II (Works 62)]
Abortive beginning (AG's title to *A Pagan's Pilgrimage*)
Untitled opening of an essay on widening one's horizons
Fragment of an essay on snobbishness
•
5 [Sims II:5]
*Black hardback notebook*
**Corn**
[written on front? — 'Article on Corn from Palestine'; unfinished essay, the rest unused; Sims calls it 'Corn from India']
•
6 on back [Sims II:6] 32 on front in LlPs handwriting
*Marbled quarto hardback notebook*
**Hedgecock and Hedgecock Memories** (*West Country Magazine* Autumn 1946)
[10pp MS; on the fly-leaf: 'T G Crippen, Christmas and Christmas Lore, from essays: Charles Lamb: The Essays of Elia; Essays & Miscellaneous; Poems, Plays and Essays']
•
8 [Sims II:8]
*Blue hardback quarto notebook*
**Egyptian Head**
[This is contained in a Sangorski box which says on the spine 'Egyptian Head'. On the cover in LlP's handwriting: 'Almost unused. Egyptian head'. In AG's handwriting: 'Begun and not finished'. The essay in the book is untitled and written in ink, 6pp.]
•
12 [Sims II:12]
*Green quarto hardback notebook, boxed* [HANLEY II (Works 40)]
**Julian the Apostate** (*Rationalist Annual* 1936)
**The Revd Henry Hardin** (1838-1904) [written at end 'Finished on July 18th 1935'] (*Congregational Quarterly* January 1936)
•
14 [Sims II:57]
*Davos black mottled quarto hardback notebook* [HANLEY II (Works 57)]
**Christmas Day 1937** [on front simply 'Christmas']
**Christmas in Dorset** ('Oh to be in Dorset — Now with Christmas Here', *Dorset Daily Echo* 24 December 1937)
**Christian Churlishness** (*Literary Guide* May 1938)

**Buffalo Intruders** ('The Two Buffaloes', *Countryman* January 1939)
•
[15] but 52 on cover [Sims II:15]
*Green exercise book* [WORKS IX]
[On cover is written 'Llewelyn Powys aged 50 and 5 months']:
**The Month of February** ('Fair Februeer', *Daily Herald* 2 February 1935)
**Meditations of a Dying Man** ('Reflections of a Dying Man', *Literary Guide* June 1935)
**St Valentine's Day** ('... To be Your Valentine ...', *Daily Mail* 13 February 1935)
•
16 [Sims II:16]
*Green quarto hardback exercise book* [HANLEY II (Works 61)]
**Nancy** ('A Vagabond', *Western Gazette* 3 July 1936)
**George Eliot** ('The Morality of a Novelist', *American Mercury* September 1936)
**Whit Sunday** [AG's title] ('Cast Those Clouts', *Daily Herald* 1 June 1936)
•
17 [Sims II:17]
*Green quarto hardback exercise book*
**Ham Hill** ('A West Country Landmark', *Western Gazette* 10 January 1936)
[Another variant version of the essay? In ink,18pp]
•
18 [Sims II:18]
*Green quarto exercise book* [HANLEY II (Works 60)]
**Thomas Hobbes** [at end: 'finished Sunday 20th August 1935'; Sims describes it as 'the final version' of this essay] (*Literary Guide* July 1936)
**Accidental Reflections** [AG's hand] (*Fig Tree* June 1936)
•
19 [Sims II:19]
*Green quarto exercise book* [HANLEY II (Works 58)]
**Threnody** [title on cover 'My Darling Bertie'] (*London Mercury* June 1936)
**Athelney** ('In the Steps of Alfred', *John O'London's Weekly* 9 October 1936)
•
20 [Sims II:20]
*Green quarto hardback exercise book* [HANLEY II (Works 59)]
**July** ('Days of Summer Pomps', *Daily Herald* 29 June 1935)
**Durdle Door** ('Llewelyn Powys Looks at Durdle Door', *Dorset Daily Echo* 25 May 1935)
**The Month of August** ('Go Away and Play', *Daily Herald* 5 August 1935)
**The White Horse** (*Manchester Guardian* 2 July 1935)
Draft of a letter in reply to one from EHJ re. Catholic doctrine
•
22 [Sims II:22]
*Black quarto Compositions book* [HANLEY II (Works 63)]
**St Bartholomew's Day** ('St Bartholomew's Day Reflections', *Dorset Daily Echo* 22 August 1936)
**Temple Targets or God's Butts** ('The Ways of Providence', *Literary Guide* September 1936)
[not published in the *Rationalist Annual* as Sims thought]
•
24 [Sims II:24]

*Davos black mottled quarto hardback notebook* [HANLEY II (Works 56)]
**Haymaking Season** ('Haymaking Months', *Reynold's News* 27 June 1937)
**August Bank Holiday, 1937**
**Easter** (*Daily Herald* 16 April 1938)
•
25a [Sims II:25?]
*Green quarto notebook* [HANLEY II (Works 21)]
**September 1st (Partridges)** ('Shooting Partridge as a Pastime', *Manchester Guardian* 28 August 1936)
**John Locke** (*Saturday Review of Literature* 19 June 1937)
**Tolerance** [AG's title]
•
25b [Sims II:26]
*Green quarto notebook* [HANLEY II (Works 18)]
**Robert Herrick** (*Saturday Review of Literature* 8 February 1936)
**Untitled** ('A Royal Failure for Whom Men of Dorset Died', *Dorset Daily Echo* 11 April 1936)
•
26a [Sims II:27]
*Green hardback notebook* [HANLEY II (Works 29)]
**Notes on Johnson** [in JCP's hand]
**For Ever in the Dust** (*Literary Guide* January 1937)
**Gloomy November** ('Lament for the Fallen Leaves', *Daily Herald* 14 November 1936)
**Downland Burden** [called 'Downland Burdens' in Sims]
•
26b [Sims II:28]
*Green quarto notebook* [HANLEY II (Works 17)]
**May**
**Nativity Ground** (*Country Life* 28 November 1936)
**Corfe Castle** (*Dorset Daily Echo* 27 June 1936)
**Midsummer Eve** ('Midsummer's Magic Eve', *Daily Herald* 23 June 1936)
•
27 [Sims II:29?]
*Green quarto notebook* [HANLEY II (Works 20)]
**Camelot** ('Love at Camelot', *Nineteenth Century and After* October 1936)
**Sir John Harrington** [published in *Somerset Essays* (1937)]
[at the back an address: 'C E Harward, Isle Hill, Ecchinswell, Newbury, Berks'.]
•
28 [SimsII:30?]
*Green quarto hardback notebook, ink* [HANLEY II (Works 37)]
**Monmouth** ('Monmouth June-July 1685', *Cornhill* June 1936)
**The Book of Ecclesiastes** (*New English Weekly* 2 July 1936)
**Untitled**, beginning 'It is interesting to learn that the Rabbinical commentators were accustomed to interpret the allusion ...' [section from 'The Book of Ecclesiastes' as above]
•
30 [Sims II:31]
*Green quarto hardback notebook* [HANLEY II (Works 32)]
In ink: **January Skates** ['Hard Weather' on the cover, LJP's original title?] ('Feb-

ruary Freeze Fingers', *Daily Herald* 1 February 1937)
**Longevity and How to Attain to it** ('Growing Old Gladly', *Reynold's News* 28 March 1937)
**St Valentine's** ('Valentine from Llewelyn Powys', *Daily Herald* 13 February 1937)
**A Little Clan** ['Mountain Valley' on the cover and in Sims's Catalogue] (*Manchester Guardian* 11 January 1937)
**Candlemass**
•
**31 [Sims II:32]**
*Small notebook* [HANLEY II (Works 6)]
**Mr Goodden**
**Exmoor** (*Manchester Guardian* 9 April 1936)
**Easter Day** ('This Lucky Thirteenth', *Daily Herald* 11 April 1936)
•
**32 [Sims II:33]**
*Green quarto notebook* [HANLEY II (Works 23)]
**Blackamore! Blackamore!**
**March Many Weathers** [called in Sims 'Month of March'] (*Daily Herald* 2 March 1935)
**Chainy Bottom** ('Llewelyn Powys Picks Up Flints', *Dorset Daily Echo* 30 March 1935)
•
**33 [Sims II:34]**
*Green hardback notebook marked 'Bush Fire and the rest unused'*
**An African Bush Fire**
[It has a note at the front: 'Type story with cc — but not until you have finished and sent back DE which I am impatient to finish'. This indicates a composition date of 1933-34. There is a sketch by LlP on the last page showing himself and a horse on a cliff edge, signed 'LlP 1917']
•
**34 [Sims II:35]**
*A quarto notebook* [HANLEY II (Works 7)]
**The Month of March** (?'March Many Weathers', *Daily Herald* 2 March 1935)
**Midsummer Night** ('Midsummer's Eve', *Western Gazette* 21 June 1935)
**Dorset Folklore** [unfinished]
**Thomas Fuller: The Cavalier Parson of Broadwindsor** [Sims calls it 'Tom Fuller, unpublished'] (*Dorset Daily Echo* 21 September 1935)
**St Swithin's Day** (a variant of 'Tomorrow is St Swithin's Day — Rain, Rain, Go Away', *Daily Herald* 14 July 1936)
**Draft of a letter**
•
**35 [Sims II:36]**
*Brown mottled quarto hardback notebook* [HANLEY II (Works 34)]
**Untitled** ('R.L.S. in the Alps', *John O'London's Weekly* 28 July 1939)
**A Footpath Way of the Senses** (*Rationalist Annual*1940)
**Town Critics and Debatable Literature** (in P. J. Foss, *A Study of Llewelyn Powys* (1991))
•
**38 [Sims II:39?]**

*Black and green quarto hardback notebook, ink* [HANLEY II (Works 41)]
Sertig
Why the Humbug of the Churches Should be Attacked and Exposed at Every
Chance ('The Humbug of the Churches', *Literary Guide* January 1938)
Whit Monday ('Throw Open the Gates', *Daily Herald* 6 June 1938)
[drawings and sketches on back flyleaf and a poem about a pipe and drinking]
•
39 [Sims II:40?]
*Brown quarto notebook* [HANLEY II (Works 22)]
From a Bath Chair Window
High Chaldon (*Dorset Daily Echo* 27 April 1935)
The Month of June ('In Leafy June', *Daily Herald* 1 June 1935)
The Month of September ('Garnering Summer's Harvest', *Daily Herald* 31
August 1935)
•
40 [Sims II:41]
*Cream quarto cloth hardback notebook*
Unpublished Notes concerned with my visit to the museum in Amsterdam to
see the relics of Wm Barents' expedition to Spitzbergen
[Title in ink, draft of 35pp., rest of book unused]
•
43 [Sims II:42]
*A quarto notebook* [HANLEY II (Works 30)]
How I Became and Why I Remain a Rationalist (*Rationalist Annual* 1937)
August Bank Holiday
Untitled ('Burton Pynsent', *Cornhill* January 1937)
[at the end a reference to 'Dorset County Chronicle and Somerset Gazette, 8 Oc-
tober 1936']
•
42 [Sims II:43]
*Green quarto notebook* [HANLEY II (Works 11)]
October Fairs [This ends with the line 'Finished September 22nd (1936) Thank
God without trouble, but in danger of a haemorrhage'; Sims calls it 'Autumn
Fairs'] ('Heigh Ho, Come to the Fair', *Daily Herald* 1 October 1936)
Fair Rosamund [dated October 1936] (*Cornhill* October 1937)
•
43 [Sims II:44]
*Red hardback(?) notebook*
Birds of a Winter Garden (*Spectator* 8 February 1935)
[Written on cover: 'Birds. Published in Spectator. Rest unused'. Also inside in-
structions for copying up; the essay covers 18pp.]
•
44 [Sims II:45]
*Brown quarto notebook*
Merton Wood's Luncheon (*New English Weekly* 15 June 1933)
[In ink on cover: 'original MSS'. Most of the pages are unused, at the end of the
MS is the draft of a letter to the prospective publisher suggesting they print 'these
scant notes' as that month was the tercentenary, and it might coincide with a talk
being broadcast on the 23rd December.]
•

45 [Sims II:46]
*Red quarto hardback notebook, boxed*
**The First Christmas Tree** *(Sunday Referee* 22 December 1935)
[This comes in a Sangorski-type case, with the sale slip where it says incorrectly that it was unpublished; the MS in ink is 14pp long, the rest unused. Sims's description gives the title as 'The First Christmas Term!']

46 [Sims II:47?]
*Grey quarto hardback notebook, ink* [HANLEY II (Works 33)]
'Not in Dorset essays' (AG's words; about the city of Tiberius)
**Confucius** *(John O'London's Weekly* 2 September 1933)
Draft of a letter about saving Lodmoor as a bird sanctuary ('Preserve Lodmoor for the Birds', *Dorset Daily Echo* 27 July 1933)
**Gypsies** *(London Mercury* December 1933)
**An Owl and a Swallow** *(Week-End Review* 19 August 1933)
Draft of a letter about preserving the bus services to Chaldon
Draft of a letter about Oliver Lodge's parody and T. S. Eliot

49 [Sims II:49]
*Marbled quarto hardback notebook* [HANLEY II (Works 28)]
**The Necrophilias** *(Cerebralist* December 1913)
Untitled [on Turnpike roads]
**The Strayed Sphinx** [in ink]
Untitled [**The Wryneck**]
[all in pencil]

[50] [Sims II:50]
*Specially bound early exercise book, therefore no number visible* [HANLEY II (Works 43)]
**The Stars**
**The Confession** [in pencil about the two brothers who plot to kill one of their wives]

[51?] 57 [possibly Sims II:51]
*Thick black quarto notebook:* [WORKS I]
250pp, dating possibly from 1919–20, containing pencilled drafts of:
**The Black Pox or How It Happens** ('How It Happens', *New Age* 8 April 1920)
**The Girl Who Understood**
**A West Countryman's Return** *(Countryman* Autumn 1956)
**Lions and Lion Trapping**
An untitled essay on hating Africa
An untitled essay on Masai
**Leopards**
**Hippopotami** [the original of 'Kiboko'] ('Kiboko, Otherwise Hippo are Peaceable and Shy ...' *New York Evening Post* 8 January 1921)
A fragment about Carew
**African Animals of Forest and Veldt**
**The African Rhinocerous**

**Betsy Cooper**
A fragment about Cornelia Fanshawe in Africa
**Thomas Bewick** (*Freeman* 9 March 1921)
1914 diary notes
A fragment about Charles Jesson
**May Hodder**
**May Seaton**
•
52 [Sims II:52]
*Red quarto notebook* [HANLEY II (Works 19)]
Untitled [essay on Montacute]
**An Old Clock Weight** ('Praise Be to My Lord …', *Dorset Daily Echo* 5 January 1935)
**Twelfth Night** [signed at end 'Llewelyn Powys, New Year 1934']
**New Year's Night** ('On This Night Through the Ages …', *Daily Mail* 31 December 1934)
**Dawn in Autumn** [called by Sims 'Death in Autumn']
•
53 [Sims II:53]
*Large blue hardback notebook, ink* [HANLEY II (Works 42)]
**Tom Deloney** ('Thomas Deloney', *Virginia Quarterly* October 1933)
**Bat's Head** (*Weymouth and District Hospital Carnival Magazine* 1934)
**Granfer Jack** [Sims has 'Granpa Jacob'] ('The Head of a Man', *Dublin Magazine* April 1935)
**Gangsters in Tudor Times**
**Hesiod** (?'Poetry and Religion', *Week-End Review* 24 December 1932)
**True Religion and Undefiled** (*New English Weekly* 16 February 1933)
•
54 [Sims II:54]
*A quarto notebook* [HANLEY II (Works 8)]
**Niccolo Machiavelli** (*Saturday Review of Literature* 24 December 1932)
**Unicorn Legends** (*Week-End Review* 12 November 1932)
**Visions and Revisions** (*American Spectator* March 1933)
**Thomas Deloney** (extended version) (*Virginia Quarterly* October 1933)
•
55 [Sims II:55]
*Red quarto notebook* [HANLEY II (Works 10)]
**The Christmas Spirit** [with earlier titles 'Christmas in the Country', 'The Christmas Spirit and the Open Country', 'Christmas Spirit in the Open Country is Best'] (*Daily Herald* 22 December 1934)
**Janet Sparkes** (*Dorset Daily Echo* 24 December 1934)
•
56 [Sims II: 56]
*A quarto notebook* [HANLEY II (Works 4)]
**A House of Correction** (*Country Life* 3 June 1933)
**Akhenaton** ('A Religious Reformer of the Ancients', *Bookman* June 1933)
**The Blind Cow** (*New Statesman and Nation* 19 August 1933)
**The Oxford Movement** (*New English Review* 13 April 1933)
**Firelighters for Sale** ('Signs of the Times', *New English Review* 25 May 1933)

The Pest of Spring Cleaning
The Music of the Spheres
•
59 [Sims II:59]
*Green quarto notebook* [HANLEY II (Works 14)]
The Month of May ('May Magic', *Daily Herald* 1 May 1935)
Easter
The Most Primitive of All Religions and the Truest [Sims calls this 'The Oldest of All Religions']
Notes in JCP's hand on hedonistic theories and Aristippus, some from a book by John Watson
May Day [at back]
•
60 [Sims II:60]
*A quarto notebook* [HANLEY II (Works 16)]
October ('Apples Be Ripe — October Month of Cider Making', *Daily Herald* 30 September 1935)
The Morality of Pleasure ('The Gentle Craft of Happiness', *Freethinker* 24 May 1936)
Abbotsbury Swannery
Lulworth Castle Park ('The Castle Park of East Lulworth', *Dorset Daily Echo* 24 August 1935)
•
61 [Sims II:61]
*Large black hardback notebook, bought at Fulton Stationery Corp., 74 Fulton St., NYC; ink* [HANLEY II (Works 44)]
A Voyage to the West Indies (In M. Elwin, *The Pleasure Ground* (1947))
Essay on Style [letter to Warner Taylor] (In Warner Taylor, *Types and Times of the Essay* (1932))
•
62 [Sims II:62]
*Red softback notebook*
The Trapped Fairy (a variant version as 'The Trapper', *Century Magazine* August 1925)
[Most pages unused. At the back is written 'Eastern Daily Press, Sat 22nd Dec. Harriett Cowper Johnson']
•
64 [Sims II:64]
*Green quarto notebook* [HANLEY II (Works 13)]
The Craft of Happiness (?another version of 'The Gentle Craft of Happiness', *Freethinker* 24 May 1936)
Untitled ('Hardy's Monument', *Dorset Daily Echo* 5 October 1935)
Aristippus (*Nineteenth Century and After* April 1936)
•
66 [Sims II:66]
*A quarto notebook* [HANLEY II (Works 5)]
Sir Thomas Browne ('The Quincunciall Doctor', *Saturday Review of Literature* 4 June 1932)
Neglected Notes [on Sir Thomas Browne]

For a Mummy's Sake [a story about a farmer called John Rug]
On the Other Side of the Quantocks (*Atlantic Monthly* January 1933)
Natural Happiness (*Rationalist Annual* 1933)
Lucian (*John O'London's Weekly* 20 August 1933)
A Locust Message (*Week-End Review* 3 September 1933)
[Sims had put 'For Pity's Sake' in place of 'For a Mummy's Sake']
•
68 [Sims II:68]
*Grey quarto hardback notebook* [HANLEY II (Works 39)]
Celsus [original title 'Great Links'] ('Celsus and Origen', *Rationalist Annual* 1934)
A Day on Dartmoor (*Atlantic Monthly* October 1933)
The Lake of Galilee ('Weymouth Bay and the Lake of Galilee', *Dorset Daily Echo* 14 July 1933 and 4 August 1933)
Draft of a letter to *Country Life* about the dog (*Country Life* 8 July 1933)
Words
•
69 [Sims II:69]
*Blue quarto notebook* [HANLEY II (Works 9)]
Untitled essay ('Clean Linen', *The Powys Journal* I (1991))
Deity in a Cur (*The Powys Journal* XII(2002))
A Gentleman from Bournemouth
Joseph Conrad [Sims says erroneously 'written for a publisher's leaflet'] (as 'Youth' in *A Conrad Memorial Library* (1929))
Review of a book by Ingersoll
Public Schools
•
70 [Sims II:70]
*Green quarto hardback notebook, in ink* [HANLEY II (Works 55)]
An Oxford Tree (*New English Weekly* 27 February 1936 and 5 March 1936)
Preface to Anthony à Wood [2pp?] (Preface to *The Life and Times of Anthony à Wood* (1932))
Untitled work in 2 parts on the Prehistory of the Downs and worked flints
•
72 [Sims II:72]
*Green quarto notebook* [HANLEY II (Work 15)]
April 1st ('This is the First Day of Aprile — Hunt the Gowk Another Mile', *Daily Herald* 1 April 1937)
Untitled (variant of 'The Steinadler', *Times* 17 May 1937)
Untitled ('Mountain Foxes', *Manchester Guardian* 29 March 1937)
Pens for Priests [this has earlier titles, viz: 'A Priest's Paradise', 'Penfold the Priests', 'What to do with the Clergy'] (*Literary Guide* July 1937)
The Mountain Climb
May Day
•
73 [Sims II:73]
*Blue quarto hardback notebook* [HANLEY II (Works 36)]
The English Prayer Book ('The Book of Common Prayer', *Cornhill* May 1934)
The Yellow Iris (*Week-End Review* 1 April 1933)

A Fairy Reserve ('The Little People in Dorset', *Dorset Daily Echo* 15 April 1933)
Heralds to Prayer ['Natural Worship'] (*Adelphi* July 1933)
Herrick's Fairies (*Spectator* 21 July 1933)
Dionysos [AG: 'not the same but similar to the one in *Rats*'] (*Aryan Path* August 1934)
T. S. Eliot ('T. S. Eliot, The Tutor-Poet', *Week-End Review* 20 May 1933)
The Shambles Fog Horn ('Listen to the Shambles Foghorn', *Dorset Daily Echo* 27 May 1933)
Self as Pot [fragment]
•
74 [Sims II:74]
*Black quarto hardback notebook [inscribed inside 'For dearest Llewelyn from Katie late but with love KP'], ink* [HANLEY II (Works 36)]
Mr Winston Churchill (review of *Great Contemporaries*)
Thoughts from Switzerland ('Wessex! Stand Firm ...', *Dorset Daily Echo*, 23 September 1939)
The Spirit of Christmas
The Christmas Spirit
Christmas Larders (*Western Mail* 22 December 1939)
Christmas Evergreens (*Western Gazette* 22 December 1939)
Children of Dorset and Christmas (originally called 'Ships') ('Christmas Memories', *Dorset Daily Echo* 23 December 1939)
Christmas Food, Christmas Lore and the Christmas Spirit ('The Groaning Boards of Our Merry Ancestors', *Western Mail* 17 December 1949)
Paracelsus [this occupies almost half the book] (*Nineteenth Century and After* October 1940)
•
75 [Sims II:75]
*Quarto hardback notebook* [HANLEY II (Works 3)]
A Fable [unpublished]
God (*New English Review* 13 July 1933)
Immortality (*New English Review* 31 August 1933)
Morality (*American Spectator* August 1933)
Reformation (*American Spectator* August 1934)
What is wrong with conventional people?
A review of a book by Colonel Colin Harding ('A Soldier in Africa', *John O'London's Weekly* 11 March 1933)
Draft of a letter to the *New English Weekly*
•
78 [Sims II:78]
*Pink and Blue marbled quarto notebook, sellotaped at back*
[Some Meditations Upon Death]
[This is 135pp long, an early MS in pencil, with variations on the death theme that later emerged into his essay about his brother, 'Death', therefore it dates from c.1912-13. A version of 'Death' begins 12 pages into the text; this also merges with a version of 'The Stunner'. On the cover is written 'Death', 'Stunner' — 'first essay published by LlP?', 'original MSS'. Sims gives the title as 'Death's Variations'] ('Death', *New Age* 10 April 1913; 'The Stunner', *Cerebralist* December

1913)
•
81 [Sims II:81]
*Sandy-coloured notebook*
**Young Man Waiting on a Platform**
[early 9-page fragment of a story about Mervyn Holbech leaving for BEA]
••
[The following Notebooks are numbered here in a separate sequence. These correspond to the residue of the archive left with Malcolm Elwin presumably after the sale of most of the MSS in the Sims Catalogue. This archive was put up for sale by Elwin's widow, Eve Elwin, in the 1970s through Bertram Rota, London, and came thence to the HRHRC. The archive was listed in a 21-page typed document called 'Llewelyn Powys Papers at Sedgebanks' got up for the sale. The enumeration comes from this Sedgebanks list.]
•
17 [Sedgebanks 17]
*Square home-made softback notebook, of woven cloth with Chinese picture on the front, on Chinese ideogrammed rice paper*
**Guests of Benison** ('Guests of Grace', *Countryman* April 1935)
[Pasted on front and back inside covers are fragments of the newspaper cutting of 'China's Homely Philosopher' from *John O'London's Weekly* (Outline Supplement), 2 September 1933. The book is much like a child's artefact]
•
20 [Sedgebanks 20]
*Blue-green quarto softback exercise book*
Untitled African Pieces
[Contains various African pieces written in pencil, including one on the shooting of a zebra, and one about his pony Rosinante]
•
21 [Sedgebanks 21; also 3 on back]
*Red diary notebook* [catalogued as DIARY 41pp]
**Conversations with Theodore on walks** [1931? AG's title] ('Conversations with Theodore Powys', Summer 1931, *The Powys Review* 4 (1978/9))
Also notes by JCP on Edward Fitzgerald etc.
[Malcolm Elwin's initials on front; described in Sedgebanks as 'diary-record of LlP's conversations with TFP, very interesting']
•
27 [Sedgebanks 27]
*Blue exercise book* [WORKS VIII]
**Footsteps**
**A Confession** [beginning 'Catherine was not the only person who suspected Carew ...']
**At the Cattle Dip**
•
[Sedgebanks 28, 29, 30]
*Three quarto softback exercise books, one pink, one blue, one pale blue*
**African novel**
[These contain an ink draft of Llewelyn's projected novel *Aliens in Africa* written at Weymouth 1919, divided into 9 chapters, as follows:
1.    Into Africa

2.    The Top Farm
3.    The Other Side of the Escarpment
4.    Black Hides
5.    Kekenuki Farm
6.    Catharine
7.    The Confession
8.    The Lake
9.    By the Dead]
•
31 [Sedgebanks 31]
*hardback notebook* [WORKS II]
[On front cover, AG: 'Long Lasting Local Names, Religion of Poetry etc'.]
**Long Lasting Local Names** ('South Somerset Memories', *Western Gazette* 4 August 1939)
**Religion of Poetry** (*Dublin Magazine* 1 January 1940)
Untitled [with alterations by Louis Wilkinson] ('Happiness Comes to Those Whose Values Are Simple', *Western Mail* 3 July 1939)
**August Bank Holiday** ('The Happiest Day of All the Year', *Daily Herald* 7 August 1939)
Untitled ('Manners False and True', *West Country Magazine* 1946)
Untitled ('Green Corners of Dorset', *Adelphi* December 1939)
•
32 [see Sims II:6]
•
39 [Sedgebanks 39]
*Pale quarto softback exercise book*
**African Story**
[Written on cover by AG?: 'melodramatic African story — unfinished'; written in pencil over 21pp]
•
40 [Sedgebanks 40]
*Notebook* [WORKS VII]
**The Lunk**
**The Dawn** (*The Powys Review* 22 (1988))
Fragment
•
41 [Sedgebanks 41]
*Pink softback exercise book*
**By the Elephant's Skull**
[this is a draft of part of the African novel involving the character Foxden; the rest unused]
•
42 [Sedgebanks 42]
*Marbled hardback notebook*
**Drafts of Untitled Essays**
[This contains a number of untitled items, all in pencil, dating from about 1913. I have identified the following:
a)    'How indelibly are printed in my mind all the various scenes and sensations associated with discovering that I was suffering from pulmonary tubercu-

losis ...' 11pp. This is an account of his experience of contracting consumption in 1909. It is not the same as 'A Struggle for Life', but much earlier.
b)   A fragment of 'The Brown Satyr'. 4pp (*Pearson's Magazine* March 1922)
c)   Another attempt at 'The Brown Satyr'. 'There is a very ancient legend ...' 11pp
d)   A fragment of 'The Strayed Sphinx' 3pp
e)   A story about his meeting with 'Angela' on holiday at Purbeck, when he was 15 years old. 'On the easterly extremity of the Island of Purbeck ...' 8pp
f)   A story involving Marjorie Brown at Cambridge. 'It was in my second year at Cambridge that I first met Marjorie Brown ...' 6pp.]
•

## 43 [Sedgebanks 43]
*Black notebook*
**The Last Request**
[This title is written in pencil on the inside of the front cover. The story, of about 33pp, is about a consumptive patient called Waddington, lying ill at Bournemouth, and based upon Wilbraham. It also contains a fragment of 'Not Guilty' on 3pp, the rest torn out, and another unfinished story beginning 'Madness, What is it?' of about 15pp. This is about a friend called Lorenzo, put away in an asylum, who falls in love with a girl called Eleanor.]
•

## 44 [Sedgebanks 44]
*Notebook, 23pp.* [WORKS V]
**Strindberg**
**Consumption** [at back of book]
**The Two Brothers**
•

## 45 [Sedgebanks 45]
*Notebook* [WORKS X]
**Regret**
**My Choice** (re. two brothers and choice of wife)
Fragments of two untitled love stories
•

## 46 [Sedgebanks 46]
*Large 1915 diary notebook*
**An African Manuscript**
[This seems to be an earlier version of the story of Carew, written in crayon, which has got wet, over 55pp. The pencilled outline reads:
i.     Home
ii.    Boat
iii.   Imaginative reactions from Africa
iv.    Sordid influences
v.     Nairobi
vi.    What does it profit a man?
vii.   —
viii.  —]
•

47 [Sedgebanks 47]
*Notebook:* [WORKS IV]
[similar material to Sedgebanks 44]
**Strindberg**
**The Confession** (about two brothers plotting to kill one of their wives)
**Death by Consumption** [beginning 'To die very slowly we none of us wish to do
that ...']
•
49 [Sedgebanks 49]
*Pale softback exercise book marked on cover in pencil*
**The Continent of Dreadful Night.**
[Containing chapters entitled: Into the Land of Darkness; Over the Escarpment;
By the Elephants Skull; Where One Least Looks for It There Starts the Hare.
The note on the front by AG says 'African Story, not typed'. This seems to be an
attempt at a novel, with the figure of Foxden]
•
50 [Sedgebanks 50]
*Brown marbled notebook with label*
**Venice 1913**
[73pp. There are two parallel versions on both sides of the pages. 'Unprinted']
51 [Sedgebanks 51]
*Dark blue notebook* [WORKS III]
[AG wrote on front of book 'The Cuckold — a dreadful story'. The inside of
back cover contains a projected contents list for the *Confessions* memoir]
**Bull's Feathers** [original title crossed out and retitled 'What to do — a Story for
Cuckolds']
**Nietzsche and the Germans**
**Africa** [a simulated diary beginning 'Sat Mar 20th. Walked over the farm and up
the empty bed of the river ...']
Fragment on Africa
•
52 [Sedgebanks 52; see Sims II:15]
•
53 [Sedgebanks 53; Sims V:3?]
*Black notebook* [WORKS VI]
**A Consumptive's Diary**, the original draft of the simulated diary published in the
*New Statesman*, 1915 ('A Consumptive's Diary', *New Statesman* 7 March 1914)
untitled version of the two brothers story
untitled version of '**Not Guilty**' (published in *Ebony and Ivory* (1923))
•
54 [Sedgebanks 54]
*Notebook* [WORKS XI]
[AG marked this as 'Diary No.11']
untitled simulated diary of his arrival in Africa ('From Montacute to Gilgil', *New
Age* 21 January 1915)
**Rubbish** (*New Age* 8 April 1915)
**Land of the Kikuyus** (Africa section of *Confessions?*)
Bits of Swahili vocabulary
•

229

55 [Sedgebanks 55; Sims V:1?]
*Black diary notebook* [catalogued as DIARY NOTEBOOK 1908-1909]
19pp
•
56 [Sedgebanks 56]
*Plain green quarto softback exercise book*
**Early African Stories**
[This contains a number of fragments of African stories concerning the figure of
Carew running to 64pp, not copied by AG]
•
57 [Sedgebanks 57; see Sims II:51]
•
58 [Sedgebanks 58]
*Black diary notebook* [catalogued as DIARY 136pp]
[On panel on back AG: 'Diary No.10. Letters about Marion Linton typed 14/2/
56. Diary as Tutor used in *Confessions of Two Brothers*. Dialogue between two
brothers on God, philosophical beliefs — Adolphus & Mervyn — JCP & LlP (not
typed) all in pencil']
136pp in notebook
At back 30pp philosophical debate between Adolphus and Mervyne c.1919? [TFP
and LlP]
('Diary of a Private Tutor' in *Confessions of Two Brothers* (1916))
•
59 [Sedgebanks 59]
*Small black horizontal notebook*
**West Indian Diary** ('Voyage to the West Indies' in *The Pleasure Ground* (1947))
Quotations from Montaigne
•
101 [Sedgebanks 101]
*Pink softback exercise book*
**Dorchester Childhood. St Austin's Well**
[a 20pp pencilled draft of a third-person autobiography, featuring Mervyn
Howard of St Austin's Well. See *Life of Llewelyn Powys*, p.82]
• •
[Other numbered Notebooks in the HRHRC collection not corresponding to
enumeration in Sims or Sedgebanks]
•
29
*Green quarto hardback notebook, ink* [HANLEY II (Works 38)]
**A Threnody: Walter Parker** (1886–1935) (*Manchester Guardian* 2 August 1935)
**November** ('Thirty Days to Remember', *Daily Herald* 31 October 1935)
•
83
*Marbled hardback notebook* [*c.1913–14*] [HANLEY II (Works 26)]
**Niccolo Machiavelli** (*Saturday Review of Literature* 24 December 1932)
Pencilled draft of the simulated 1911 diary of his stay at Chaldon
Drafts of two letters: one to William Heinemann, asking whether he would be
interested in publishing his stories. He says he has published in three magazines
already, one of them being 'The Occult Review'; the other a letter to T. N. Foulis,
recommending an imaginative work by his brother.
•

85
*Marbled hardback notebook*
**Nicholas Culpeper, Gent, Astrologer and Herbalist**
[A 28pp MS, with the last 2½ pages finished by JCP. A note on the front cover
says 'unpublished', but it was published in the *Freeman*.]
(*Freeman* 28 December 1921)
•
90
*Large thick black quarto notebook* [HANLEY II (Works 54)]
**Spheric Laughter** (published in *Ebony and Ivory* (1923))
**Forster's Starvin'**
**The Strayed Sphinx** [AG: 'publ. In USA']
**The Brown Satyre** (*Pearson's Magazine* March 1922)
**The Stunner** (*Cerebralist* December 1913)
[This is an early notebook, Llewelyn wrote date 'October 1912' in black ink; the
contents on the front written by AG, on the first page by LlP]
• •
[The following Notebooks are unnumbered]
•
*Sangorski-bound notebook*
**A Ride in the African Night**
[This notebook having been rebound, is minus its covers and numbered label. It
contains: 'A Ride in the African Night', 'The Poetry of Edna St Vincent Millay',
'The Old Town of Mombasa', 2pp, and 'A Negro's Writing', about Merishu, possi-
bly material used in the *Freeman*. On the latter AG has written 'used in BL'. Date
c.1921?]
(? 'The Poetry of Edna St Vincent Millay', *Double Dealer* June 1921)
•
*Red notebook* [mentioned under Sims I:5]
HANLEY II (Works 1)
**Notes for proposed book on Henry Hudson, June 1926**
**House Breaking at White Nose** ('An Intruder at White Nose', *Dorset Press Ball
News* 21 February 1939)
•
*Black foolscap hardback notebook*
HANLEY II (Works 2)
'Wenda Weir' by John Cowper Powys
**Henry James**
**Nathaniel Hawthorne**, these latter dated to September 1908
[The story was written at Llewelyn's behest in 1908, the two lectures were dic-
tated by JCP to LlP and delivered by him in America in 1909]
•
*Thick black notebook called 'Diary No.9'*
HANLEY II (Works 12)
**Sheepman's Diary** (*Dial* April 1920)
**Monday**
**Black Magic**
**Return to Montacute**
**West Countryman's Return** (*Countryman* Autumn 1956)
**New York — impressions**

PETER J. FOSS

**African Moods**
**The Black Pox** ('How it Happens', *New Age* 8 April 1920)
**Black Parasites** (published in *Ebony and Ivory* (1923))
**Black Gods** [with original title 'The Gods of Lake Elmenteita' and 'Meditations from Africa'] (*New Statesman* 10 July 1920)
Fragment of a 1915 diary
**Black Magic** (repeated)
[These are all in pencil, some at the back of the book; the writings date from 1918 to 1920]
•
*Sangorski-bound notebook of c.1913*
HANLEY II (Works 24)
Untitled story about Suckey Fowler, a Betsy Cooper figure [this is not 'Nancy Cooper' as the spine says]
Another version about 'Nancy Vernon', an old mad woman [a variant of 'Forster's Starvin'']
A variant of **The Strayed Sphinx**
**Thomas Hardy — The Poet** [written to the dictation of JCP?]
[all in pencil]
•
*Marbled quarto hardback notebook, very decrepit, boxed*
HANLEY II (Works 25)
**An Old English House** (*Atlantic Monthly* April 1925)
**Heroes Out of the Past** (*Western Gazette* 24 May 1935)
**The Sea! The Sea! The Sea!** (*Manchester Guardian* 28 September 1924)
**A Rector of Durweston** ('An English Parson', *Spectator* 30 November 1934)
•
*Plain brown hardback notebook*
HANLEY II (Works 27)
Untitled ('Ancient Mountain Pieties', *New English Weekly* 12 May 1938)
**Witcombe** ('Thoughts of Home', *Western Gazette* 20 May 1938)
**The Fairest Flowers of the Season** (*Dorset Daily Echo* 23 April 1938)
Untitled, beginning 'The other day I received as a present an enormous photograph of my old home ...'[about Miss Sparkes] ('The Village Shop', *Manchester Guardian* 6 May 1938)
•
*Large format red hardback notebook, in ink*
HANLEY II (Works 31)
**Paracelsus** (*Nineteenth Century and After* October 1940)
**Christmas Cakes from Switzerland**
**Welshmen and Their Love of Walking** ('The Cymro's Impulse is to Walk', *Western Mail* 17 November 1939)
**That Island of England**
**The Aebi Wood** (*Literary Guide* January 1940)
**Children of Switzerland** (published in *Swiss Essays* (1947))
**Soul Windows** ('A Soul Window', *Manchester Guardian* 19 July 1939)
[on flyleaf, the address of 'Percy Griffiths, 4 Ayton Terrace, Rhymynnin, Glamorgan, S.Wales']
•

232

*Green hardback exercise book, patched up on spine with white tape*
HANLEY II (Works 45)
Untitled essay about Weymouth (?'Llewelyn Powys Sees Weymouth Harbour ...',
*Dorset Daily Echo*, 23 January 1937)
Notes on Marmots, foxes etc.
**Carling Sunday** ('Carlings for Mothering Sunday', *Yorkshire Post* 6 March 1937)
**Cuckoo Week**
**Clavadel**
**Steinadler**
**Piers Plowman**
[this has an address at the back of the book: 'Fehrenstrasse 20, Traufeuberg,
Zurich 7']
•
*Green hardback exercise book*
HANLEY II (Works 46)
**Tintinhull Memories** [opposite LlP had written a note about Death being his
first published piece] (*New English Weekly* 7 October 1937)
**Steinadler** (*Times* 17 May 1937)
untitled essay on Priests
•
*Green quarto hardback exercise book*
HANLEY II (Works 47)
**Language**
**Easter** ('Its an Old pagan Custom Too', *Daily Herald* 25 March 1937)
**Andreas**
**In the Hour of Death** (*New English Weekly* 22 July 1937)
•
*Davos black mottled quarto hardback notebook, in ink*
HANLEY II (Works 48)
**Paracelsus** [abortive beginning]
**Mountain Flowers** ('Flowers of Switzerland', *Atlantic Monthly* December 1939)
**The Religion of Poetry** (*Dublin Magazine* January 1940)
•
*Davos black mottled quarto hardback, in ink*
HANLEY II (Works 49)
**Wedding Customs in Switzerland**
**Mountain Tops** (*Manchester Guardian* 29 October 1937)
**What I Believe** (*Forum* August 1939)
Untitled essay (?'Hay of the Mountains and of the Meadows', *Dorset Daily Echo*
24 July 1937)
•
*Davos black hardback notebook*
HANLEY II (Works 50)
Untitled [re. 'The Simple Cobbler of Aggawam']
**Sertig** ('Happy Valley of Sertig', *Atlantic Monthly* June 1939)
[essay for a Welsh magazine]
**St Valentine's Day** ('Happy Days Again (After Tomorrow)', *Daily Herald* 13
February 1939)
•

PETER J. FOSS

*Davos black quarto hardback notebook*
HANLEY II (Works 51)
**The Swiss Family of Moilliet** (published in *Swiss Essays* (1947))
**The Montacute Mill** [on the cover 'Montacute Hill'] ('Delights of Somerset Mills', *Country Life* 24 May 1941)
**The Chesil Beach** (*Time and Tide* 12 August 1939 )
**Cringing and Crematoriums** (*Literary Guide* July 1939)
•
*Davos black quarto hardback notebook*
HANLEY II (Works 52)
**In the Dischmatal** ('The Steinhuhn', *Country Life* 4 February 1939)
**The Autumn**
**Dorset Place Names**
**Immortal Breath**
•
*Davos black quarto hardback notebook*
HANLEY II (Works 53)
**Chamois** ('Notes on Chamois', *Countryman* October 1937)
**Whitsuntide**
**Midsummer Night**
**Larch Trees** ['Men and Trees'?] (published in *Swiss Essays* (1947))
**Marmots** (*Country Life* 25 June 1938)
**Tusser** ('Farmer's Wisdom', *Western Gazette* 23 July 1937)

---

(i) IN THE DEPARTMENT OF SPECIAL COLLECTIONS, THE UNIVERSITY OF <u>CALIFORNIA</u>, LOS ANGELES, CALIFORNIA, USA:

---

667
1 [Sims III:1]
*Small yellow hardback notebook*
Essay on partridges? (?'Perdix Perdu', *Country Life* 10 September 1932)
[other notes and items, but no more information available. Sims recorded an essay with the title 'The One Thing Needful'. California have one other unnumbered notebook, which seems to be purely notes, mainly on Dorset folklore and Whit Sunday]

KATE KAVANAGH

# 'In View of Glastonbury' and writers' views on JCP
*The Powys Society Conference 2002*
*August 16th—18th at Millfield, Somerset*

Millfield, famed as the ultimate luxury school, has a campus of assorted modern buildings placed among winding paths, trees, playing fields, lawns and large modern sculptures. The conference rooms were in the Music building (a room with overtones of chapel and Arts and Crafts, according to Iain Sinclair). Between fifty and sixty people attended for the whole conference. 'In View of Glastonbury' was the conference title and from the back of the meeting room there was indeed a fine view of that persuasive Tower. On the first evening the opening talk, introduced by David Gervais, was by **Lawrence Mitchell** on 'T. F. Powys and John Death' — on TFP's own stoical death, notably, as LM read from the closing section of his biography in progress.

The three following speakers, all concentrating on JCP, were good examples of different personal approaches. David Goodway introduced the first, **Colin Wilson**, who last came to the JCP centenary conference in 1972. On that occasion he expressed some criticism of his audience, and they of him, but thirty years on he seemed more indulgent and accessible, staying for the whole conference with his wife Joy. Wilson's talk ran through his meeting with Angus Wilson in the British Museum, leading to encounters with Powys books while staying in Wilson's cottage; and his writing *The Outsider*, themes of which he later linked with JCP — such as T. E. Hulme's idea of original sin, as something wrong in human nature that needs changing; and the 'peeper in the hotel room' of Henri Barbusse's *L'Enfer* — a person existing through others. He had been at first irritated (as a T. S. Eliot man) by what seemed to him the excessive enthusiasm of *Pleasures of Literature*, but came to recognise this as a necessary part of JCP's multi-mindedness and identification with his subjects. He had already tried but not much liked *Glastonbury*, but then reread it (in a 5/- copy) with total concentration, in a car on the way to Cornwall, escaping from the wave of publicity brought by *The Outsider*. The chapter on Stonehenge and Mr Evans hooked him: as did JCP's total honesty (which he also found in *Autobiography*), his intense subjectivity and his courage. In *Glastonbury* he saw him as a great puppet-master, an example of Keats's 'negative capability', absorbing the experience of others.

In *Jobber Skald* what attracted Wilson was the sexual element between Magnus Muir and Curly Wix: sex as revelation, as intense concentration, as states of ecstasy; with the related problems of not focussing on the personal. But JCP's lack of self-assertion, his apparent lack of deep self-belief, his presentation of himself as a failure, Wilson found puzzling, and when he then read *Wolf Solent* he was rather disappointed. It was only later that he saw its greatness, in the 'mythologizing' of the self. Before that, the way Wolf Solent is presented as disappointing and failing everyone seemed to contradict the power of mythologizing, and also to negate the magical powers that JCP famously found in himself.

Wilson sees JCP as a subjective Romantic poet — like the early Yeats. JCP's constant travelling, he thinks, was a spur to his creativity, as hard work generates strength (relating to Gurdjieff's 'intentional suffering') and leading to *growth* (something many people don't achieve); it provided a spiritual discipline that he could use without needing to force it (as Wilson was forced to make himself write). Another spur to JCP's imagination must have been the dual consciousness of living in America and thinking about England; *Maiden Castle*, written without this, Wilson found less impressive.

But it is clearly the magical element in JCP that most interests Wilson — as in the story of JCP's extra-body 'appearance' to Theodore Dreiser. JCP also fits in with Wilson's theory of the 'robot' in us. If our normal state is 50% robotic — that is, automatic activity, boredom — Blake's 'Spectre' or negative self — we need to focus, to concentrate, not to let the robot become 51%; to work on our mind to condition it to achieve 'peak experiences'. This needs luck, skill, and a talent for enjoyment. JCP's 'mythologizing' — descending into oneself, into concentration — made him a master of the Peak Experience, and this is reflected in his fiction. Wolf Solent's rejection of suicide and acceptance of ordinary life didn't cancel his ability to mythologize — looking at the buttercup field, illuminated by it, he ends in an objective state of mind equivalent to JCP's when creating the world of *Glastonbury*. JCP, living in the early days of psychical research, is an example of power of the mind — whether of extra-body experience, or of concentration controlling experience. Hence the title of Colin Wilson's talk — 'To Live in Two Worlds'.

John Hodgson introduced the next speaker, **Iain Sinclair**, linking him to JCP by speaking of their 'congruent imagination', their psycho-geography, the 'transfigured landscapes' of Sinclair's books on London. In contrast to JCP's Wolf Solent or even minor figures like Lord Carfax, even the Man on the Waterloo Steps, Sinclairian figures are disturbingly elusive, and his spirit of place hard to pin down. But as novelists they share close-packed scenes, and the 'peripatetic mode' — JCP the lifelong walker, Sinclair's books based on walking (his latest is a circuit of the M25 London ring road).

Iain Sinclair saw Glastonbury as a mirror image, across the Bristol Channel, of the Welsh border country where he grew up — the sea between being a negative space. Among his influences he listed the view of a Multiverse, seen through the writing of Michael Moorcock; the energy (vs. narrative) of comic-strips; Pantheism, and the art of sketch and movement learnt from Kerouac; William Burroughs's satirical/ misogynistic view; William Carlos Williams's poem *Patterson*; Charles Olsen in Gloucester, Mass.— and JCP in exile interpreting sacred sites in England. Hackney, Sinclair's part of London, is built on rubble, on history. He worked for the Council there, marking football pitches. This ended with the entry of Jeff Kwintner into his life, bringing publishing and unpredictable literary assignments ... hence the title of his talk, 'Powys, Place, and the White Lines on Hackney Marshes'. Sinclair's Whitechapel (White Chapel) novels dug into London's past: a park with the outline of a church destroyed; melted lead, coffins. But he felt *drawn to the West* ... He planned a series of novels based on significant places: Whitechapel; Wales (his last, *Landor's Tower*); Montacute (a 'Romance') and its hill from which you can see Glastonbury Tor.

Sinclair sees JCP's writing in terms of relationships between people and places, and people and things. In *Glastonbury*, what he noticed was the importance of *clothes*, as part of characters: Mr Evans's long black coat; Sam's heavy tweeds. And the landscapes of the mind: clouds, weather: 'psychopathic geography'. Walking, with JCP, *activates* place: it can be the same walk with small changes. His focussing through configurations (of people, of things) is a planetary consciousness. JCP's lecturing was a form of ventriloquism, speaking through his subjects. His language is unprocessed, like breathing.

Like JCP, Sinclair feels drawn to *significant places*. He walked to Glastonbury with Brian Catling. For him Warminster is a UFO capital; Glastonbury a place for de-energising: a place for meeting oneself, seeing one's older double — as the lone reader in a pub.

On Saturday evening Timothy Hyman and P. J. **Kavanagh** discussed *Glastonbury* with **Margaret Drabble**. This was more a novelists' view and about literary technique. Admired passages were read, discussing how JCP got his effects; the general agreement being that his virtues are what he is often criticised for: his lack of the conventional qualities, neat plots, or social comment. All that, the material of other novelists, he undercuts, or avoids. He writes about what other writers leave out. He is never predictable, so always interesting ... He can be placed in the early-C20 literary scene of long saga-like books, but always as an organic, rather than organised, creation.

Next day, Richard Graves introduced **Chris Woodhead;** a special pleasure to invite, he said, because Richard's grandfather Graves was also an Inspector of Schools and an educational theorist. Woodhead's talk, '*Wolf Solent*, the Enduring Appeal', began like the others with an account of discovering Powys — in his case the Penguin 1960s edition of *Wolf Solent* which (as others did too) he bought for its attractive cover (Graham Sutherland's 'Entrance to a Lane'). He found it hard to define what appealed in the book, because the reader that he was then fused with the text he read, identifying with Wolf /JCP struggling with his manias, as when Wolf is compelled to rescue a dead leaf from the pavement (which then blows into a worse fate).

In *Wolf Solent* Woodhead feels questions gnawing as if the reader is their prey: the importance of *pity* conveyed in the book and simultaneously, the feeling in Wolf himself that pity is a cruel trap — he wants to kill pity. The 'man on the Waterloo steps' represents all martyrs to life, as if one unhappy person could kill all the happiness in the world.

But is Wolf's view Powys's? Woodhead thinks not. Wolf would like to believe that we enjoy *because* pain exists. But the dying Malakite commands 'forget', as Wolf can't; and Christy too rejects his sympathy. The book *is* Wolf's meditations and through him the book sets ethical questions: confrontation or evasion? Sympathy or detachment? Words 'making sense' or words as a substitute for action?

Wolf is 'sublimely egotistical'; this is justified by existence being bounded by consciousness — by what one person believes to be real. He's alone; and when he can't decide he retreats into this. Nevertheless this aloneness is *true* — hence its appeal. JCP forces us to confront whether this is an adequate human stance, or whether it's an ultimately insoluble dilemma.

There are three conditions for appreciating the book, Woodhead finds. First, you have to feel as Wolf says at the start that the 'real world' (i.e. the social world of other novels) is commonplace, tedious, sickeningly clever:

you have to share his sense of the unreality of the 'worldly' world. Second, you have to understand his 'mythologizing' — his sinking into his soul — and see the ambivalence of this in human terms: against both the 'normality' of Lord Carfax and 'Gaffer Barge''s un-egotistical willingness to please. Third, you need to be *interested* in this constant battle. How many are?

Among other enduring enjoyments in *Wolf Solent*, for Woodhead, are the minor characters: in *Glastonbury* there are too many of them; in *Wolf Solent* they're important, and rich with incidental discoveries. Another is JCP's way with nature, the nostalgia for pre-modern England (and its links with Hardy). Finally, the *sanity* of the book despite the neurotic states it presents (the ending, the escape from the fair to the field) — all its interpretations appeal in *human* terms.

In discussion, points brought up were Wolf's similarity to Hamlet; and the technique of dispersing neurosis into nature: the concept of the novel both as a philosophical web and as therapy, through combinations of life-description and life-techniques, defences against pity and exposed nerves. These are, of course, the themes of JCP's non-fiction ('philosophical' or 'self-help' books, whichever you like to call them), that are transfer to his invented characters. We share Wolf's vulnerability, and also his determination to survive.

CHARLES LOCK

# On Biographical Proportions: A review-essay

**Fisherman's Friend: A Life of Stephen Reynolds**
CHRISTOPHER SCOBLE
*Tiverton: Halsgrove, 2000. xiv, 817pp.* £25

**A Poor Man's House**
STEPHEN REYNOLDS, edited by CHRISTOPHER SCOBLE
*Tiverton: Halsgrove, 2001. xxii, 223pp.* £19.95

**The Life and Work of Robert Gibbings**
MARTIN J. ANDREWS
*Bicester: Primrose Hill Press, 2003. xii, 426pp.* £45

Christopher Scoble's expansive biography of Stephen Reynolds (1881–1919) appeared three years ago, and would have been reviewed at an earlier date had its bulk either invited or excused skimming. That the book is disproportionately massive in view of the diminished standing of its subject goes without saying; it is a judgement that might precede a reading, but is unlikely to be supported thereby. Reynolds is known today only through his one successful book, *A Poor Man's House* of 1908, much reprinted through the following thirty years and revived as an Oxford paperback in 1982. This account of life in a fishing community in Devon has achieved status as a 'minor classic', and as a document of working-class culture, a pioneering contribution to the construction of a history of the working-class. (The 1982 edition carries an introduction by Roy Hattersley.)

To students of the Powys family Reynolds is also known as the man to whom Katie Powys devoted herself, with disastrous consequences. Katie's agonies of unrequited devotion, her sense of inexplicable rejection, led to a breakdown during which she was placed under institutional care. Her bewilderment cannot have been eased by — and may even be largely attributed to — the suppression of the explanation: Reynolds' homosexuality was never to be mentioned. As late as 1994 it could be stated by Oliver Wilkinson (innocently repeating the family's version of events) that Katie had met Reynolds in Sidmouth, that 'they had been in love' and that at one time Reynolds 'had been very much in love with Katie'. (See *Jack and Frances, The Love Letters of John Cowper Powys to Frances Gregg*,

ON BIOGRAPHICAL PROPORTIONS

ed. O. M. Wilkinson, 193, 252.) Katie had first visited Sidmouth in 1908 with her parents and two of her sisters, Marian and Lucy; enchanted by the town, the family returned in June 1909, and on this visit Katie met Reynolds and, to cite Scoble, 'fell instantly in love, a love that was to survive unblemished until her death … more than fifty years later.' (Fisherman's Friend, 282–3)

John Cowper had been most intimate with Frances Gregg in 1912–13, the period of Katie's breakdown, and their correspondence furnishes contemporary evidence of the family's opinion on her condition. One of the reasons given at the time for Katie's breakdown was that she had been reading Walt Whitman. This might well be taken as a coded way of saying what could not be said. However, it is reported by John Cowper in August 1912 that their sister Gertrude 'blames me for ever having given Katie that fateful Walt Whitman' (Jack and Frances, 30). Whether Gertrude's allegation has a cryptic point is not now to be determined. Katie in her mid-twenties was not permitted to know the reason why her love for Reynolds was unrequited. Almost one hundred years later, his secret and her ignorance — making victims of them both — would explain, in part, why Reynolds should have regained our interest and gained our sympathetic concern.

It should be said that Fisherman's Friend is not in any obtrusive way a contribution to 'gay studies', and it certainly offers no scandalous disclosures. Scoble is himself a retired civil servant, and the book is remarkably even in tone through all its passages: indeed, Scoble is far from tedious when treating of Reynolds' work on the Inshore Fisheries Committee. Reynolds was not a committee man, and Scoble gives a most informative account of the workings of committees when the fullness of bureaucracy was still a project on its own drawing-board.

Throughout the near-700 pages of text runs a narrative of stubbornness and sacrifice. It is that conflict that keeps the reader engaged and alert, wondering how Reynolds will respond to the next frustration of his cruelly limited life: he died, aged 37, in the influenza pandemic, just three months after the Armistice. On that occasion Reynolds had written: 'the intense relief of today's news seems to be swamped for me in a kind of backwash — the thought of who and what will never be any more — the inadequacy of the end compared with the horror of getting there. So that the festivity in the streets gives one the feeling of witnessing an orgie in a graveyard.' (FF, 656)

The phrasing is characteristic, and characteristically discordant: a hard-bitten refusal to get excited, together with a strenuous aspiration towards the imaginative metaphor. Of the former, Scoble is right in seeing (and hearing) Reynolds as a precursor to Orwell. After Reynolds' death one of his many distinguished admirers, T. E. Lawrence, was keen to see his other books, not only A Poor Man's House, brought out in cheap editions. (FF, 677) One might say that Seven Pillars of Wisdom approaches success in its metaphorics, and stumbles over the actualities; Lawrence seems to have favoured those aspects of Reynolds' writing

241

that others have found somewhat pretentious, and those of his works in which the dominant impression is that of straining for literary effect.

Lawrence particularly objected in Reynolds to his 'irritating sense of the difference between a complicated man and a worker' (*FF*, 775) and that points to the antithesis on which both Reynolds and Orwell would shape their polemics: there is little mysterious about their image of the working man, as there is, abundantly, about the Arabs among whom Lawrence chose to live. *A Poor Man's House* is a notable articulation of that antithesis: the fishing community of Sidmouth is presented as tough and sane and wise, free of the impediments and fripperies of the middle class to which Reynolds had been born.

Yet it is not the case that Reynolds (any more than Orwell) renounces or inhibits his own learning, or his own sophisticated powers of observation. Reynolds applies his learning to the justification of unlearning. Those of us who have acquired a distaste for the terminal 'like' will find bracing Reynolds' defence — and find ourselves perhaps also in the company of Arnold Bennett for whom 'In the whole book nothing charmed me more than the extraordinarily fine excursus ... on the vulgar use of the word "like" at the end of a sentence' (*FF*, 248):

> The cause of the uneducated man's use of the word like is interesting....
> "The world's a bubble, like, and the life of man less than a span, like."
> *Like*, in fact, with the poor man as with the poet, connotes simile and metaphor. The poor man's vocabulary, like the poet's, is quite inadequate to express his thoughts. Both, in their several ways, are driven to the use of unhackneyed words and simile and metaphor; both use a language of great flexibility: for which reason we find that after the poet himself, the poor man speaks most poetically. (*Poor Man's House*, 57–8)

And thus terminal *like* is to be redeemed as the promise of a comparison itself unachieved. It is a detail of linguistic observation, of what we might call idiomatic compassion, that is not without condescension, which at once puts Reynolds on the same side as the poor, and sets him apart. As he confesses astutely of Tony, his friend who, hardly articulate, 'is always pathetically eager to make himself plain':

> But it is just because I am fond of him that I am able to feel with him and to a certain extent to divine his half-uttered thoughts; to take them up and return them to him clothed in more or less current English which, he knows, would convey them to a stranger, and which shows him more clearly than before what he really was thinking. That seems to be one of my chief functions here — thought-publisher. (*PMH*, 59)

Reynolds thus confesses to giving a voice to the voiceless, to putting his words into their mouths. It is an ambiguous enterprise, and one that has had plenty of detractors. In 1919, after his death, Reynolds was described by C. F. G.

Masterman in terms that surely allude to Lawrence of Arabia: 'He appeared to me then, as he appeared ever afterwards, a literary man disguised as a fisherman, and greatly enjoying the adventure.' (*FF*, 253) Both in his edition of *A Poor Man's House* and in the biography, Scoble draws our attention to comparable accounts of working-class life presented by educated persons who chose to immerse themselves, rather than to observe from above in the late Victorian manner of Charles Booth or Seebohm Rowntree. Reynolds was specifically encouraged by two books published in 1907: Miss Loane's *The Next Street but One* and Lady Bell's *At the Works: A Study of a Manufacturing Town*, both of which, he claimed, supported his view that 'the poor make a better thing of life, and are evolved in a more balanced manner, than the other classes.' (*FF*, 159) To these two, Scoble adds W. H. Davies's *The Autobiography of a Super-Tramp* of 1908 (exactly contemporary with *A Poor Man's House*) and George Sturt's *The Wheelwright's Shop* of 1923; it appears striking — now — that W. H. Hudson, a friend of Reynolds though forty years his senior, did not publish *A Shepherd's Life* until 1910. Another book published that same year (a very different sort of pastoral) is *Mad Shepherds*, by L. P. Jacks. All of these are attempts by educated men and women to give representation to those who are illiterate. As late as 1908 Ford Madox Hueffer (Ford) could thus celebrate Reynolds' achievement in *A Poor Man's House*: 'It is astonishing how little literature has to show of the life of the poor.' (*FF*, 259)

In 1911 Reynolds published a second book on the Woolley family of Sidmouth, *Seems So!: A Working-Class View of Politics*, this one concerned with their opinions on social, political and economic matters. Reynolds had planned to have the book appear under their names as well as his, as he told Arnold Bennett: 'My two fishermen partners and myself are getting out a book this Autumn, to be called "Seems So". If I'm not mistaken, it's the first appearance of the illiterate in literature, as authors!' (*FF*, 379: of this book, 'by Stephen Reynolds and Bob and Tom Woolley', a new edition is awaited.) Unfortunately this sort of 'writerly ventriloquism' involves a modification and dilution of Reynolds' own 'voice', providing us with something less than what another of his older admirers, Joseph Conrad, distinguished as 'first rate literary Reynolds'; this is glossed by Scoble as 'clear English in full Orwellian mode', a claim supported by the introduction to *Seems So!*, by Reynolds alone:

> In a country where, being poor, one may not sleep under the sky without money in one's pocket, the economic difference tells most…. (*FF*, 377)

This gives some indication of the strengths of Reynolds' prose, and of the ideological conviction that drove him to a sacrificial assimilation of his own voice to that appropriate to the representation of illiterate fishermen. (The Biblical parallels are so obvious as to be left tacit.) In 1912, when he was just thirty-one, Reynolds seems to have renounced writing in his own person. Between 1906 and 1912 he had published no fewer than seven books; henceforth there would be no more, and Reynolds' voice would be submerged in those of either fishermen or committees, or both. His death in 1919 is not then to be understood as having cut short a career of brilliant promise. That career had already fallen victim to Reynolds' scruples about writing; to his identification with those who could not write; and to his determination to put his educational advantages to the benefit of fishermen by serving on Government committees. If there was no way to avoid the charge that he was 'a literary man disguised as a fisherman', it was better not to be thought of as a writer at all.

What part Katie Powys' crisis of 1912 played in that renunciation is not clear; it is clear that Reynolds considered himself much misunderstood. With one's readers, one can try one's best. With Katie he was simply not permitted to make himself understood. His readers would take him amiss precisely insofar as he was a writer; Katie mistook him because he was a man.

The most intriguing of all Reynolds' writings may be an essay published in 1906 under the curious composite title of 'Autobiografiction'. Reynolds claimed to have identified a new literary genre, compounded of fiction, autobiography and the essay, and he explains why it should be emerging now, in the years that would later be distinguished in literary history under the label of Modernism:

> A man, usually of an introspective nature, has accumulated a large body of spiritual experiences. He feels that he must out with it.... Fiction is impracticable. He does not wish, or is not able, to invent such a complicated apparatus for self-expression. Besides, the story's the thing in fiction. To use that medium would be to scatter and sink precisely the spiritual experience which he wants to record. Formal autobiography would present much the same difficulty – the large amount of (for his purpose) extraneous matter .... Essays, again, would be too disconnected and would scarcely admit of an attitude frankly egotistical enough. ... He invents a certain amount of biographical detail, or ... he selects from his life the requisite amount of autobiographical material, adding perhaps a quantity of pure fiction, and on that he builds the spiritual experience, with that he dilutes it, and makes it coherent and readable. The result is autobiografiction, a literary form more direct and intimate probably than any to be found outside poetry. (*FF*, 135–6)

This was written one year before the publication (anonymously and amidst growing curiosity and controversy) of *Father and Son*. In April 1907 Reynolds and Edmund Gosse met for the first time, and talked, among other matters, about Devon, in which county the unnamed narrator of *Father and Son* had had had his difficult upbringing. It is a refined disjunction in literary history that Reynolds should have known Gosse personally, but would never learn the identity of the author of *Father and Son*, a book for which his own essay and his coinage 'autobiografiction' seemed to have provided the blueprint.

Though some critics (Peter Keating, David Trotter) have paid attention to 'autobiografiction', the broader significance of the term has not been adequately estimated. John Cowper's and Llewelyn's *Confessions of Two Brothers* and T. F. Powys's *Soliloquies of a Hermit* (both appearing in 1916) may be taken as part of this emerging genre; Llewelyn's *Skin for Skin* (1925) is an assured masterpiece of the kind. By contrast, Llewelyn's only novel, *Apples be Ripe* (1930), shows how antithetical narrative can be to a certain form of prose–writing. The avoidance of narrative is a pressing question in the early twentieth century (Yes — oh dear yes — the novel tells a story, runs E. M. Forster's celebrated groan of 1927), and it is for once perhaps more than a conventional lapse that Reynolds should speak not inclusively but only of 'a man'. Llewelyn's one novel appeared in the same year as Katie's only novel, *The Blackthorn Winter*: the sad difference between them is of course that this was Katie's only book. When were women permitted to write autobiografictions? One could argue that Virginia Woolf's novels have all the constituents specified by Reynolds, and yet contain them in the guise of fiction; Woolf is thus constrained to write novels, albeit with a minimum of narrative continuity. A similar sort of generic conservatism can be seen in the 'novels' that hold and frame the extraordinarily free meditative associational prose of Dorothy M. Richardson.

We (and not only Powysians) would treasure an autobiografictional account by Katie Powys, but what we have, in her stories and poems and the archly 'poetical' prose of *Phoenix* (unpublished), is confined to the conventional genres. Yet any of the Powys sisters would have been adept at autobiografiction, as would Phyllis Playter, Frances Gregg, Alyse Gregory, Gamel Woolsey, to mention no others. We could even suggest that autobiografiction ought to have been a distinctively feminine genre; it renounces the ordering of narrative and with that, more importantly, explanation, the conventions of causality and consequence. It appeals to those who are less interested in explaining themselves or their lives than in celebrating or recording their experience outside of the framework (and the solvent) of narrative explanation.

Reynolds achieved his only lasting success with *A Poor Man's House*, a work that fits into none of the traditional genres, and has therefore been consigned to the periphery. Yet as long as it continues to be read, it will speak for those silenced by circumstance, law and shame. On first reading, *A Poor Man's House* left an indifferent impression on me. Scoble's biography gives one an overpowering sense of the constraints under which Reynolds lived, of the compulsions of both law and conscience by which he was driven. One would not wish to suggest that a reading of *Fisherman's Friend* be a prerequisite for an appreciation of *A Poor Man's House*, for that would only place another obstacle in front of readers. But it must be said that this biography, in virtually all its detail, is eminently justified. At a crucial period of English life Reynolds apprehended what was at stake in being a writer. He dedicated the talents attained through his education to helping the poor, while lamenting that the poor would lose their distinctive culture, their more authentic mode of being, as a consequence of the improvements in their condition. That conflict has been a staple of working-class reflection over the past sixty years, and is presented with complex dignity in the works of Richard Hoggart and Raymond Williams. Reynolds' choice of silence is exemplary; after the silence *A Poor Man's House* continues to be heard, an echo, a trace, a witness not only to the poor but to that fisherman whom we might mistake for its writer.

Much of the sustaining interest of Scoble's biography is derived from Reynolds' associates and admirers. From Conrad and Edward Thomas to Galsworthy, Hugh Walpole and sundry Garnetts, the Edwardian literary world seems to surround and embrace Reynolds. Prominent figures, from Edward Carpenter to Cecil Harmsworth, figure prominently, but only by virtue of their closeness to Reynolds. Members of the Powys family make their appearances, but seem already, as early as 1912, disconnected from any circle but their own.

Robert Gibbings (1889–1958) enjoyed a very different destiny, though these days he and Reynolds might well be sharing a corner of obscurity, or a neglected shelf in a second-hand bookshop. For fifty years Gibbings was acknowledged as one of the greatest of English wood-engravers; in the 1950s he was a national celebrity, frequently in the press and to be heard on the BBC. His renown was such that an intemperate reviewer could round on Gibbings' last book, *Till I End My Song* (1957), with allusive ease: '... to tell the truth he has been coming down the Thames and the Lee and the Seine and the Wye and making those exquisitely meaningless wood engravings quite long enough.' (*Robert Gibbings*, 368) That this should not be the final verdict is the premise of Martin Andrews, whose biography of Gibbings runs to over 400 pages. As many of these pages are filled with those engravings, the biography poses no monumental challenge to the reader, nor does it set out to make large claims.

The engravings tell the story eloquently. In 1920 Gibbings produced one of the most ingenious and optically challenging of all English wood-engravings, 'Clear waters'. The outline of the girl's body is given by shadows falling behind it and, as Andrews explains, 'the eye naturally completes the shape by implication' (*RG*, 41). The technique was suggested to Gibbings by 'the "dazzle" effect of camouflage paint on warships'. His engravings of the early 1920s have significance even in a European context. And then, gradually, the charm sets in. The jacket illustration for *Mark Only* by T. F. Powys (1924) is oddly unremarkable. In 1932 Llewelyn Powys and Alyse Gregory visited Gibbings in his Berkshire home. In the words of Patricia Empson, Llewelyn and Gibbings 'found themselves in close accord.' In 1937 Llewelyn became godfather to Gibbings' daughter Tiare. (*RG*, 223: a detail supplied by Andrews but not mentioned in Gibbings' reminiscences of Llewelyn which, with an introduction by Patience Empson, can be found in *The Powys Journal* III (1993).)

*Glory of Life* (1934) and *The Twelve Months* (1936) are the enduring result of their collaboration. The former was printed by the Golden Cockerel Press, owned by Gibbings between 1925 and 1935; while the latter appeared under the imprint of the Bodley Head, it had been designed for the Golden Cockerel, and was produced entirely under the direction of Gibbings. As examples of book-making these titles belong to an exclusive company.

Llewelyn died in 1939, Eric Gill in 1940. One could suggest that Gibbings was made vulnerable by the loss of these two figures, one a writer on natural and local themes who yet resisted the rural idyll, the other a printer and engraver of principle as well as genius. With the publication in 1940 of *Sweet Thames Run Softly* Gibbings became a memorialist of English pastoral, and one of very considerable value to the propaganda effort during the Battle of Britain and the Blitz. If he is remembered at all, it is that image that has stuck. Yet behind the bluff jesting and the complacent corpulence we can find in Gibbings' writings some evidence of a quite remarkable eye.

In 1937 Gibbings rigged up some elaborate diving-gear so that he could not only explore the marine life of the West Indies but also — a waterproof surface being created by a colleague at Reading University — make drawings while under water. The results are as extraordinary as Gibbings' observation: 'The strange thing was that when I came to the surface I found that during my time below I had forgotten all rules of perspective ... and that I had drawn everything in the proportion of its importance to me ... . This suggests a parallel with primitive art ... .' (*RG*, 211) Twenty years later, Gibbings is still trying to achieve in wood engraving something of the stylized quality of primitive art, as if behind all in Gibbings that tempts one to sentimental reverie there remains a serious modern artist: 'Now, with the years, I incline to austerity of outline in combination with formalized texture. I would like my engravings to partake somewhat of the quality of the low relief stone carvings from Assyria in the British Museum ... .' (*RG*, 365) One could claim of Gibbings that he never wholly abandoned that exceptional deployment of whiteness, of negative spacing, that characterize his best engravings of the years after 1918. When we look at Gibbings we see a vanished England, but that might be our problem at least as much as his, for it is our tendency 'to complete the shape by implication', to see depths where there are surfaces and outlines where there are only lines. In Gibbings — this is his mastery over wood, and over the wood's gouged absence — there may be not more but rather less than meets the eye: less than the eye is trained to see.

# REVIEWS

## Unquiet world: The Life of Count Geoffrey Potocki de Montalk
STEPHANIE DE MONTALK
*Wellington: Victoria University Press, 2001, ISBN 0-86473-414-X, $NZ39.95*

Stephanie de Montalk has written the first full account of the life of Count Geoffrey Wladyslaw Vaile Potocki de Montalk, a poet, printer and pamphleteer, and claimant to the throne of Poland and Hungary. De Montalk, who is Potocki's cousin, has based this work on taped interviews, correspondence, her own diaries, Potocki's own poetry and prose, and access to his vast archive of papers and correspondence, which she dutifully cleaned and catalogued after his death in April 1997 at Draguignan, Provence. An internet website called 'The Lost Club Journal' has a section headed: 'I've spent my life being me'. This phrase refers to Potocki and indeed, in three hundred plus pages de Montalk reveals the life of a man who was extraordinarily individualistic and who, despite controversies, has remained forever on the margins. In truth, the qualities he possessed are not the ingredients for mass culture.

Readers of the works of the Powys brothers will be familiar with Count Potocki. His natural daughter was adopted by T. F. Powys and his wife Violet and called Susan. In later life she became Theodora Gay Potocka, and readers will remember her recollections of T. F. Powys under the name of Theodora Scutt in *The Powys Review* 9 and 10 (1981 and 1982), further reminiscences in *Potocki: A Dorset Worthy?* (Typographeum, Francestown, New Hampshire, 1983), and in *Cuckoo In The Powys Nest* (Brynmill, 2000). This Dorset period also resulted in *Dogs' Eggs*, Potocki's vitriolic four part series subtitled *A Study in Powysology*, and published by his own Mélissa Press in 1968. De Montalk quite rightly remarks that these digressive near-libellous pieces, and other publications such as *Mel Meum* (poems, 1959), *The Fifth Columnist* (a satire by Jim Goodleboodle, 1960), *The Whirling River* (poems, 1964), and *Let the Rhodesians Not* (1977) have attracted collectors of rare and unusual books.

Potocki was born in New Zealand in 1903 of Polish and Scottish ancestry. He belonged to the generation of early New Zealand poets such as A. R. D. Fairburn, R. A. K. Mason and D'Arcy Cresswell. In 1927 he left 'the butter republic' of New Zealand because 'Poets are badly treated in this land of white savages and All Blacks [the national rugby team]'. It was in 'Merrie England' that his destiny was to be fulfilled, a place where 'they [Poets] are feted and laurelled and crowned'. Unfortunately this was not to be. In 1932 he produced a number of his own poems and translated versions of works by Rabelais and Verlaine that were classified as obscene. In court, Potocki's refusal to swear on the Bible, his attire — long hair, cloak and sandals — and perhaps his answer of 'several years in Buckingham Palace' to Sir Ernest Wild's question of 'can you suggest what punishment you think you deserve?', further provoked the Recorder. Potocki was given six months in prison. W. B. Yeats described it as a 'criminally brutal sentence' and the affair produced a number of supporters such as Leonard and Virginia Woolf, H. G. Wells and T. S. Eliot. The appeal was unsuccessful. However, from these events, Potocki produced *Whited Sepulchres* and *Snobbery with Violence*, two pamphlets on the trial, and his jail experience. The latter is Potocki's best work.

After his release, and in the spring of 1933, Potocki travelled via France and Italy to Poland. In 1935, he was back in England and with financial assistance from Aldous Huxley and Brian Guinness he obtained his first printing press. Thus began a long tradition of journeyman work and self-promotion. He started his own ultra-monarchist journal the *Right Review* and produced both poetry and political pamphlets. The appearance of *The Unconstitutional Crisis* in December 1936, a pamphlet prompted by the abdication of King Edward VIII, saw Potocki again in jail briefly. On 14 September 1939 Potocki proclaimed himself 'Wladislaw 5th King of Poland, Hungary and Bohemia, Grand Duke of Lithuania, Silesia and the Ukraine, Hospodar of Moldavia, etc etc, etc, High Priest of the Sun', and in July 1940, there was the 'Battle of Claverton Street' which had started over a summons for an alleged black-out offence during the Blitz. For this, Potocki served two months in Wandsworth Prison.

With a growing dislike for the 'english', that 'Kingdom of the Half Mad', Potocki moved to Draguignan, Provence, in 1949. At his 'Villa Vigoni', an old cottage that he painstakingly repaired, he spent some twelve years. It was a frugal life, one of much self-sufficiency and very little income. In 1959 he obtained another press, and began printing again. Frederica, his long-time lover, claimed that he got into trouble having a press and she didn't want him to have another one. Potocki's quip was: 'That's not the case. I got into trouble through *not* having a press.' One attribute that shines through this book is Potocki's humour and wit. He was also a natural mimic, witness his takeoff of the Woolfs in his satirical *Social Climbers in Bloomsbury*, printed in his *The Right Review* (1938). It is extremely funny.

Draguignan was where he drove around the countryside in his Citroën 2CV, flying the Polish Royal Standard. He was eccentric, but a well-liked local figure. It was home (except for those years in Dorset) until his return to New Zealand in November 1983. While in New Zealand, he mixed with family members, met many hand-craft printers and writers, and enjoyed meeting younger people, to whom he was something of a personality. His last years were spent commuting, living in a small flat in the provincial town of Hamilton and his house in France.

De Montalk's book contains lively accounts of Potocki's thoughts on poets, politics, women, the literary establishment, longevity (the answer: rye bread and naked sun bathing), and his own egotism. There is much unwritten history. My personal experience with this extraordinary man validates this truism. I had corresponded with the Count prior to his arrival in New Zealand and he stayed at my house in Auckland while he acclimatised to the changes after an absence of fifty-six years. His remarkable survival skills were quickly evident. After helping him buy his car, which was like a large land crab in comparison to his smaller Citroën, he hopped in it, and without any hesitation, drove off into the sunset — on the left hand side of the road, which, of course, for antipodeans, is the right one. Amazingly he (and the other drivers) survived. On another occasion, after complaining loudly about America and the Americans, he went next door to telephone his daughter. He was gone for an age and I was worried about 'The Chief', as we affectionately called him. Perhaps he had fallen into a ditch and was hurt. I eventually went next door and found him ensconced on a plush green lazy-boy rocking chair, eating pizza, and watching a television documentary about John F. Kennedy. A strong inner-world resourcefulness matched a keen ability to adapt. And I believe he liked the changes he experienced. He was amazed at bacon and egg sandwiches (a New Zealand delicacy), combined hot and cold shower taps, and eateries, like the Indian restaurant we dragged him to. It was there that he met my friend Michael O'Leary, our own famed aristocrat the 'Earl of Seacliff'. I believe he quite enjoyed talking to another 'Pretender'.

Stephanie de Montalk must be congratulated for undertaking this first full work on Potocki. There are excellent photographs and a useful checklist of books by and about him. Unfortunately, it could have been a better book. Indeed, what started out as an exercise in a creative writing course has resulted in an extended memoir. It suffers from this. There is an idiosyncratic arrangement of chapters and there could have been greater editorial control on the text. The reader who is interested in Potocki, his activities as a printer-cum-pamphleteer, or the history of censorship, and his position in the literary stream of England in the mid-1900s will demand more. In time a well-documented biography will appear; something that he does deserve.

Donald Kerr

## Wet Leaves
PATRICIA V. DAWSON
*Hub Editions, Lincolnshire, England, 2002, paper 58pp.*

Reading Patricia Dawson's poems in *Wet Leaves*, her fourth book from HUB Editions, I was struck by the fact, as an American poet, that I don't often get the chance to read older poets. America is a youth culture, our movies are about kids falling in love, our song are mostly about dating and erotic urge; our novels are about first love or about thirty-something's falling out of love. Our poets are fresh out of writing schools and are just testing the water in most books. Truth is, however, we are an aging culture in America, with the majority of citizens now past thirty-five and possessing most of the spending power, but with little incentive to go to the mall. We need poets our own age, with some savvy and grace, and a bit of humor against the excesses and foolishness of the times we live in.

Dawson, who is English, a painter by trade, and now in her late seventies, writes vividly of her life in the golden years. She's had her heart aches: a friend recovering from a stroke, the passing away of old comrades, her own aches and pains at growing older. But she lives in a culture that still thinks about maturity and life after forty, and she weaves her ironic impressions in and out of commentaries on painters, gallery shows, gossipy snippets and haikus, a form that grows in appeal as one ages. Those simple, three-line vignettes she writes are particularly suited to a painter, since they depend much on seeing a few objects or a natural event in the landscape, and writing as if you had a brush, not a pen, in your hand. The haiku, especially makes you shut up the chattering monkeys of the verbal imagination and push all your brains out into your eyes, as in

Six o'clock sunrise
and the celandines
not yet open —

Two gourds in a bowl
one white, one orange
lie skin to skin

The latter haiku, from 'Autumn Haiku', is Dawson's trademark, a slightly rueful, ironic observation on familiarity, even intimacy, without eros.

Her repertoire includes four and five-line observations, a few notes on things that amuse her, some longer, skilfully rhymed poems that are tightened up by a dry humour, and the mildly mocking lyric poem like 'The Museum'

The museum, built
to conserve the works of God
and man, has failed
to preserve itself.

Her social commentary can be astringent, as well — as in the poem 'Shopping' where she notes that a recent poll has declared 'the nation's favorite/ occupation's shopping' after taking us on a stroll along a gallery hung with paintings of dukes who enjoyed another age, now almost completely faded. And again, in 'I Wooed Her on the Net' a poem about love in cyber space, and all the treacheries of an intermediated, hopelessly abstract life filtered through technology.

Among her more imposing lyrics, those daring to express more personal emotions, is 'Drawing Lady Gregory', a moving tribute to one of Ireland's great patriots, but the beauty that broke Yeats' and others' hearts. The title is ironic; she is drawing her out of memory, as well as rendering her with a pencil, as she talks directly to her subject, asking questions that zero in on beauty, female youth, the poets own longings for that time and the blunt knowledge that it's all gone, the tower at Ballylee now 'empty/ but for one blue wooden chair.' She draws a ghost, she tells us, among the colours of a summer night recollected from 'forty years ago in County Clare'.

My impression is that Dawson thinks in prose, then writes it down as poetry. She is plain almost to the bone, rarely ever letting go with a bit of reckless verbal riffing. When she does ease up on her pen, she's fine, even elegant, wary perhaps of losing control and always reining herself in abruptly. She's a painter, but she is also a very smart observer, and her ear is sensitive. In the short lyric poem, 'The Fall', she pulls off one of the best imitations of Robert Frost I have read in years. The sounds, the humour, the dry eye scanning the New Hampshire twilight are pure Frost, and the rhymes are terse, bitten-off line endings of the sort you most expect from the New England bard. And yet, Dawson is there too, working out her own love poem:

> He read me lines by Robert Frost
> In Suffolk fields, among the crops
> Of ripening corn. That way we lost
> The hounds of war

'Wet Leaves'. The title of this little collection is apt and tells us this is a book about aging, memories, about growing older, making peace with this fact of the body. The poems are sharp-edged, reserved, one wants to say delicate, if the word has not been too damaged in this age of overkill. Delicate lyrics, many of them inviting silence, or wedging into silent hours. The clock ticks in the background, the English countryside is all around, and her thoughts move unhurried across the page. These are the fallen leaves, but their wetness tells us they are still growing, turning into something else, alive even in their disintegration.

Paul Christensen

## James Hanley: Modernism and the Working Class
JOHN FORDHAM
*Cardiff: University of Wales Press, 2002, hardback, £25, xxii, 315*
*ISBN 0 7083 1755 3*

James Hanley was born of Irish-Catholic, immigrant parents and grew up within sight of the sea, close to the Liverpool docks. His father was an engine-room greaser on various ships, and Hanley himself went to sea on a cargo vessel in 1915, when he was thirteen. Subsequently, he experienced the horrors of war while serving on troopships, as described powerfully in *The Hollow Sea* (1937), and later while in the Canadian Army from April 1917, after lying about his age. After the war he briefly returned to the sea, but then undertook a variety of jobs, though railway porter seems to have been the main one, prior to starting his career as a full-time writer, in 1930.

Despite these credentials neither Hanley nor his family were typical members of the working class. His father, according to Hanley's 'autobiographical excursion' *Broken Water*, had been born in prestigious Meirion Square, Dublin, and might have worked in a law office, if he had not gone to sea. Hanley's mother came from the famous Irish seaport of Cobh, Cork, and amongst her ancestors, according to her son, were sailing boat captains. Hanley's father was also a serious reader of such authors as Dickens and Thackeray, and Hanley records in *Broken Water* going to see Shakespeare's Richard III in the 1920s, with his parents. During the 1920s Hanley himself undertook a rigorous programme of self-education, and bought himself a piano on which to play classical music. However, as Jonathan Rose's *Intellectual Life of the British Working Classes* reminds us, there has been a long tradition of working-class people who have been interested in self-improvement and so-called high culture. Fordham, however, sees the Hanley family as having undergone a loss of status, or proletarianization, upon leaving their more prosperous Dublin origins, and becoming immigrants in England.

Hanley wrote a great variety of works, including five semi-autobiographical novel about the Fury family of Liverpool, novels of the sea, novels set in Wales, Marseilles, London and Ireland. His novels especially deal with men and women in extreme situations. *Levine* (1956), for example, has a Polish protagonist who is part of the flotsam from war-torn Europe, and *Ocean* (1941) deals with a World War II shipwreck. Hanley also published many short stories, and wrote extensively for BBC radio and television.

While Fordham explicitly denies that he is writing a critical biography, what makes this book especially interesting is the fact that he is not just concerned with the books that Hanley wrote, but also with the man, and the tensions that developed in him, when he became a professional writer, between his working-class roots and middle-class and modernist values. His writing brought him into association with publishers, with BBC and theatre producers, journal editors, as well as with authors such as E. M. Forster, T. E. Lawrence and John Cowper Powys. Other modernist writers influenced him too, for Hanley was an Irish-man of the generation that followed James Joyce, and an admirer of William Faulkner. Fordham is also interested in the effect on Hanley, who began his career writing about the workers and sailors from Liverpool, of living in isolated, rural Wales. Above all, Fordham is concerned with the struggle of this working-class writer to remain loyal to his Liverpool working-class, and seafaring roots, under such social, intellectual and — with a wife and son to support — economic pressures.

While Fordham makes effective and lucid use of left-wing critical theory, to

REVIEWS

re-examine the relationship between modernism and working-class writing, the
theory is used to give depth and structure to the discussion so that the book is
not burdened with superfluous critical jargon. Hanley the man and writer
remains always at the centre. Thus while Fordham makes use of Adorno's
aesthetic theory in relation to Hanley's works, he is also interested in the
possible affect on Hanley's writing of his marriage in 1931 to a member of the
aristocracy, Enid (Timothy) Heathcote, and of moving into a veritable mansion
with five acres in 1935.

Fordham thoroughly researched Hanley's background for the University of
Middlesex Ph.D. thesis from which this book developed, scrutinizing BBC and
publishers' archives, and unpublished letters, and conducting numerous interviews, that range from Hanley's son Liam Hanley and friends of Hanley to
people from the Welsh village of Llanfechain, where the Hanleys lived from late
1940 until 1963.

Hanley was an important writer about life at sea, and Fordham thoroughly
examines Hanley's place within this tradition. He includes a discussion of
Hanley in relation to Melville, whom Hanley greatly admired, along with
references to Eugene O'Neill, B. Traven, H. M. Tomlinson, and others. His
discussion of Hanley's response, as a former seaman from the lower deck, to the
Polish aristocrat — and modernist novelist — master mariner Joseph Conrad, is
most interesting. Added depth is given to this analysis of Hanley's books on the
sea and ships by Fordham's use of autobiographies by working-class sailors.

Liverpool of course is at the centre of Hanley's novels in the 1930s, and
another interesting dimension of Hanley's writing explored by Fordham is
Hanley's relationship to the modernist tradition of writing about cities. Included in Fordham's book is a useful historical and cultural context for Hanley's
Liverpool novels, along with a consideration of his relationship to such important literary precursors as Balzac and Dostoievsky.

This is a book that is fired by Fordham's own political commitment, as well as
by his strong sense of the social and political responsibility of writers within
society. In his introduction, Fordham refers to the recent Liverpool dockers
strike, as well as to 'the renaissance in working-class writing from Scotland',
both of which he sees as

> a clear indication that class consciousness continues to be central to the
> way people live their actual lives, particularly within those communities
> in traditional areas of British industry which have been economically
> devastated since the consolidation of Conservative power during the
> 1980s.

*James Hanley: Modernism and the Working Class* (2002) was published thirty-
eight years after the only other full-length study of this important working-class
novelist, *The Novels of James Hanley* (1964) by Edward Stokes appeared in New
Zealand. Curiously, the only other important work, *James Hanley: A Bibliogra-*

*phy* (1980) by Linnea Gibbs, was published abroad too, in Canada. Harvill Press, however, republished *Ocean*, in 1999, and *The Voyage and Other Stories*, in 1997. Some out-of-print titles of Hanley can — at times — still be purchased at fairly reasonable prices, and there are rumours that further works may republished. In addition Chris Gostick has prepared an edition of the correspondence between John Cowper Powys and James Hanley, which it is hoped Cecil Woolf will eventually publish. He is also working on the official biography, with the encouragement of Liam Powys Hanley, James Hanley's son, and John Cowper Powys's godson.

In a December 1997 review of James Hanley's *Last Voyage and Other Stories*, in *The Independent*, Alberto Manguel pondered 'why one of the major 20th-century writers' has been so neglected. As with John Cowper Powys, this is not the first, and will not be the last, time this question will be asked. John Fordham's book, however, shows, especially because of the enthusiasm and thoroughness that he brings to this study of Hanley's works, why important writers ranging from E. M. Forster and John Cowper Powys, to Antony Burgess, C. P. Snow, and Doris Lessing have praised Hanley. *James Hanley: Modernism and the Working Class* is an invaluable addition to Hanley criticism as well as to the whole subject of working-class writing. The University of Wales Press is to be congratulated for publishing an important book on an unjustly neglected writer.

Robin Wood

# NOTES ON CONTRIBUTORS

MELVON L. ANKENY is a Reference Librarian and Assistant Professor on the Faculty of The Ohio State University Libraries in Columbus, Ohio.

PAUL CHRISTENSEN is a Professor of English specialising in twentieth-century poetics. His most recent books are a memoir of his writing life in the Southwest, *West of the American Dream: An Encounter with Texas* (Texas A&M Press, 2001) and *Blue Alleys* (Stone River Press, 2001), a collection of prose poems.

PETER J. FOSS is currently Honorary Secreray of The Powys Society. He has published in the fields of History and Literature, particularly in the area of his expertise, Llewelyn Powys. His work on Llewelyn Powys's early diaries is on-going, and his definitve *Bibliography of Llewelyn Powys* is under consideration by Oak Knoll Press and The British Library.

KATE KAVANAGH is Editor of *The Powys Society Newsletter*. She is married to the poet P. J. Kavanagh and has worked with him on a number of anthologies.

DONALD KERR is the Special Collections Librarian at the University of Otago, Dunedin, New Zealand.

CHARLES LOCK is Professor of English Literature at the University of Copenhagen. Recent publications include articles on William Cowper, Joyce Cary and Geoffrey Hill.

J. LAWRENCE MITCHELL is a Professor and Head of Department of English at Texas A&M University. A specialist in linguistics, he has published widely, and continues to work on a biography of T. F. Powys.

STEPHEN POWYS MARKS is an architect, editor and writer, and was the Hon. Treasurer of The Powys Society until last year. He has been responsible for the production of much of the Society's publication work, and has himself contributed extensively to Powys studies, especially the history of the Powys and other related families, in the Society's *Newsletter*, *Journal* and *Review* and in volume IX *of Bath History* (2002).

ANDREW NASH is Lecturer in English at the University of Reading. He has written several articles on J. M. Barrie and edited a collection of his works, and also published essays on other aspects of Scottish literature and Victorian and early twentieth-century publishing.

BARBARA OZIEBLO teaches in the Departmento de Filologia Inglesa, Universidad de Malaga, Spain. She is the author of a critical biography of Susan Glaspell published by the University of North Carolina Press in 2001.

JACQUELINE PELTIER has been a member of The Powys Society since 1982, and has contributed articles to *The Powys Review* and to the Society's *Newsletter*, mostly on John Cowper Powys, and articles on Alyse Gregory and Frances Gregg to the American *Powys Notes*. She wrote a monograph on Alyse Gregory, *A Woman at her Window*, in the Cecil Woolf Powys Heritage Series. Since 2000, she has been the Editor of *la lettre powysienne*, a twice-yearly French-English bulletin of 52 pages on the Powyses.

SUSAN RANDS has published many articles in *The Powys Review* and the Society's *Newsletter*, mostly on John Cowper Powys. She contributes frequently to *Somerset and Dorset Notes and Queries* and occasionally to *Devon and Cornwall Notes and Queries* and to the *Frome Year Book*. Her latest publication is *John Cowper Powys, the Lyons and W. E. Lutyens* (Cecil Woolf, 2000).

ROBIN WOOD recently took early retirement from the English Department at Memorial University, Newfoundland, Canada.